SHAW'S PEOPLE

SHAW'S PEOPLE

Victoria

to

Churchill

Stanley Weintraub

The Pennsylvania State University Press
University Park, Pennsylvania

Library of Congress Cataloging-in-Publication Data

Weintraub, Stanley, 1929–
    Shaw's people: Victoria to Churchill / Stanley Weintraub.

        p.   cm.
    Includes bibliographical references and index.
    ISBN 0-271-01501-4
    1. Shaw, Bernard, 1856–1950—Friends and associates.   2. Shaw,
Bernard, 1856–1950—Contemporaries.   3. Shaw, Bernard, 1856–1950
—Contemporary Great Britain.   4. Dramatists, Irish—19th century
—Biography.   5. Dramatists, Irish—20th century—Biography.
6. Great Britain—History—19th century—Biography.   7. Great
Britain—History—20th century—Biography.   I. Title.
PR5366.W42   1996
822′.912—dc20
    [B]   95-15481
                                                                    CIP

Frontispiece: Bernard Shaw in a 1928 photograph he inscribed to Frank Harris. From
the author's collection.

for Gladys Weintraub Greenfield

". . . there is no friend like a sister."

—Christina Rossetti, in *Goblin Market*

Other books by Stanley Weintraub about Bernard Shaw

SHAW: *The Annual of Bernard Shaw Studies*, vols. 1-10, ed.

An Unfinished Novel by Bernard Shaw, ed.

Private Shaw and Public Shaw: A Dual Portrait of Lawrence of Arabia and G.B.S.

The Court Theatre, ed.

Cashel Byron's Profession by Bernard Shaw, ed.

Shaw: An Autobiography 1856–1898, ed.

Shaw: An Autobiography 1898–1950. The Playwright Years, ed.

Saint Joan by Bernard Shaw, ed.

Journey to Heartbreak: Bernard Shaw 1914–1918

Bernard Shaw's Nondramatic Literary Criticism, ed.

Saint Joan: Fifty Years After—1923/24–1973/74, ed.

The Portable Bernard Shaw, ed.

Heartbreak House: A Facsimile of the Original Typescript, ed. with Anne Wright

The Playwright and the Pirate: Bernard Shaw and Frank Harris, a Correspondence, ed.

The Unexpected Shaw: Biographical Approaches to G.B.S. and His Work

Bernard Shaw, The Diaries 1885–1897, ed., 2 vols.

Bernard Shaw on the London Art Scene, 1885–1950, ed.

Bernard Shaw: A Guide to Research

Contents

Preface

Over ninety-four years, Bernard Shaw's life intersected with an enormous number of interesting people. One, the formidable lady who was Shaw's sovereign during the first forty-five years of his life, never even knew him—very possibly never even heard of him. Yet each of the personalities viewed through my lens in this volume reveals another facet of that complex creature, G.B.S., who in his lifetime possessed the most famous initials in the world.

A man of more contradictions than most of us, he is seen here in each relationship as a somewhat different Shaw. And with the cantankerous Irish expatriate as mirror, each subject reflects a character not quite what we may have expected.

The dozen Shavian relationships described here represent the researches of thirty or more years. Not all the chapters have appeared in print before. Some of those published earlier have been updated or rewritten. I have chosen as "Shaw's people" those whose encounters with him have intrigued me most. In a few cases these are individuals whom Shaw never met—or saw seldom indeed. However, even his fabled relationship with Ellen Terry (not included here since it has often been examined at great length) was largely epistolary. He met her perhaps half a dozen times aside from seeing her onstage. In one case the relationship was entirely epistolary and indirect, yet with profound result.

In another case—Queen Victoria—even correspondence would have been quite impossible. Yet again, Shaw's imagined relationship was not only profound, but lifelong.

The Shavian relationships that have remained most memorable to me over a lifetime are replete with paradoxes. How could Shaw, the redbearded young Irish radical, have found anything to admire in Queen Victoria, then or later? Or in the passionately evangelical "General" William Booth of the Salvation Army? What possible connections could there be between Shaw, the passionate socialist, and the Tory titan Winston Churchill, who seemed to represent everything G.B.S. should have rejected and despised?

The paradoxes arise just as dramatically on the literary level. Why did H. L. Mencken, the feisty Baltimore critic who was one of Shaw's earliest American fans, turn against his hero at the peak of his transatlantic reputation? Why was James Joyce more interested in his fellow Irishman, Shaw, than he cared to confess except through his own cranky codes? How could Shaw and W. B. Yeats, who seemed to have nothing in common but their large egos and their Irish ancestry, not only gain inspiration from each other but become a mutual admiration society? And how could Shaw, whose fastidiousness recoiled from Oscar Wilde's lifestyle, have become his champion? And how did they happen to borrow from each other, Shaw even writing his own *The Importance of Being Earnest* after, in one of his least perceptive theater reviews, damning the play?

Why, too, did Shaw tolerate so many insufferable types in his life, and—seemingly—encourage many of them? Their names are legion, although only a representative pair, Frank Harris and Siegfried Trebitsch, appear here. Not in these pages are the German spy and propagandist George Sylvester Viereck, whom Shaw indulged, or his incompetent French translator Augustin Hamon, whom Shaw refused to jettison and whom he later pensioned. The list could have included his cadging Polish translator Floryan Sobienowski and a parasite of Shaw's old age, his selfstyled "bibliographer and remembrancer," Fritz Erwin Loewenstein.

A book of Shavian parasites could also include the harridan poetess Erica Cotterill and the ungifted but charming actress Molly Tompkins, to whom Shaw played Henry Higgins, and perhaps more, in the 1920s, but some of these intruders into Shaw's life have been written about elsewhere. Such a collection would be dreary fun, but even a sampling shows that indulging, even encouraging, parasites is clearly an element of Shavian psychology worth exploration—if not to Shaw's advantage. I have looked here at his long relationship with his one-time editor, the outrageous Frank Harris, and his patience (and impatience) with his plodding and insufferable German translator, the Viennese playwright Siegfried Trebitsch. In neither case was he indulging genius (other than his own), but the matter of Sean O'Casey was different. However cranky and contrary O'Casey was, even at cost to his own career, Shaw stood by him. There was goodness and possibly greatness in the man, even if O'Casey's personality stood in the way of his own potential.

Only one other woman—besides Victoria—appears here, and only briefly, befitting her abortive role in Shaw's life. It would be easy to identify other women more important in Shaw's life, all of them well documented—

Florence Farr, Annie Besant, Stella (Mrs. Pat) Campbell, Ellen Terry, and Lady Astor, among others. But the timid Shaw, reluctant, when still unmarried, to follow up a case of authentic sex-appeal, except after the fact and on paper, reveals a different G.B.S. lost in the shadows of his later—and public—reputation. Missing the opportunity in life, he possessed the mysterious and exotic Edith Adams on paper, in a play.

In a few cases I have written elsewhere at length about a Shavian relationship, as in the dual biography *Private Shaw and Public Shaw* (1963). Yet even there I failed to realize some of the subtleties of Shaw's understanding of the "other Shaw"—T. E. Lawrence—until afterward. I thought then that G.B.S. had exploited "Lawrence of Arabia's" personality in two dramatic roles. It turns out—and it appears to be a case of split personality—to be three. Shaw knew his surrogate son well and could not tell all at the time. True respect for one's relationship to another may lie in reticence about it.

One could easily choose twelve very different people as lenses through which to look at Shaw, or at the lives that are illuminated through the ways that they touched his. In some cases, as with William Morris, an entire book might be needed. When he died, Shaw wrote, "You can lose a man like that by your own death, but not by his." Morris was a father figure to Shaw, whose own failure of a father embarrassed him. Or I might have written about Shaw and Sidney Webb—"my oldest and best friend as well as my political partner," he explained to Trebitsch. "You think I saw him every day. As a matter of fact, though he lived within a three hours motor drive from me I did not see him for years before his death; and we exchanged very few letters. But our feelings were quite unchanged. . . ." Oldest and best friend—and yet, Shaw confessed, "I never shook hands with Webb in all my life."

Shaw's people in these pages are here because at some point they interested me for themselves as well as for their roles in G.B.S.'s life. Over the years I also thought of Janet Achurch, Eleanor Marx, William Archer, Granville Barker, and others as candidates. They are still available. I recommend, too, Gene Tunney and Mark Twain. The Shavian portrait gallery is full of paradoxes and stretches on and on.

Stanley Weintraub

EXASPERATED ADMIRATION

Bernard Shaw on Queen Victoria

In 1882, Cetewayo, King of the Zulus, was captured by the British. Brought to London to be impressed by English might at its peak before being restored to his diminished throne, he appeared tall and broad, and considered himself, at fifty-two, an "old man." That August he had an audience with Queen Victoria, arriving in what the Queen called "a hideous black frock [coat] and trousers" over a colorful native tunic. Writing his fourth novel then (publishers had rejected the first three) in the quiet of the great domed British Museum Reading Room, a twenty-six-year-old Irishman with literary aspirations named Bernard Shaw put the Zulu king into his story, inventing a Colonial Office dilemma as to how to entertain Cetewayo.

In the novel *Cashel Byron's Profession*, where the hero's profession is the socially unacceptable one of prizefighting, Cetewayo is taken to the ring to see what Cashel and his opponent—allegedly the two brawniest Englishmen—could endure. Shaw's Zulu chieftain fears for his health in the polluted air of London, "filthy with smoke," and fears for his life when he learns that European monarchs are the shooting targets of their citizens—that even "the queen of England, though accounted the safest of all, was accustomed to this variety of pistol practice."[1] The episode was Shaw's first published reference to Queen Victoria. In his allusion to Victoria's having become "accustomed" to assassination attempts—there had been seven of them—a tone of awe on the part of the young Socialist and republican was palpable. Shaw might not admire the Queen's politics or the institution she symbolized, but he recognized that Victoria was a formidable lady. He would become the only Marxist member of her admiration society.

When preparations began to mark Victoria's Golden Jubilee in 1887, Shaw found himself suddenly writing again about his Queen. By the autumn of 1886 his five novels had all failed, only *Cashel Byron* managing a meager commercial success—not enough to warrant further attempts in fiction. The fifth, *An Unsocial Socialist*, with a Marxist republican hero, was hardly noticed when published. To support himself, Shaw had taken to literary journalism, writing anonymous art reviews for *The World* and anonymous book reviews for the *Pall Mall Gazette*. The payment was meager— sometimes only a few shillings—but it kept him alive. He also wrote execrable political doggerel that no one would publish—at least not until the afternoon *Star* sought material. But whether Shaw published anonymously or pseudonymously, Queen Victoria would not hear of him, and although he was famous by the time she died at the turn of the century, almost certainly he was still unknown to her. Yet Shaw would be, throughout a life even longer than her own, a perceptive commentator on her life and reign.

Anticipating the Jubilee, the autumn publishing season in 1886 spawned book after book on the Queen. One, *Fifty Years of a Good Queen's Reign*, by A. H. Wall, was offered to Shaw for an unsigned notice in the *Pall Mall Gazette*.[2] As assignments went, it was one of his better ones—he was sometimes asked to make a paragraph out of a bushel of privately printed poetry or out of forgettable novels with such titles as *Fatal Bonds* and *The Evil Genius*. The Queen, at least, was a real human being, although Shaw found her fast disappearing into myth. "With her merits," he wrote sardonically in his *Gazette* review,

> we are all familiar, and may expect to be more so before the last Jubilee bookmaker has given the throne a final coat of whitewash. We know that she has been of all wives the best, of all mothers the fondest, of all widows the most faithful. We have often seen her, despite her lofty station, moved by famines, colliery explosions, shipwrecks and railway accidents; thereby teaching us that a heart beats in her Royal breast as in the humblest of her subjects. She has proved that she can, when she chooses, put off her state and play the pianoforte, write books, and illustrate them like any common lady novelist. We can all remember how she repealed the Corn Laws, invented the steam locomotive, and introduced railways; devised the penny post, developed telegraphy, and laid the Atlantic cable; how she captured Coomassie and Alexandria, regenerated art by the Pre-

Fig. 1. Queen Victoria in a portrait photo by Bassano in 1885 just prior to her Golden Jubilee in 1887. Courtesy the Royal Archives, Windsor Castle.

Raphaelite movement, speculated in Suez Canal stock, extended the franchise, founded the Primrose League, became Empress of India.

This adulation, Shaw exaggerated, lacked authenticity and credibility. If the Golden Jubilee were to be a success, he ventured, "the sooner some competent cynic writes a book about Her Majesty's shortcomings the better." The problem was, as Shaw knew and did not say, that the radical press had been going that route for decades and had failed to find much republican sentiment to exploit. Still, Shaw thought, people were moving away from passive reverence, and much of the public fulsomeness paid the Queen, he predicted anonymously, "will be pure hypocrisy. . . . Yet there must be much genuine superstitious loyalty among us. . . . Were a gust of wind to blow off our Sovereign's head-gear tomorrow, 'the Queen's bonnet' would crowd Bulgaria out of the papers. Clearly the idea of Royalty is still with us; and it is as the impersonatrix of that idea that the Queen is worshipped by us. That feeling is the real support of thrones."

Irishman though he was and Marxist though he claimed to be, Shaw discovered himself one of the Queen's admirers, however reluctant, and he would conduct a curious love affair with her in print all his life. As art critic of *The World*, he reviewed, in January 1887, an exhibition of a portrait of the Queen, twice her own tiny size, painted from a photograph by Alexander Bassano for the government of the Punjab. Rather than vent some sarcasm at the grotesque nine-by-six dimensions of the picture, Shaw contented himself with comments about the camera being "as attentive" to the Queen's lace as to the Queen, which left the work as painted without a focus. Still, Shaw concluded, it was "by no means unsuccessful."[3] He felt much the same in March about Blake Wirgman's *Peace with Honour*, a canvas of no great distinction (it "will serve its turn") showing Victoria receiving the Treaty of Berlin from Disraeli in 1878. In the old-fashioned Great Power way of arranging things, Prince Bismarck and the Earl of Beaconsfield had settled a Balkan war between Russia and Turkey, Britain receiving Cyprus for its pains. Wirgman's title had come from Disraeli's triumphal statement on his return to London.

As a playwright eleven years later, Shaw would recall this phrase ironically in *Caesar and Cleopatra*. Now only an anonymous and unimportant art critic, Shaw merely described "Her Majesty, mildly self-conscious, [who] sits at one end of a table, and Lord Beaconsfield condescends to her from the other, in a 'genteel apartment' pervaded by peace with honour. The old-fashioned furniture helps to give the picture an air of being a family portrait.

. . . No one will guess that two such unassuming personages are Empress and Earl."[4]

Later in the Jubilee year Shaw was less kind, not surprisingly since he was acting for a socialist committee. To prepare themselves for the hoped-for day when a socialist party might emerge into power and members of the three-year-old Fabian Society might then hold high office, a number of Fabians took an active part in the "Charing Cross Parliament." The mock legislature was a popular late-Victorian institution, following the extension of suffrage, and women participants were anticipating its further extension. The Charing Cross Parliament was named for the railway hotel in which it took place, where the Strand poured into Trafalgar Square below Charing Cross Road. It was more than a charade of forming an imaginary socialist government, for considerable research went into the preparation of the addresses and draft legislation and of the conduct of debate.

On 15 July 1887 the pretended Parliament chose the militant Henry Hyde Champion as prime minister, with scholarly Sidney Webb as chancellor of the exchequer. The notorious advocate of free love and birth control, Annie Besant, became home secretary; the womanizing Hubert Bland was foreign secretary; the schoolmasterly Graham Wallas was president of the Board of Trade; and Bernard Shaw was president of the Local Government Board. Since the real Parliament was traditionally opened by an address from the throne, Shaw drafted a "Queen's Speech," which Annie Besant then published in her magazine *Our Corner* in August 1887. In effect it was the first long speech that Shaw, the playwright-to-be, had drafted for a female character.

In her *Autobiography* Mrs. Besant recalled that the mock Parliament "debated with much vigour the 'burning questions' of the day. We organized a compact Socialist party, defeated a Liberal Government, took the reins of office, and—after a Queen's speech in which Her Majesty addressed her loyal Commons with a plainness of speech never before (or after) heard from the throne—we brought in several Bills of a decidedly heroic character. G. Bernard Shaw . . . and I . . . came in for a good deal of criticism in connection with various drastic measures."

Annie Besant was wrong about the Queen's plainspokenness. Victoria in her own person used a directness of speech that Shaw could adopt without artificiality. She minced no words, not even with her prime ministers, once telling one of them that his putting off decisions "in the vain *hope* that matters will mend" was irresponsible, and when he pointed to the need for economies in the midst of a colonial war, she snapped, "This appears hardly the moment to make savings on the Army [budget] estimates." What was different about the words which Shaw gave her was the content. What Shaw gave her to say was nothing she did not know; they would have disagreed only about the solutions. "I have summoned you," the Shavian Victoria told her Parliament, her royal *We* having escaped Shaw,

> to meet in this, the Jubilee year of my reign, for the transaction of business of great importance, unfortunately delayed these many years, and now become indispensable. The state of my nation is such as must fill the most hopeful with anxiety. Owing to the operation of economic conditions which no application of the existing law can thwart, the vast wealth produced daily by the labor of my people is now distributed not only unequally, but so inequitably that the contrast between the luxury of idle and unprofitable persons, and the poverty of the industrious masses, has become a scandal and reproach to our civilisation, setting class against class, and causing among the helpless and blameless infants of my most hardworking subjects a mortality disgraceful to me as head of the State, and unbearable to me as a woman and mother. And since this is in nowise due to any stint of the natural resources whereby my oppressed people may better themselves if you apply yourselves to their enfranchisement with due diligence and honesty, and without respect to persons; and since, too, every day of avoidable delay is a day of avoidable and unmerciful suffering to millions of innocent persons throughout the realm, there will forthwith be submitted to you a series of measures for the redress of their heavy and crying wrongs. And . . . I perceive that the main source of these wrongs has been the misdoing or neglect of those stewards to whom I and my predecessors gave the land that they might faithfully administer it for the welfare of the realm.

Shaw's Queen went on to enumerate an ambitious program of social legislation, from redistribution of land and conferring the franchise upon every adult man and woman in Britain, to the establishment of publicly owned utilities, free public education, a graduated income tax, and the abolition of all private charities in order to get at the causes of suffering rather than the symptoms that charities strove to alleviate. Further, the Speech promised the elimination of religious oaths, reduction of waste in government departments, a review of the salaries of Cabinet officials, and self-rule for Ireland. Only Justice, she concluded, was the "safeguard of order, prosperity, and stability."[5]

Shaw's Victoria, unlike the aloof real one, was an ideal queen, a Platonic philosopher sovereign; and in years to come he would create several monarchs in that image—Caesar, Charles II, and the invented King Magnus of a futuristic Britain among them. Using Victoria herself would have been impossible since the censorship laws forbade dramatizing the life of a reigning monarch or of one whose near kin were alive. He could only comment upon her in print, as he did again in 1888, the next year, in reviewing what he called "a colossal statue of the Queen," outsized, but without "deception"—the likeness was "faithful and characteristic."[6] When the likenesses were not, he would complain about the misrepresentation.

Although Victoria's Jubilee was the occasion for national self-examination as well as pride, Socialists largely took the former route. One of Shaw's friends, J. F. Oakeshott, a government employee at the Public Record Office, used the occasion of the fiftieth anniversary of the Penny Post—the first nationwide postal system—to write an anti-Victoria diatribe. He offered it to *Truth*. The proprietor, Henry Labouchere, a Radical M.P., was one of the noisiest anti-monarchists in the realm.

Before taking it to Labouchere, Oakeshott showed it to Shaw, who declared that it was unprintable and offered to improve it. Oakeshott had represented the anniversary in the guise of a translation of rediscovered Egyptian hieroglyphics that suggested strong parallels of past with present. Shaw turned the language of the satire into a pastiche of King James Bible prose-poetry. Victoria, one learns, becomes a patron of the postal celebration as "her heart was stirred within her; for she said, 'For three whole years have I not had a Jubilee.'" The executives of the Post Office had mingled with the socially prominent at a "conversazione" in the South Kensington Museum on 2 July 1890 while the workers themselves, who already had made the bureaucracy legendary in its efficiency, were uninvited—in Shaw's version, "They of Tag and Rag that had been cast out were utterly forgotten; so that they were fain to cry aloud, saying 'How long, O ye honest and upright in heart, shall Snobs and Nobs be rulers over us, seeing that they are but men like unto us, though they imagine us in their heads to be otherwise?'"[7]

Every appearance of the venerable Queen was now a jubilee of some sort, but Shaw was not involved again until 1893, when Victoria officially opened the Imperial Institute, a sprawling monument to the Empire on the South Kensington site informally known as Albertopolis, the burgeoning realization of Albert's dream of a huge cultural and educational complex in South Kensington. *The Star* assigned three reporters to cover the events both inside and outside the Institute with the intention, as an afternoon newspaper, to publish its accounts the same day. Whether Shaw did it for the money, which was not much—only thirty shillings—or was genuinely curious is unknown. His diary for 10 May 1893 only notes that he was to be inside the hall by 11:45 for the ceremonies that were to begin at noon.

As he walked to the Institute from his Fitzroy Square flat he could see the crowds gathering. Londoners had flocked to Buckingham Palace by early morning and filled the broad streets of South Kensington, parting only for the royal procession. "Horsetralian Lancers" and a column of sailors from the *Excellent* appeared early in the parade, and Her Majesty's six cream-colored horses, with their colorful trappings, drew the royal coach near the end of the progress. *The Star* man alongside had the most sensational news to report: the Queen's veil fell off as her carriage rumbled along, exposing Victoria's "cheerful healthy countenance." (It seemed a fulfillment of Shaw's prediction about the Queen's bonnet far back in 1886.) Outside the Institute another reporter took up the narrative, and when Victoria entered at noon to inaugurate the enterprise for which she had laid the first stone during her 1887 Jubilee, the music critic for *The World*—once, as Corno di Bassetto, the critic for *The Star*—took up one of the few news reporting jobs of his writing life.

The anonymously written "Inside Ceremony" had the characteristic Dickensian resonances and musical allusions that marked it unmistakably as Shaw's. He was also unmistakably in the palm of Victoria's hand. The Queen's poise as the principal actress on the national stage, and her bell-like voice—which he admired and recalled all his life—caused most of his Socialist antipathy to thrones to vanish. In part, one can assume that Shaw was writing in the warm, gently satirical tone called for by his editor so that the three reports would be consistent in approach to people and events. Yet he was also consistent with what he would say elsewhere and often.

To Shaw, the Queen was, in her active post-Jubilee years when she symbolized England, the best actress in the realm despite her age and frailty. As she was helped up the steps to the stage by her sons Bertie and Alfred, the band playing "God Save the Queen," Shaw wrote, giving his sentiments away beneath the irony, "Everyone is affected: the *Star* man WEEPS WITH LOYALTY."

The portly Prince of Wales, Shaw observed, had little "artistic turn for the platform. . . . When he was done, the Queen, seated, shows him the proper way to do it. There is not an actress on the English stage who could have done it better—tone, style, all are of the best. The *Star* man's artistic instincts get the better of him; he feels that it is a pity that so able an artist should be wasted on a throne." A gold key is presented to the Queen, who examines it dubiously, then turns a lock that electrically sets bells ringing, and a royal salute follows from the artillery in the Park. "Finally the Queen, using her walking stick a little, is helped down the steps by the Prince, [who is] President of the Institute, and [Prince Alfred,] the Duke of Edinburgh. The moment she reaches level ground she starts gaily off to shake hands with the Indian princes, like the Honorable Samuel Slumkey at the Eatanswill election.[8] A wave of bobbing, curtseying and salaaming passes down the banks as she flows through them; the Court scampers off the platform and closes up in her wake; the band plays the March from 'Le Prophète,' and the *Star* man vanishes from the hall and is at Stonecutter St. before the Queen is half-way to the main entrance on her way home."[9]

While typesetters were working on Shaw's report, which he had written in the hall as things happened, he went to a vegetarian restaurant nearby, the Central, and lunched. Then he returned to the *Star* to correct his proofs and walked home.

Eventually there would be an end even to Victorian jubilees, but not until 1897 had passed, and with it the Queen's sixtieth anniversary on the throne. No legal or journalistic compulsion forced Shaw's hand, and he chose the unlikeliest of events as his excuse, but again he found a way to write about Victoria, using the springboard of a *Saturday Review* drama column on a production of Ibsen's most vilified play, *Ghosts*. "The Jubilee and Ibsen's *Ghosts*!" he began his 3 July 1897 column:

> On the one hand the Queen and the Archbishop of Canterbury: on the other, Mrs Alving and Pastor Manders. Stupendous contrast! how far reflected in the private consciousness of those two august persons there is no means of ascertaining. For though of all the millions for the nourishment of whose loyalty the Queen must submit to be carried through the streets from time to time, not a man but is firmly persuaded that her opinions and convictions are exact facsimiles of his own, none the less she, having seen much of men and affairs, may quite possibly be a wise woman and worthy successor of Canute, and no mere butt for impertinent and senseless Jubilee odes such as their perpetrators dare not, for fear of intolerable domestic scorn and ridicule, address to their own wives or mothers.

"I am myself cut off by my profession from Jubilee," he lied, "for loyalty
in a critic is corruption. But if I am to avoid idolizing kings and queens in
the ordinary human way, I must carefully realize them as fellow-creatures."[10]
And so, while the nation was saluting Victoria at a naval review at Spithead,
he told his readers, he was wondering, returning home from a performance
of *Ghosts*, whether the Queen had been confronted at any stage in her life
with the stark lessons imposed upon Ibsen's Mrs. Alving. Both had grown
up in the early nineteenth century, he explained, and Mrs. Alving, an
intelligent and principled woman, had learned that life was corrupted not so
much by the vices she was taught in her youth to reject, "but by the virtues
it was her pride and uprightness to maintain."

"Suppose then," he asked,

> the Queen were to turn upon us in the midst of our jubilation, and
> say, "My Lords and Gentlemen: You have been good enough to
> describe at great length the changes made during the last sixty years
> in science, art, politics, dress, sport, locomotion, newspapers, and
> everything else that men chatter about. But you have not a word to
> say about the change that comes home most closely to me? I mean
> the change in the number, the character, and the intensity of the
> lies a woman must either believe or pretend to believe before she can
> graduate in polite society as a well-brought-up lady." If Her Majesty
> could be persuaded to give a list of these lies, what a document it
> would be! Think of the young lady of seventy years ago, systemati-
> cally and piously lied to by parents, governesses, clergymen, servants,
> everybody; and slapped, sent to bed, or locked up in the bedevilled
> and beghosted dark at every rebellion of her common sense and
> natural instinct against sham religion, sham propriety, sham decency,
> sham knowledge, and sham ignorance. Surely every shop-window
> picture of "the girl Queen" of 1837 must tempt the Queen of 1897
> to jump out of her carriage and write up under it, "Please remember
> that there is not a woman earning twenty-four shillings a week as a
> clerk today who is not ten times better educated than this unfortunate
> girl was when the crown dropped on her head, and left her to reign
> by her mother wit and the advice of a parcel of men who to this day
> have not sense enough to manage a Jubilee, let alone an Empire,
> without offending everybody." Depend on it, seventy-eight years
> cannot be lived through without finding out things that queens do
> not mention in Adelphi melodramas.

Ibsen's heroine learned from life, too, Shaw insisted, but her luck was worse. We had to "guard ourselves," he thought, "against the gratuitous, but just now very common, assumption that the Queen, in her garnered wisdom and sorrow, is as silly as the noisiest of her subjects, who see in their ideal Queen the polar opposite of Mrs. Alving, and who are so far right that the spirit of Ghosts is unquestionably the polar opposite of the spirit of the Jubilee. The Jubilee represents the nineteenth century proud of itself. Ghosts represents it loathing itself."*

When Shaw began *Caesar and Cleopatra* not long afterward he seems consciously to have written the play on two levels of time—the historical past and his own century. The young Cleopatra was sixteen in Shaw's rewriting of history. Eighteen in reality, she was as old as Victoria at her accession. And the most powerful man in Cleopatra's Egypt, Julius Caesar, was—in his early fifties—almost exactly the age of Victoria's first prime minister, Viscount Melbourne. Was Victoria in love with her mentor? Rumor had it so, perhaps because Victoria had yet no husband and was largely innocent of men, and Melbourne was handsome, devoted, and avuncular. In one of the Victorian reverberations of the play, an elderly courtier, Pothinus, accuses the young Cleopatra of having been altered by her intimacy with the attractive Roman. "Do you speak with Caesar every day for six months: and you will be changed," she says.

It is "common talk," he goes on, that she is infatuated "with this old man." If by "infatuated" one meant "made foolish," Cleopatra counters, it was not so:

CLEOPATRA: Now that Caesar has made me wise, it is no use my liking or disliking: I do what must be done. . . . That is not happiness; but it is greatness. If Caesar were gone, I think I could govern the Egyptians; for what Caesar is to me, I am to the fools around me.

POTHINUS: Is Cleopatra then indeed a Queen, and no longer Caesar's prisoner and slave? . . . Does he not love you?

---

*An irony unknown to Shaw was that after a command performance of Victorien Sardou's *Dora* (1877) in the English version, *Diplomacy* (1878), by B. C. Stephenson and Clement Scott, at Balmoral Castle in 1893, the Queen's impresario Alec Yorke suggested to Ibsen actress Elizabeth Robins that the next time she played before Victoria she could do Ibsen: "The play I'm most anxious to do is *Ghosts!*"

Marie (later Lady) Bancroft was horrified at the idea of exposing the Queen to Ibsen: "It's not a proper thing to do before Her Majesty." And it would not be done. (Elizabeth Robins, "A Close-Up View of Queen Victoria and the English Stage in 1893," typescript memoir, Fales Library, NYU.)

CLEOPATRA: Love me! Pothinus: Caesar loves no one. . . . His kindness to me is a wonder: neither mother, father, nor nurse have ever taken so much care of me, or thrown open their thoughts to me so freely.
POTHINUS: Well: is this not love? . . . I should have asked, then, do you love him?
CLEOPATRA: Can one love a god?[11]

Shaw's Caesar has Melbourne's mannerisms and vanities, his eagerness to instruct, and his tendency to coin cynical aphorisms. Shaw's Cleopatra has Victoria's youth, innocence, terrible temper, and ambition to be more than a figurehead. (Foreign-policy issues deliberately echo those of a later Victorian decade—the English 1870s.) Perhaps it was as closely as one could comment on the Victoria-Melbourne relationship in an age when the Lord Chamberlain's Office censored plays for their politics and their allusions to the sovereign.

To Victorian diarist Charles Greville, Clerk of the Privy Council, the relationship of Queen and prime minister was unhealthy because "while she . . . does everything that is civil to all the inmates of the Castle, she really has nothing to do with anybody but Melbourne, and with him she passes (if not in tête-à-tête, yet in intimate conversation) more hours than any two people, in any relation of life, perhaps ever do pass together. . . . He is at her side for at least six hours every day—an hour in the morning, two on horseback [in midafternoon], one at dinner, and two in the evening."[12] Such a "monopoly" of her time was injudicious and inconsistent with social usage. "But it is more peculiarly inexpedient with reference to her own future, . . . for if Melbourne should be compelled to resign, her privation will be all the more bitter on account of the exclusiveness of her intimacy with him." In fact, Victoria would later thrive in her independence from Melbourne, while Shaw has Cleopatra—hardly a constitutional queen—plot to rid herself of external impediments to personal rule, Caesar among them.

For Cleopatra, both impediment and accomplice are joined in the person of a devoted slave who is paradoxically her most powerful courtier. In *Caesar and Cleopatra* there is a grim drama in the duel between Caesar and the Queen's lifelong nurse and servant Ftatateeta, a formidable foe whose life only has meaning, and is fully used up, in loyalty to Cleopatra. Again there are Victorian resonances since the character is not historical, but only a Shavian invention, and Victoria had an imperious and utterly devoted personal nurse and servant, Louise Lehzen. The Baroness Lehzen would do, and did, anything for Victoria—at least until Victoria married Albert and he contended with Lehzen for power. Coming to the throne when barely eighteen, Victoria, in her inexperience, had depended upon Lehzen, who acquired a proliferation of duties and responsibilities in the Royal Household. As London gossip knew, Lehzen had a bedroom in Buckingham Palace next to Victoria's, with an entrance cut through the wall at the young Queen's direction in the summer of her accession. As Greville remarked in his diary (published, to Victoria's indignation, in Disraeli's time), when any of the Queen's Ministers came to see her, "the Baroness (Lehzen) retires at one door as they enter at the other, and the audience over she returns to the Queen."

Prince Albert's term for the Baroness was "the House Dragon." Like the dragoness Ftatateeta, Lehzen had to be eliminated, as Prince Albert realized. His contention with Lehzen, with the hasty and passionate Victoria caught between them, emerged quickly into public knowledge. By Shaw's time, when Victoria was an old woman, it was already remote history.

Even Caesar's tendering the island of Cyprus to the boy king Ptolemy as a sop to compensate for the loss of Egypt to Cleopatra is a Victorian reference. Impatiently, the boy's adviser, Pothinus, dismisses the offer with the complaint, "Cyprus is no good to anybody."

"No matter," says Caesar. "You shall have it for the sake of peace."

And Caesar's English slave Britannus (another Shavian unhistorical invention) adds, *"unconsciously anticipating a later statesman,"* Shaw notes in his stage directions, "Peace with honor, Pothinus."

Shaw's "later statesman" was Victoria's favorite prime minister, Disraeli, credited with the remark by people who had not realized that he was quoting a predecessor, Lord John Russell. Shaw, as his stage directions made clear, was again deliberately recalling the Victorian age. The Victorian empire in its sunset years was Shaw's aging Roman Empire, as we see again in the closing scene, where Shaw once more recalled his stint in the late 1880s and early 1890s as an art critic. It was not the heyday of English art. Just as its best drama was being produced by Irishmen, its best visual art was being imported from France and Italy or created by expatriate Americans. "I leave the art of Egypt in your charge," says the departing Caesar to Cleopatra's art dealer, Apollodorus. "Remember: Rome loves art and will encourage it ungrudgingly."

"I understand, Caesar," says Apollodorus in lines suggesting late-Victorian England. "Rome will produce no art itself, but it will buy up and take away whatever the other nations produce."

"What!" Caesar exclaims, "Rome produce no art! Is peace not an art? Is

Fig. 2. "New Crowns for Old Ones!" *Punch*, 15 April 1876.
Quoting from "Alladin," Disraeli offers Victoria the title he had
pushed through Parliament for her, Empress of India.

war not an art? Is government not an art? Is civilization not an art? All these
we give you in exchange for a few ornaments. You will have the best of the
bargain." In places a "Victoria and Melbourne," "Victoria and Albert," or
"Victoria and Disraeli," *Caesar and Cleopatra* is more than Shaw's look
back at Rome.

     In the last scene, Cleopatra appears suddenly at Caesar's leave-taking,
"cold and tragic, cunningly dressed in black, without ornaments or decoration of any kind, and thus making a striking figure among the brilliantly
dressed bevy of ladies as she passes. . . ." The Queen is in ostensible
mourning for the loyal Ftatateeta, but if Shaw were playing his dramatized
history lesson on two levels she may also have been representing the English

queen who dressed resolutely in black for the thirty-nine years she lived after Albert's death, well aware of the distinctive impression she would make among the fashionable dresses of aristocratic women and the brilliant court dress and uniforms of the men about her. In later years, Victoria loaded her mourning garb with jewels and diamonds, but Shaw would have known better than to make his parallel too obvious. Subliminal in places, mockingly direct in others, his teasing look at the Victorian age still fascinates.

The writing of *Caesar and Cleopatra* preceded only by months the beginning of the Boer War, and the play seemed art anticipating history in that a great power found itself bogged down and suffering military embarrassments in a colonial enterprise very far from home. Unlike most of his Fabian friends, Shaw refused to support the underdog, viewing "Oom Paul" Kruger's Afrikaners as uncivilized fundamentalist throwbacks. Further, Shaw, always quick to applaud decisive leadership where he thought he saw it, perceived in Victoria, now past eighty, an active symbol of determination to win. Although the Queen threw her weight about in order to get the inept bureaucracy moving, Shaw later offered her more credit than was her due, given her constitutional limitations, in observing, in 1915, "It was fresh in my recollection that in the South African War we were both disgraced in the field and swindled in the Commissariat until Queen Victoria, in desperation, insisted on sending out Lord Roberts and getting rid of the worn-out and hopeless incapables whom the mob were cheering as madly as if they had been so many Nelsons and Napoleons."[13] The Queen could not insist, but she had belabored the sluggish War Office into sending Roberts, who had been stationed uselessly in Ireland.

In the gloom of "Black Week" in December 1899, when the war was going badly, Victoria had told the despondent Lord Balfour, whom Shaw knew, "Please understand, there is no one depressed in this house; we are not interested in the possibilities of defeat; they do not exist." A few months later, when she made a progress through London to rally her people, Shaw was offended at what he interpreted as listless crowd behavior. "The Queen has just passed," he wrote to Charles Charrington in March 1900. "A street full of rampant Fenians would have cheered her more heartily, if only out of . . . sentiment towards an old woman. These patriots have no guts in their bawling."[14]

In an even earlier play than *Caesar*, Shaw observed later, pleased with himself, he had anticipated Victoria. For Christmas 1899 the Queen had sought a symbolic present to send to her troops in the field as something special from her. Soon, ships were bringing every soldier in the field a flat

tin box of chocolates with the Queen's head embossed on the lid, a profile
that Kipling pictured as her troops might have:

> 'Ave you 'eard of the Widow of Windsor
>   With a hairy gold crown on 'er 'ead?
> She 'as ships on the foam—she 'as millions at 'ome,
>   An' she pays us poor beggars in red.

Every soldier in South Africa and in transports on the high seas was to
receive such a box, bound in red, white, and blue ribbon, and had to sign a
receipt for it. A hundred thousand slabs of chocolate went south, and
legends grew about their efficacy. Some soldiers would not touch a morsel,
determined to take the sacred gifts home. Sean O'Casey's brother Tom
returned to Dublin, "the Queen's coloured box of chocolate in his kit-bag
still full of the sweetmeat, for what soldier could eat chocolate given by
a Queen?"[15]

More than one box was reputed to have stopped a bullet. An authentic
example was sent to the Queen by the medical officer treating Private James
Humphrey of the Royal Lancasters on 28 February 1900. The forwarding
note from the military hospital at Frere explained that the box had been in
the soldier's haversack. The bullet had gone through it and lodged in the
chocolate rather than in Private Humphrey's spleen. Victoria's Private
Secretary suggested that the Queen "would doubtless wish another box be
sent to Private Humphrey."

The gift was highly prized—a rare if not unique contact, the troops felt,
with Her Majesty. Men refused £5—two months' pay for a private soldier—
for the Queen's chocolate. On visits to hospitals, Victoria carried additional
tin boxes, and one legless soldier declared gallantly, "I would rather lose a
limb than not get that!" Widows and bereaved mothers were often sent the
boxes together with the personal effects of a soldier buried far from home.

Shaw's *Arms and the Man* (1894), later musicalized by Oscar Straus
without Shaw's permission as *The Chocolate Soldier,* includes an early scene
in which Captain Bluntschli confides that where other troops have kept
cartridges, he had secreted supplies more valuable to a soldier—chocolate.
For that and other reasons, Shaw explained to his German translator,
Siegfried Trebitsch, in 1905, "the play was received, except by a few people,
as an *opera bouffe* without music. The notion that soldiers ate chocolate was
taken as a silly joke, and it was not until the South African War reminded

the English of what war was really like, and Queen Victoria presented all the troops with boxes of chocolate, that *Arms and the Man* was justified."[16]

When Victoria died in January 1901, Shaw was indignant at the extended obsequies, during which the Queen's tiny, withered body lay in state for a fortnight before the lengthy funeral in London and burial at Windsor. Always hostile to what he called the grotesque mummeries of traditional funerals, and particularly unhappy at what he perceived as the maltreatment of the dead Queen, he wrote a letter to the editor of the *Morning Leader*.

Sir

I am loth to interrupt the rapture of mourning in which the nation is now enjoying its favorite festival—a funeral. But in a country like ours a total suspension of common sense and sincere human feeling for a whole fortnight is an impossibility. There are certain points in connection with the obsequies of Queen Victoria which call for vigorous remonstrance.

Why, may I ask, should the procedure in the case of a deceased sovereign be that which has long been condemned and discarded by all intelligent and educated persons as insanitary and superstitious? To delay a burial for a fortnight, to hermetically seal up the remains in a leaden coffin (and those who are behind the scenes at our cemeteries know well what will happen to that leaden coffin), is to exhibit a spectacle, not of reverent mourning, but of intolerable ignorance perpetuated by court tradition long after it has been swept away in more enlightened quarters. The remains of the Queen should have been either cremated or buried at once in a perishable coffin in a very shallow grave. The example set by such a course would have been socially invaluable. The example set by the present procedure is socially deplorable.

If at such a moment the royal family, instead of making each other Field Marshals, and emphasizing every foolish unreality and insincerity that makes court life contemptible, were to seize the opportunity to bring its customs into some sort of decent harmony with modern civilization, they would make loyalty much easier for twentieth century Englishmen. (*Collected Letters 1898–1910*, pp. 216–17)

Shaw was using Victoria's obsequies less to protest the insensitivities toward her person than to wage war on outmoded rites and practices, and

Ernest Parke, proprietor of the *Morning Leader* and an old friend of Shaw's, understood and politely declined the letter, declaring, "I am not anxious to run counter to [public] loyalty in its most solemn expression." Then writing *Man and Superman*, Shaw would put into the Devil's major speech in the "Don Juan in Hell" play-within-the-play a lengthy denunciation of the English love of funerals. "Their imagination glows, their energies rise up at the idea of death; these people: they love it."

Victoria in death remained as important to Shaw as in life. However exasperated he may have been at her regressive concepts about government and society, he remained full of admiration for her person. When a selection of her letters through 1861 was published in 1907, Shaw quickly acquired the three volumes, writing to a young actress, Frances Dillon, who was to play Ann Whitefield in *Man and Superman* on tour, that a study of the late Queen's letters would teach her how to remain ladylike yet dominate men, and how to remain majestically in mourning yet do what she pleased. "I strongly advise you," he wrote to her on 21 November 1908,

> to read the letters of Queen Victoria through from beginning to end. Then try to imagine yourself Queen Victoria every night in the 1st Act. You will notice that Queen Victoria, even when she was most infatuatedly in love with Prince Albert, always addressed him exactly as if he were a little boy of three and she his governess. That is the particular kind of English ladylikeness in which you are deplorably deficient. An English lady in mourning is a majestic and awful spectacle. No matter how improperly she may behave, an English lady never admits she is behaving improperly. Just as there are lots of women who are good-hearted and honest and innocent in an outrageously rowdy way, so are there ladies who do the most shocking things with a dignity and gentility which a bishop might envy. Ann is one of the latter sort; and this is what you have not got in Ann. Ann's dignity, her self-control, her beautifully measured speed, her impressive grief for her father, which absolutely forbids her to smile until she is out of mourning, a sort of rich, caste, noble self-respect about her which makes you feel that she belongs to carriage folk and is probably very highly connected, must be splendidly and very firmly handled on the stage in order to give effect to her audacity. (*Collected Letters 1898–1910*, p. 817)

Shaw had written *Man and Superman* in the years just after Victoria's death, and one can see in his Ann Whitefield and in her mythic incarnation

Doña Ana the shrewd utilization of mourning to achieve strategic ends. Like Victoria, Doña Ana wears mourning all her life and reveres a statue of the deceased she has had erected (the Queen, of course, had Albert statues erected wholesale around England).

The "carriage-folk audacity" that Shaw put into his Ann Whitefield went as well into his mourning widow of a few years later, Jennifer Dubedat of *The Doctor's Dilemma*, and is also given to the upstart heroine of *Pygmalion*. In lines added for the film, Shaw has Eliza Doolittle exclaim to Professor Higgins after the ball at which she has triumphed, "I don't think I can bear much more. The people all stare so at me. An old lady has told me that I speak exactly like Queen Victoria. I am sorry if I have lost your bet. I have done my best; but nothing can make me the same as these people."

"You have not lost it, my dear," Colonel Pickering assures her, understanding the phenomenon of her superiority. "You have won it ten times over."

Shaw emphasized the point to the actress Dorothy Dix in 1914, when he coached her in the role for a touring company. Eliza should not, he warned, produce "the effect of giving herself airs by imitating a lady badly. She is not imitating at all: she is pronouncing as Higgins has taught her; and his Miltonic taste must be assumed to be first rate. And she must be very much in earnest. . . . Play it as if you were reciting Shakespeare for a prize in fine diction—classical English, like Queen Victoria's (she spoke extremely well)—not smart drawingroom English."[17]

Victoria's voice rang through Shaw's memory all his life. When, in the infancy of radio, he advised Cecil Lewis, a BBC producer, on broadcasting "the invisible play," he pointed out how the medium might use effectively talents robbed by age from the live theater. "Many actors and actresses who have lost their place on the stage through losing their youth, their good looks, and their memory, could do admirable work for broadcasting. Queen Victoria had a beautiful voice and first rate delivery at an age when she could not have played any part on the stage presentably except the nurse in *Romeo and Juliet*" (*Collected Letters 1911–1925*, p. 881).

But Victoria remained, to Shaw, more than a voice. She was, in his view, a dominating personality who made use of character as compensation for her miseducation. For *Back to Methuselah*, written in the last years of a war that proved how little men had learned about governing themselves, Shaw composed a post–World War I conversation between a philosophical writer and two politicians. H. H. Lubin, the ex-prime minister, is a thinly veiled caricature of H. H. Asquith, who took England into the war in 1914; Joyce

Fig. 3. Her Majesty the Queen Empress Victoria on the promenade at Cimiez on the Riviera. A "Guth" drawing for the Diamond Jubilee number of *Vanity Fair*, 17 June 1897.

Burge, his successor, is an equally unconcealed Lloyd George, who finished out the war at Downing Street. "Have you read the recent political autobiographies?" Franklyn Barnabas asks, those which reveal the true inside workings of the Victorian England they inherited.

LUBIN. I did not discover any new truth revealed. . . .
BARNABAS. What! Not the truth that England was governed all that time by a little woman who knew her own mind?

. . . .

LUBIN. That often happens. Which woman do you mean?
BARNABAS. Queen Victoria, to whom your Prime Ministers stood in the relation of naughty children whose heads she knocked together when their tempers and quarrels became intolerable. Within thirteen years of her death Europe became a hell.
BURGE. Quite true. That was because she was piously brought up, and regarded herself as an instrument. If a statesman remembers that he is only an instrument, and feels quite sure that he is rightly interpreting the divine purpose, he will come out all right, you know.
BARNABAS. The Kaiser felt like that. Did he come out all right?

Even then, in the reflection of Shaw's sardonic mirror, Victoria appears as an enduring reproach to the character and quality of the statesmanship that came after her, and even to much of it that she endured in her own time.

Almost certainly thinking of Victoria, Shaw had written to Sylvia Brooke, the Ranee of Sarawak (wife of the "White Rajah"), in 1913, "Women make the best sovereigns. The Salic law is a mistake: it should be the other way about. Constitutional monarchy is not a man's job: it is a woman's. The relation of a king to his ministers is intolerable: the relation of a queen to them is much better."[18] But that Victoria, raised as she was, could bring it off was to him a triumph of character. As he put it in *The Intelligent Woman's Guide*, his political handbook of the late 1920s, "Nowadays a parlormaid as ignorant as Queen Victoria was when she came to the throne would be classed as mentally defective." Yet, he added, "Queen Victoria managed to get on very well in spite of her ignorance" because "civilized life and highly civilized life are different: what is enough for one is not enough for the other." Later in the book he noted the limits of her pragmatism. For example, "Queen Victoria shewed her practical common sense when she said that she would not give a title to anyone who had not money enough to keep it up; but the result was that the titles went to the richest, not to the best."[19]

Two years later, in his 1930 preface to his prophetic political play *The Apple Cart*, he observed how Victoria's combination of keenness of mind and continuity of office sometimes made it possible to prevail over her constitutional limitations and her elected officials: "George the Third and Queen Victoria were not, like Queen Elizabeth, the natural superiors of their ministers in political genius and general capacity; but they were for many purposes of State necessarily superior to them in experience, in cunning, in exact knowledge of the limits of their responsibility and consequently of the limits of their irresponsibility: in short, in the authority and practical power that these superiorities produce."

The play itself borrowed a lesson from Victoria. Shaw explained his device a decade later, after an authentic abdication had rocked Britain. In *The Apple Cart*, a king brings about the resolution by threatening to abdicate. "And note well . . . how natural and reasonable and probable the [action in the] play is, and how improbable, fantastic, and outrageous the actual event was. There was not a single circumstance of it which I should have dared to invent. If you could raise Macaulay or Disraeli from the dead to see *The Apple Cart* just to ask him 'Could this thing actually happen?' he would have replied 'Oh, quite probably. Queen Elizabeth threatened to abdicate; and Queen Victoria used to hint at it once a week or so.'" She would abdicate, Victoria once told her Private Secretary, Henry Ponsonby, who was her conduit to Gladstone, "rather than send for or have any *communication* with that *half-mad* firebrand who wd soon ruin everything & be a *Dictator*. Others but herself may submit to his democratic rule, but *not the Queen*."

Particularly when trying to get her way with Gladstone, Victoria would threaten to step down in favor of Bertie, the aging playboy Prince of Wales. It was a consummation which even the prime minister hoped devoutly would be delayed. Gladstone had often urged the Queen to offer the portly prince more to do, in order to learn the job that would inevitably be his, but only the extreme radicals in his party pressed for the Queen's exit. "If only our dear Bertie was fit to replace me!" Victoria would confide. Shaw's King Magnus offers to abdicate in favor of his son Robert, Prince of Wales. "He will make an admirable constitutional monarch," Magnus explains. "I have never been able to induce him to take any interest in parliamentary politics."

A Cabinet Minister agrees. "Personally I get on very well with the Prince;

but somehow I do not feel that he is interested in what I am doing." And the other Ministers agree that the King's good sense and interest in government, even when they disagree with him, are preferable to the unpredictability of Prince Robert. A very different monarch and princely successor in a very different time, the royal pair in *The Apple Cart* are nevertheless a Shavian tribute to a stratagem by which Victoria attempted to stretch her waning powers as sovereign.

Dignified good sense was something Shaw associated with Victoria both seriously and in fun, his kind of fun represented by lines an outraged bishop would sputter in the 1938 play of European politics, *Geneva*. His grandson at Oxford, he moans, has joined a "Communist club." And his granddaughter has become a nudist. "I was graciously allowed to introduce my daughters to good Queen Victoria. If she could see my granddaughter she would call the police." On the other hand, Shaw would have been glad to call in the police to remove the art that continued to clothe Victoria in the ungainly regalia and poses of royalist pomp and respectability. In 1919, when the *Arts Gazette* asked readers to identify the ugliest statue in London, Shaw was quick to respond that there was no single candidate for the dubious honor, yet he perceived a single subject. "As an old Victorian," he wondered

> what crime Queen Victoria committed that she should be so horribly guyed as she has been through the length and breadth of her dominions. It was part of her personal quality that she was a tiny woman, and our national passion for telling lies on every public subject has led to her being represented as an overgrown monster. The sculptors seem to have assumed that she inspired everything that was ugliest in the feminine fiction of her reign. Take Mrs. Caudle, Mrs. Gamp, Mrs. Prig, Mrs. Proudie, and make a composite statue of them, and you will have a typical memorial of Queen Victoria. Now if this were a bold republican realism which disdained courtly sycophancy, it would be at least courageous, if unkind. But it is pure plastic calumny. Queen Victoria was a little woman with great decision of manner and a beautiful speaking voice which she used in public extremely well. She carried herself very well. All young people now believe that she was a huge heap of a woman. . . . How could they think anything else, with a statue at every corner shrieking these libels at them? The equestrian statue in Liverpool is the only one that is not an act of high treason, and even it makes her commonplace in size.[20]

Just as the ugly statues were "lying reproaches," so the aging Shaw felt were the outmoded perceptions of the Queen. In a Socialist lecture in 1918 he suggested that the spread of public education had so standardized British attitudes, from the nursery to the dinner table, from the pulpit to the jury box, that "Even Queen Victoria is now too liberal for us."[21] The reason? Victoria remained to him the prime example of the successfully self-educated person. The experience gave her, he thought, advantages not only over most formally educated people, but particularly over her university-educated Parliamentarians and Prime Ministers. To the later Shaw, she could do little wrong. He recalled in 1913 and again in 1930 that she had "stood up valiantly for Wagner when the Philharmonic Society, in a moment of madness, engaged him as conductor for a season; but she could [not] save him from the wrath of the critics and the professional musicians."[22] Again she was the inspired, self-educated Shavian amateur. Like Shaw himself, we might infer.

In 1937, in the post-Strachey period—a time, as Shaw put it, "when the writings of Sigmund Freud had made psychopathy grotesquely fashionable"—"Everybody was expected to have a secret history unfit for publication except in the consulting rooms of the psychoanalyst. If it had been announced that among the papers of Queen Victoria a diary had been found revealing that her severe respectability masked the daydreams of a Messalina, it would have been received with eager credulity."[23] But not by Shaw. Even in 1940, discussing London hotels with his German translator, when Shaw suggested two comfortable establishments that were not "smart," Victoria was his touchstone. "Smartness," he went on to explain, "was not considered respectable by the old Queen" (*Letters to Trebitsch*, p. 394).

Well into his ninth decade, he felt no need to explain who "the old Queen" was. He may have claimed all his days to be an unreconstructed Marxist, but he knew the truth of the matter was that he was really, as he had confessed on occasion himself, "an old Victorian."[24]

Notes

1. *Cashel Byron's Profession* (London: Modern Press, 1886), ch. 7.

2. Shaw, "The Year of Jubilee," anonymous rev. of A. H. Wall's *Fifty Years of a Good Queen's Reign*, in *Pall Mall Gazette* (16 November 1886), p. 6. Reprinted in Brian Tyson, ed., *Bernard Shaw's Book Reviews* from the *Pall Mall Gazette* (University Park: Pennsylvania State University Press, 1991), pp. 213–18.

3. Shaw, unsigned and untitled paragraph in the "What the World Says" column, *The World* (26 January 1887), p. 15.

4. Shaw, anonymous review, "Spring Picture Exhibitions," *The World* (23 March 1887), pp. 9–10. An engraving of the canvas now hangs in the Prince of Wales Hotel, Niagara-on-the-Lake, Ontario, Canada.

5. *Our Corner* 10 (August 1887): 125–27.

6. Shaw, unsigned and untitled paragraph in the "What the World Says" column, *The World* (10 October 1888), p. 17.

7. "A Curious Hieroglyphic," *Truth* 27 (10 July 1890): 68.

8. An allusion to *Pickwick Papers*.

9. "The Queen Shows Herself to Her Subjects in London and Gets Loyal Cheers" (unsigned report, part 3: "The Inside Ceremony"), *The Star* (10 May 1893), pp. 2–3.

10. Reprinted in *Our Theatres in the Nineties* (London: Constable, 1932), 3:177–78; and in Bernard F. Dukore, ed., *The Drama Observed* (University Park: Pennsylvania State University Press, 1993), 3:886–87.

11. Quotations from the play are from *The Bodley Head Bernard Shaw: Collected Plays with Their Prefaces*, vol. 2 (London: Max Reinhardt, 1973). Unless otherwise noted, all quotations from Shaw's plays are from this edition (7 vols.).

12. Quotations from Greville are from Weintraub, *Victoria, An Intimate Biography* (New York: Dutton, 1987), p. 104.

13. "The Need for Criticism," letter to the editor, *Everyman* (16 July 1915), p. 266.

14. In Bernard Shaw, *Collected Letters 1898–1910*, ed. Dan H. Laurence (London: Max Reinhardt, 1972), p. 152.

15. Sean O'Casey, *Drums under the Windows* (London: Macmillan, 1956), quoted in Weintraub, p. 609.

16. In Samuel A. Weiss, ed., *Bernard Shaw's Letters to Siegfried Trebitsch* (Stanford: Stanford University Press, 1986), p. 77.

17. In Bernard Shaw, *Collected Letters 1911–1925*, ed. Dan H. Laurence (London: Max Reinhardt, 1985), p. 248.

18. Shaw to Sylvia Brooke (identified only as "Sylvia"), 16 October 1913, in the Sotheby sale catalogue of 15 December 1986, item 79.

19. *The Intelligent Woman's Guide to Socialism and Capitalism* (New York: Brentano, 1928), p. 71.

20. "The Ugliest Statue in London," *Arts Gazette* (31 May 1919), p. 273.

21. "Socialism and Culture," in Louis Crompton, ed., *The Road to Equality* (Boston: Beacon Press, 1971), p. 293.

22. "A Neglected Moral of the Wagner Centenary" (orig. in *The New Statesman* [31 May 1913], unsigned); and "Old Men and New Music" (BL fragment, Add. Mss. 50662, ff. 5–10, ca. 1930), in Dan H. Laurence, ed., *Shaw's Music* (New York: Dodd, Mead, 1981), 3:643, 749.

23. "The Casement Documents," *Irish Press* (11 February 1937), reprinted in Dan H. Laurence and David Greene, eds., *The Matter with Ireland* (New York: Hill & Wang, 1962), p. 132.

24. "Ugliest Statue in London," *Arts Gazette*.

"THE HIBERNIAN SCHOOL"

Oscar Wilde and Bernard Shaw

When Oscar Wilde in May 1893 thanked Bernard Shaw "for Op[us] 2 of the great Celtic school," he was referring to a presentation copy of Shaw's first play, *Widowers' Houses*.[1] Wilde had already opened, to acclaim, what he labeled Opus 3, *A Woman of No Importance*, at the Haymarket Theatre. He called on Shaw for the Celtic School's Opus 4.

Earlier, in sending Shaw *Lady Windermere's Fan*, his first major play, Wilde had described the comedy as "Op. 1 of the Hibernian School." The joke was more than half in earnest since the two were the first Irish playwrights in decades to make a major impact upon the London theater. However different their personalities and lifestyles, their relationship was, and would continue to be, mutually useful.

Exempt from the Hibernian School, apparently, was Wilde's *Salomé*, which had been mailed to Shaw in February. Wilde had written *Salomé* in French for Sarah Bernhardt and then published an English translation of his biblical melodrama. Somehow, it seemed wrong to refer to it in Irish terms. By 28 February Shaw had not yet received it, explaining to Wilde, "Salome is still wandering in her purple raiment in search of me, and I expect her to arrive a perfect outcast, branded with inky stamps, bruised by flinging into red prison [Post Office] vans, stuffed and contaminated. . . . I hope to send you soon my play Widowers' Houses which you will find tolerably amusing."

That *Salomé* arrived soon after is obvious from the purple prose of Shaw's letter of 3 March to actress Janet Achurch, with whom he was infatuated. "I can write nothing beautiful enough for you. And I can no longer allow myself to be in love with you: nobody short of an archangel with purple and gold wings can henceforth be allowed to approach you."

By that time, Shaw had known Wilde for nearly fifteen years and had been aware of the family even longer. Oscar's father, Sir William Wilde, a Dublin ophthalmologist, had operated on Shaw's father to correct a squint, Shaw remembered, "and overdid the correction so much that my father squinted the other way all the rest of his life." To Frank Harris in 1916 Shaw recalled seeing the Wildes at a concert in Dublin. The goatish Sir William "was dressed in snuffy brown; and as he had the sort of skin that never looks clean, he produced a dramatic effect beside Lady Wilde (in full fig) of being, like Frederick the Great, Beyond Soap and Water, as his Nietzschean son was [later] beyond Good and Evil. [Sir William] was reported to have a [bastard] family in every farmhouse; and the wonder was that Lady Wilde didn't mind. . . ."[2]

"Speranza"—the name she used for her poetry—did mind, but in double-standard Victorian society she could do nothing about it. When Sir William died, however, leaving little more than his debts, Lady Wilde escaped to London, first to a too-expensive house at 116 Park Street off Grosvenor Square, then to 146 Oakley Street, Chelsea, near the Albert Bridge. At her Saturday and Wednesday afternoon salons, where the curtains were drawn early for the cosmetic effect of gloomy gaslight on Speranza's stoutness and wrinkles, Shaw came to know the family, probably through his sister Lucy, "then a very attractive girl who sang beautifully, [who] had met and made some sort of innocent conquest of both Oscar and [his brother] Willie."

Shaw's first visit to Lady Wilde's at-homes in Park Street was in November 1879, where he met Mrs. Lynn Linton, a veteran novelist. These were forlorn years for Shaw, then working briefly for the Edison Telephone Company and spending off-hours at the British Museum writing hopelessly unpublishable novels. For the good-hearted Lady Wilde, Shaw recalled to Harris, the at-homes were "desperate affairs," attempts to gain entrée into Society but failing, usually, to draw more than has-beens or young people, aspirants for whom she predicted, encouragingly, future fame. "I once dined with her in company with an ex-tragedy queen named Miss Glynn, who having no visible external ears, had a head like a turnip. Lady Wilde talked about Schopenhauer; and Miss Glynn told me that Gladstone formed his oratorical style on Charles Kean."

Shaw's first meeting with Oscar, a self-dramatizing, already mildly notorious literary man two years older than Shaw and sophisticated by Trinity College (Dublin) and Oxford, was awkward for the younger Irishman, a school dropout who had been nowhere. Wilde, Shaw remembered, "spoke to me with an evident intention of being specially kind. . . . We put each other out frightfully, and this odd difficulty persisted between us to the very last, even when we were no longer mere boyish novices and had become men of the world with plenty of skill in social intercourse. I saw him very seldom, as I avoided literary and artistic society like the plague, and refused the few invitations I received to go into society with burlesque ferocity, so as to keep out of it without offending people past their willingness to indulge me as a privileged lunatic." Shaw's diary through 1885 is marked with invitations to Lady Wilde's salons, many of which he avoided, even when it meant spending his after-five hours alone at home playing the piano.[3] The last reference to Lady Wilde's is 18 July 1885, when he met J. S. Stuart-Glennie, a historian and folklorist who would become a good friend. After that the invitations disappear, Speranza's interest in Shaw cooling as she perceived him more as socialist activist than as promising author. As a novice music critic, however, Shaw had already observed of a Bach Choir concert that the majestic *Mass in B Minor* "disappointed some people, precisely as the Atlantic Ocean disappointed Mr. Wilde" (*Dramatic Review*, 28 March 1885).

Shaw was already seeing Oscar elsewhere, although later he could recall to Frank Harris only six meetings and was certain that there were not many more. By the next year he was encountering Wilde at the homes of émigré Irish writers who were mutual friends. One was novelist Fitzgerald Molloy. At Molloy's, Shaw noted in his diary on 14 September 1886, Oscar Wilde and novelist Richard Dowling watched as a "chiromantist," Edward Heron Allen, "told my character by reading my hand very successfully." That the reading of Shaw's palm led to Wilde's story "Lord Arthur Savile's Crime," published in three parts in the *Court and Society Review* in May 1887, seems likely from Oscar's care in sending Heron Allen a copy of the numbers with a reference to "the chiromancy of the story."[4] No G.B.S., however, the demonic Sir Arthur Savile has his palm read by the fat, coarse Podgers, who finds a streak of blood in Savile's palm that embodies his sanguinary future as well as that of Podgers, who must be murdered if Sir Arthur is to purify the evil within himself. Shaw may exist in it only in the stature of the tall and attractive Savile. After the palm reading, according to Wilde, Shaw aired his idea of a new magazine that would proselytize for socialism across the breadth of Britain. Recognizing the unreality of the dream, Wilde interrupted and observed, so he recalled, "That has all been most interesting, Mr. Shaw, but there's one point you haven't mentioned, and an all-important one—you haven't told us the *title* of the magazine."

"Oh, as for that," Wilde quoted Shaw as replying, "what I would want to do would be to impress my own personality on the public—I'd call it *Shaw's Magazine*: Shaw—Shaw—Shaw!" He punctuated his enthusiasm by banging his recently read fist on the table.

"Yes," Wilde exclaimed, punning on *pshaw*, "and how would you spell it?"

At Molloy's on 4 October, with Oscar again present, there was more palm reading, a popular late-Victorian pastime. This time it was accomplished by MacGregor Mathers who, as an occultist, was interested in Molloy's novel *A Modern Magician*, then being written. (Shaw would review the book in the *Pall Mall Gazette* in December 1887.) Mathers, very likely a model for Molloy's hero, would become a great friend of Yeats who, upon seeing Mathers in the British Museum Reading Room "in a brown velveteen coat, with a gaunt resolute face, and an athletic body," thought this was how "might Faust have looked in his changeless aged youth."

Reviewing for the *Pall Mall Gazette* would be an occupation that Wilde and Shaw would have in common, but since Wilde was already a public personality, Shaw had the license to refer to him, as he had already done, in humorous asides in reviews. In the socialist *Our Corner* (February 1886), Shaw had done it again. Reporting a lecture by Edmund Russell, he had noted that Russell had worn "a colored silk neckcloth instead of the usual white tie," resulting in paragraphs comparing Russell with Oscar Wilde—not, Shaw noted, "the staid and responsible Oscar Wilde of to-day, but the youth whose favorite freak it was to encourage foolish people to identify him with the imaginary 'aesthete' invented [for *Punch*] by Mr. [George] du Maurier." By then, Yeats remembered, Wilde had coined an observation that even Shaw would quote, since it was impossible to forget— that "Bernard Shaw hasn't an enemy in the world; and none of his friends like him." It made Yeats feel "revenged upon a notorious hater of romance, whose generosity and courage I could not fathom."[5]

For several years, beginning in 1886, Wilde and Shaw would pass each other in the *Pall Mall Gazette* office, picking up review copies of new books or submitting copy for anonymous publication. Each reviewed three or four books a month, as did William Archer and George Moore. In a letter to *New Review* editor Tighe Hopkins, Shaw recalled their

> barbarous amusement of skinning minor poets alive . . . ; and an *auto da fé* took place once a month or so with a batch of them, the executioner being sometimes Oscar Wilde, sometimes William Archer, sometimes myself. As only our elementary vices were

Fig. 4. Oscar Wilde as drawn by "Ape" for *Vanity Fair*, 14 May 1884.

brought into play; and as the literary manifestations of these are much alike in all men at a couple of pounds a column, there was no saying, in the absence of signatures, which was the real torturer on these occasions; and to this day there are men who hate me for inhumanities perpetrated by Archer or Wilde. . . . The tendency of men to ascribe injuries to persons who know them led to each of us being credited, within his own circle of acquaintances, with the reviews of the whole three.

All the reviews "of a distinctly Irish quality during the 1885–1888 period," Shaw confessed to Dublin newspaperman David O'Donoghue, "may, I think, be set down to either me or to Oscar Wilde, whose reviews were sometimes credited to me. His work was exceptionally finished in style and very amusing."

One wonders how many readers of a review of W. E. Norris's novel, *My Friend Jim*, on 2 September 1886, could have guessed the identity of the critic who excoriated a "barbarism" at the end of the tale. "A whole railway train is wrecked to get rid of Lord Bracknell. This is burning down the house to roast the pig. Why should a number of innocent passengers be maimed, slain, or delayed in their travels merely to kill a man who might have been removed without any such sacrifice of life or rolling-stock?" Wilde would later appropriate the peer's surname in *The Importance of Being Earnest* for his Lady Bracknell, but the reviewer was Shaw.[6]

Certainly Fitzgerald Molloy might have wondered whether any of his Irish cronies in London had laid hands on a review copy of his novel, *A Modern Magician*, in 1887. Both Wilde and Shaw had been at his house when the talk was of occult matters. The critic in the *PMG* on 5 December 1887 characterized Molloy amusingly as "the Bobadil of fashionable mysticism." Molloy was "a pretentious bungler: his syntax is inconceivable, his dialogue impossible, his style a desperately careful expression of desperately slovenly thinking, his notions of practical affairs absurd, and his conception of science and philosophy a superstitious guess: yet he has an indescribable flourish, a dash of half-ridiculous poetry, a pathetic irresponsibility, a captivating gleam of Irish imagination. . . ." Molloy remained on speaking terms with Shaw, apparently guessing—erroneously—that his reviewer was Wilde.

By 1888 Shaw was no longer a guest at Lady Wilde's at-homes, but he owed her something. Oscar could not fairly review his mother's books, so Shaw took on the duty, writing a notice of *Ancient Legends of Ireland* that appeared on Shaw's thirty-second birthday, 26 July 1888. Had she known it was by Shaw, his invitations might have been renewed. She must have sensed a friendly mediator, someone who confessed to not affecting "impartiality" because Lady Wilde's "position, literary, social, and patriotic," was "unique and unassailable." The book could have been dull in another's hands, Shaw wrote anonymously, but "Lady Wilde can write scholarly English without pedantry and Irish-English without vulgarity or impracticable brogue phonetics. She has no difficulty in writing about leprechauns, phoukas [*sic*], and banshees, simply as an Irishwoman telling Irish stories, . . . with a nursery knowledge at first hand of all the characteristic moods of the Irish imagination. Probably no living writer could produce a better book of its kind."

Oscar could not have written those lines, but some writers reviewed in the *PMG* assumed unhappily from internal evidence that either Wilde or Shaw had made short work of them. That concern emerges in a letter from William Michael Rossetti to Dr. Frederick James Furnivall complaining to his sympathetic friend about the amusingly adverse *Pall Mall Gazette* review of Rossetti's biography of Keats. Dismissing the book as ponderous, ill-chosen verbiage, the critic had written, after citing chapter and verse, "There is no necessity to follow Mr. Rossetti further as he flounders about through the quagmire that he has made for his own feet." The entire notice was devastating. "As I understand it," the unhappy biographer confided to Furnivall, "Shaw is the writer of that critique: though I have more than once been told that notices . . . which I supposed to be by Shaw, are in fact by Oscar Wilde. Apart from seeing and hearing Shaw at the Shelley Society etc., I don't know him: but [I] shall be equally well pleased to encounter him hereafter, and hear what he has to say—which I always find clever and telling, and the reverse of commonplace."[7] The review was by Wilde.

Unkindness, as Yeats understood, was not characteristic of either Wilde or Shaw, and for Shaw what really established his friendly feelings toward a colleague accused of wielding a poisonous pen was the affair of the Chicago anarchists in 1887. The Haymarket Riots of the year before had led to death sentences for the imprisoned Radicals, whose guilt in the matter had been dubiously proved. "I tried to get some literary men in London, all heroic rebels and skeptics on paper, to sign a memorial asking for a reprieve of these unfortunate men," Shaw wrote. His diary notes on 6 November 1887 his failure to convince William Archer to sign, "which he did not care to do." Shaw tried other friends of liberal persuasion; all shied away. "The only signature I got was Wilde's. It was a completely disinterested act on his part; and it secured my distinguished consideration for him for the rest of his life."

On 17 November, Lucy Shaw was married, and although Shaw furnished the whisky and cake he did not turn up at the church in Fitzroy Square, going off instead to Willis's Rooms, where artist and critic Selwyn Image was lecturing, then returning to wedding "tea" at St. John's Church, "where," Shaw noted in his diary, "I had a talk with Wilde. . . ." Shaw thought that still another meeting with Oscar at about that time occurred in Fitzrovia, at the home of Scottish architect A. H. Mackmurdo, but the encounter, on 15 December, actually occurred at Herbert Horne's house. Horne edited the Century Guild's magazine, *The Hobby Horse*, with which Mackmurdo was associated. The talk was stimulating, and Shaw did not leave until one in the morning.

"A stream of visitors all the afternoon, mostly chatterboxes," Shaw wrote about another semi-social occasion. "Oscar Wilde was there." It was the first of June 1888, a Sunday, and Shaw was visiting Miss Charlotte Roche, in Cadogan Gardens, to be photographed. Hobbyist portrait photographers— "Lewis Carroll" had been one—were often very good, and Shaw knew Miss Roche through artist and typographer Emery Walker and musician Felix Moscheles. Although Wilde was deaf to music, he remained with Shaw while Natalie Janotha played a Chopin scherzo, and the conversation afterward was of art and—inevitably—how socialism would metamorphose it.

The talk when Shaw was present was often about how socialism would alter the way that art was created as well as how and by whom it was consumed. When illustrator Walter Crane spoke in July 1888 at the Fabian Society's monthly meeting at Willis's Rooms, and his subject was "The Prospects of Art under Socialism," the afternoon paper *The Star* reported on 7 July,

> Mr. Crane believed that art would revive under these new socialistic conditions. Mr. Oscar Wilde, whose fashionable coat differed widely from the picturesque bottle-green garb in which he appeared in earlier days, thought that the art of the future would clothe itself not in works of form and colour but in literature. . . . Mr. Herbert Burrows contended that the masses loved good art, a fact which Mr. George Bernard Shaw deplored, as he said it proved that the lower classes were following the insincere cant of the middle classes. Mr. Shaw agreed with Mr. Wilde that literature was the form which art would take, pronounced [John] Bunyan the tinker a supreme genius, and voted Beethoven rather vulgar, saying that if a middle-class audience were told that "Pop Goes the Weasel" was a movement from Beethoven's Ninth Symphony they would go into ecstasies over it.

Wilde and Shaw continued the discussion after the meeting broke up. "He parted from us," Shaw noted in his diary, "in St. James's Square, and the rest of us—Carr, Webb, and Wallas—walked together as far as the corner of Grafton St. in Tottenham Court Rd." Later Wilde told Robert Ross, who told Shaw, that Wilde's *Soul of Man under Socialism* (*Fortnightly Review*, February 1891) had its origin that night.

Wilde was back the next week for another of the Arts and Crafts lectures, this one, on printing, by Emery Walker, as Shaw reported in an Art paragraph in *The World*.[8] William Morris spoke, and Joseph Pennell, but Wilde, Shaw noted, remained only a spectator. Still, some ideas generated by the Fabian series, and by Shaw in particular, stuck, although socialism meant something different to Wilde. Like Shaw he foresaw with approval the end of property, family, marriage, and covetousness. Like Shaw he clothed his concepts in aphorisms peppered with paradoxes. But for Wilde, the best government an artist could have was no government at all, which suggested anarchism more than socialism.

To Wilde in *The Soul*, altruism was "unhealthy." Encouraging "charity, benevolence and the like," altruism was an impulse that "degrades and demoralizes." Charity was responsible for "a multitude of sins."[9] It was a paradox that Shaw understood, and that would be central to his 1905 play *Major Barbara*. Poverty, both agreed, could not be solved that way. "The proper aim," Wilde wrote, "is to try and reconstruct society on such a basis that poverty will be impossible." Socialism, he prophesied, would change all that. "There will be no people living in fetid dens and fetid rags, and bringing up unhealthy, hunger-pinched children in the midst of impossible and absolutely repulsive surroundings." Once everyone shared "in the general prosperity and happiness of society," Wilde continued in another paradox that he found congenial, however unrealistic to readers of the *Fortnightly Review*, socialism would "lead to Individualism." Only under socialism could people cultivate their personalities, for without material well-being, each person was "merely the infinitesimal atom of a force that, so far from regarding him, crushes him."

Like Shaw, Wilde never accepted the cliché that the impoverished were automatically more virtuous than the rich. "There is only one class in the community that thinks more about money than the rich, and that is the poor. The poor can think of nothing else." Further, "what are called criminals nowadays are not criminals at all. Starvation, and not sin, is the parent of modern crime." The apostle of Aestheticism was sounding more like Shaw in his Sunday streetcorner addresses, or "General" William Booth of the Salvation Army, than those that knew Oscar could have imagined, but the familiar figure reappeared in the closing paragraphs. There, Wilde predicted that under socialism—the philosophy was William Morris's—machinery would no longer compete with man, but would serve him. And, while Art could then be enhanced, "Art should never try to be popular. The public should try to make itself artistic." Art that by conventional standards was considered immoral and unhealthy was really the opposite. "The work of art is to dominate the spectator; the spectator is not to dominate the work of art." Individualism, Wilde concluded, would have its greatest opportunities under socialism, "whether it wills it or not."

When Shaw relinquished regular art criticism for *The World*, he nominated his friend Lady Colin Campbell as his replacement. In the course of her reviewing, Lady Colin began encountering Wilde. She found him physically disgusting, his paleness accentuated by teeth blackened from mercury doses he had taken for syphilis and often hidden while he talked by an oversized hand clapped across the mouth. She described him to Shaw as "that great white caterpillar."[10] Shaw explained—not that it helped—that he thought Oscar's bigness was pathological. "You know," he observed to Frank Harris, and very likely earlier to Lady Colin Campbell, "that there is a disease called gigantism, caused by"—and Shaw quoted from what he had looked up in an encyclopedia—"a certain morbid process in the sphenoid bone of the skull, . . . an excessive development of the anterior lobe of the pituitary [gland]." The overproduction of the growth hormone created the condition Shaw described as acromegaly. He saw the evidence in Lady Wilde as well as in her son. "I never saw Lady Wilde's feet; but her hands were enormous. . . . And the gigantic splaying of her palm was reproduced in her lumbar region." In adult life, after cessation of normal growth, acromegaly—the overgrowth of hands, feet, and face rather than full gigantism—results from pituitary imbalance. In Wilde, Shaw thought, acromegaly led not only to coarseness and enlargement of the face, nose, and jaws, but also to an impairment of mental ability that emerged in sexually sinister fashion. It was questionable as medical diagnosis, and even more questionable as causal analysis, but, Shaw contended, "I have always maintained that Oscar was a giant in the pathological sense, and this explains a good deal of his weakness."

A later lecture by Shaw seems to have had its impact on Wilde—Shaw's 1890 talk to the Fabians, "The Quintessence of Ibsenism." The next year Shaw sent a copy of the book version to Wilde. Where Shaw accepted, in his early extreme phase of socialism, Pierre Proudhon's contention that property is theft, Wilde preferred the more amusing paradox that the possession of private property was "very often extremely demoralising. . . . In fact, property is really a nuisance." In *The Quintessence*, Shaw began with the necessity for "the repudiation of duty," a "gloomy tyranny" that impeded the progress of humankind. Apparently adopting the concept—it fit in with his predilections—Wilde in *Soul of Man* turned Adam and the apple into the paradox that disobedience was "man's original virtue. It is through disobedience that progress has been made. . . ." Another concept that seems to parallel, if not emanate directly from, *Quintessence* is Wilde's charge "that Individualism does not come to man with any sickly cant about duty, which merely means doing what other people want because they want it. . . ." However, "Selfishness is not living as one wishes to live, it is asking others to live as one wishes to live."

The opening sections on Idealists and Realists, in which Shaw used the term *Idealist* to characterize people who clung to outworn and untenable "masks" shielding them from disagreeable truths, may have had an immediate effect on Wilde as a playwright. In *Lady Windermere's Fan*, Opus 1 of the Hibernian School, the innocent Lady Windermere confides to Mrs. Erlynne, "a lady with a past"—and her mother, although Lady Windermere will never know that secret—"We all have ideals in life. At least we should have. Mine is my mother."

"Ideals are dangerous things," Mrs. Erlynne warns—but cautiously. "Realities are better. They wound, but they are better."

Shaking her pretty head, Lady Windermere rejects the notion. "If I lost my ideals, I should lose everything." What drives the play are such hazards of "Idealism."

Perhaps a later echo emerges from *The Importance of Being Earnest* when Gwendolyn tells Jack, who has just proposed to her, "We live, as I hope you know, Mr. Worthing, in an age of ideals. The fact is constantly mentioned in the more expensive monthly magazines, and has reached the provincial pulpits, I am told: and my ideal has always been to love someone of the name of Ernest." Shaw may have taken this as a playful poke at the "idealists" he had excoriated in the *Quintessence*.

Only after Wilde's *Salomé* was banned by the Censor of Plays did he respond to Shaw about *The Quintessence of Ibsenism*, enclosing a just-published copy of the purple-bound melodrama. "You have written well and wisely and with sound wit," he noted in February 1893, "on the ridiculous institution of a stage-censorship: your little book on Ibsenism and Ibsen is such a delight to me that I constantly take it up, and always find it stimulating and refreshing: England is the land of intellectual fogs but you have done much to clear the air: we are both Celtic, and I like to think that we are friends: for these and many other reasons Salome presents herself to you in purple raiment. Pray accept her with my best wishes. . . ." Another copy went to Shaw's friend William Archer, already a drama reviewer of some influence. "I have not forgotten," Wilde explained, "that you were, with the exception of George Bernard Shaw, the only critic of note who upheld me at all against the Censorship."

Just before *Widowers' Houses* opened in December 1892, Shaw had published anonymously, as publicity for the play, an "interview" he had written himself for the afternoon newspaper *The Star* (29 November), in which the supposed reporter had asked whether audiences might "anticipate some of your unrivalled touches of humor. . . ."

"Certainly not," said Shaw (to Shaw).

> . . . Being an Irishman, I do not always see things exactly as an Englishman would: consequently some of my most serious and blunt statements sometimes . . . create an impression that I am intentionally jesting. I admit that some Irishmen do take advantage of the public in this way. Wilde, unquestionably the ablest of our dramatists, has done so in *Lady Windermere's Fan*. There are lines in that play which were put in for no other purpose than to make the audience laugh. . . . However, I do not blame Wilde. He wrote for the stage as an artist. I am simply a propagandist.[11]

Although Wilde had written that he liked to think that he and Shaw were friends, they had seen little of each other since the *Pall Mall Gazette* days. Wilde had become famous, if not infamous, while Shaw had secured his small niche in the press with music reviews as "Corno di Bassetto" and as "G.B.S." As a playwright, Shaw in 1893 hardly counted. Of his three plays, the first, *Widowers' Houses*, had managed two unrewarding performances in December 1892, while *The Philanderer* had frightened away producers and *Mrs Warren's Profession* had been proscribed by the Censor.

At a performance of *As You Like It* opening the Shaftesbury Theatre in October 1888, Shaw had chatted with Wilde between the acts. Their "shyness of one another," Shaw recalled to Frank Harris, "made our resolutely cordial and appreciative conversation so difficult that our final laugh and shake-hands were almost a reciprocal confession." It was a confession, he did not need to add, that their worlds were moving even farther apart. On 5 February 1889 Wilde had been in the audience when the Rev. Stewart Headlam's Church and Stage Guild—an effort to bring the two professions closer together—presented a talk by Shaw with the paradoxical title, "Acting, by one who does not believe in it; or the place of the Stage in the Fool's Paradise of Art." It was received, Shaw told actress Janet Achurch, the first Nora in Ibsen's *Doll's House* in England, "with inexpressible indignation by all the members of the profession who happened to be present." When Shaw edited his remarks for publication in Headlam's journal, *The Church Reformer*, he noted that he had intended to spur the audience into "fierce discussion," but, he summed up, "the discussion did not get beyond a volley of questions and fragmentary remarks from Mr. William Archer, Mr. Oscar Wilde. . . ."

On 14 February 1890, while still a music critic, Shaw noted in his diary, "Go to Military Exhibition and see whether there is any music there." Afterward he added, "Met Oscar Wilde." "It was," he recalled to Frank Harris, "some exhibition in Chelsea: a naval exhibition, where there was a replica of Nelson's Victory and a set of P. & O. cabins which made one seasick by mere association of ideas. . . . The question of what the devil we were doing in that galley tickled us both." That incongruity set into motion "Oscar's wonderful gift as a raconteur."

The cramped cabin reminded Wilde, Shaw recalled, "of a young man who invented a theatre stall which economized space by ingenious contrivances. . . . A friend of his invited twenty millionaires to meet him at dinner so that he might interest them in the invention. The young man convinced them completely by his demonstration of the saving in a theatre holding, in ordinary seats, of six hundred people, leaving them ready and eager to make his fortune." Unfortunately, in his enthusiasm the young genius, who also had a fanatical gift for calculation, went on to extrapolate "the annual saving in all the theatres in the world; then in all the churches of the world; then in all the legislatures; estimating finally the incidental and moral and religious effects of the invention until at the end of an hour he had estimated a profit of several billions." By then the worried millionaires had "folded their tents and silently stole[n] away, leaving the ruined inventor a marked man for life."

Wilde hit it off with Shaw "extraordinarily well," because Shaw only had to listen, and with an audience of one, Wilde was not tempted into his pompous public pose. "We did not talk about Art, about which, excluding literature from the definition, [Wilde] knew only what could be picked up by reading about it. He was in a tweed suit and low hat like myself . . . instead of pontificating in his frock coat. . . . And I understood why [William] Morris, when he was dying slowly, enjoyed a visit from Wilde more than from anybody else. . . ."

Years later the claimed visits were called into question since Morris actually died during Wilde's time in prison; but Shaw remembered that Morris had long been failing, and that even in Oscar's heyday of fame, after *Lady Windermere's Fan*, Wilde would take time off to amuse the old man to whom he owed ideas about decoration that Oscar promoted in such lucrative lectures of the 1880s as "The House Beautiful."

Shaw had seen *Lady Windermere's Fan* in the company of the lady then in his life, actress Florence Farr, at a St. James's Theatre matinee on 6 April 1892. The play had opened in February and would run for 197 performances—not long enough for Shaw to metamorphose into a drama critic. He would be professionally stalking the concert halls for two more years. When Shaw did become a play reviewer, however, he tucked into a review, in a musical metaphor, his observation that Wilde had "written scenes in which there is hardly a speech which could conceivably be uttered by one real person at a real at-home; but the deflection from common sense is so subtle that it is evidently produced as a tuner tunes a piano; that is, he first tunes a fifth perfectly, then flattens it a shade." The play had succeeded despite the acting, Shaw told Janet Achurch in a letter (21 April 1892): "There is one actress supported by a crowd of people not one of whom is better than a fairly good walking gentleman or lady. . . ."

Although Shaw had endured his fill of Victorian fallen women rehabilitated by suffering and repentance or abandoned by polite society, it is possible that something of the former demimondaine Mrs. Erlynne and the daughter who does not know her echoes in *Mrs Warren's Profession*, which Shaw began on 20 August 1893 and which focuses upon a similar pair. Wilde's next play, *A Woman of No Importance*, also features a woman who yields to a wicked aristocrat and is left with a child she raises in penury and sorrow, but Shaw would have cut through the sentimentality to the fact that Mrs. Arbuthnot refuses, like Mrs. Warren, to repent.

Shaw's diary notes his plan to attend *A Woman of No Importance* on 26 April 1893, but also the cancellation of the matinee. When he did see it—it ran for 113 performances—he neglected to record the fact, but later wrote (1 March 1895) to Charles Charrington, Janet Achurch's husband, in the vein of someone who had seen the play. Commenting upon Wilde's purported facility of dashing off dramas with lazy ease, Shaw alluded to "the Wilde who makes notes on his shirtcuffs" skeptically, "as if A Woman of No Importance could be produced in any such silly way . . . without the solid detail of humanity underneath. . . ."

By then Shaw had produced his newest work in the Hibernian School, *Arms and the Man*, set in an underdeveloped Balkan country that might just as easily, given its backwardness at the time, have been Ireland itself. He made sure that the manager of the Avenue Theatre sent first-night tickets for 21 April 1894 to two Irishmen, Oscar Wilde and George Moore. No reaction from Wilde survives, but while several critics deplored Shaw's wit as "second-hand Gilbertism," Oscar might have seen his own influence at work. In many ways it was "low-Society Wilde." Wilde-like absurdities enliven the play, culminating in the social vanity of the heroine's mother's boasting to her daughter's suitor, "The Petkoffs and the Saranoffs are known as the richest and most important families in the country. Our position is almost historical: we can go back for twenty years."

Shaw was on the aisle as a theater critic for Frank Harris's *Saturday Review* when Wilde's *Ideal Husband* opened on 3 January 1895, and his notice (12 January 1895) was only his second for Harris's paper. Sadly, Henry James's *Guy Domville* competed for attention that week, and Shaw, while giving it first place in his columns and praising its artistry, recognized that it would not survive on the commercial stage. Wilde's comedy, on the other hand, was certain to make money, although Shaw warned that Wilde was hazardous for most critics. "They laugh angrily at his epigrams. . . . They protest that the trick is obvious, and that such epigrams can be turned out by the score by anyone lightminded enough to condescend to such frivolity. As far as I can ascertain, I am the only person in London who cannot sit down and write an Oscar Wilde play at will. The fact that his plays, though apparently lucrative, remain unique under these circumstances, says much for the self-denial of our scribes."

Wilde, Shaw concluded, "was our only thorough playwright. He plays with everything: with wit, with philosophy, with drama, with actors and audience, with the whole theatre. Such a feat scandalizes the Englishman, who can no more play with wit and philosophy that he can with a football or a cricket bat." Confronting the contention that Wilde's artistry was somehow slothful or slack, Shaw added, "Mr. Wilde, an arch-artist, is so colossally lazy that he trifles even with the work by which an artist escapes work. He distils the very quintessence, and gets as [his] product plays which are so unapproachably playful that they are the delight of every playgoer with twopenn'orth of brains." But it was "useless" to sum up a play that had no point other than play. "The six worst epigrams are mere alms handed with a kind smile to the average suburban playgoer; the three best remain secrets between Mr. Wilde and a few choice spirits." Yet Shaw saw "a modern note" (perhaps out of Ibsen) in the hero's "assertion of the individuality and courage of his wrongdoing as against the mechanical idealism of his stupidly good wife, and in his bitter criticism of a love that is only the reward of merit."

Wilde's mocking curtain speech as author was condemned in the press. He had been accused of insolence before when, after the curtain came down on *Lady Windermere's Fan*, he had congratulated the audience on its good taste in applauding his play. Shaw ignored the controversial aftermath of *An Ideal Husband* in his review, but when his young friend Reginald Golding Bright, aspiring to become a critic himself, objected to it, Shaw loyally wrote (30 January 1895), "You are really too hard on Wilde. His 'I have enjoyed myself very much' was an Irishman's way of giving all the credit to the actors and effacing his own claims as author."

Oscar, however, was hell-bent toward personal disaster and, in an arrogance far more dangerous than his curtain-call remarks, was busily flaunting his relationship with Lord Alfred Douglas and less pretty boys. Six weeks later, when Wilde opened *The Importance of Being Earnest* (G.B.S. went on the fourth night, 18 February 1895), Shaw was disappointed by what he saw as its coldness and suggested in the *Saturday Review* (23 February 1895) that it must have been an earlier work, now refurbished, "because it was too clever and too decent." Two plays in two months was too much even for Shaw. One had to have been manufactured earlier, and he took the second comedy's apparent lack of surface seriousness as its core, failing to realize that it satirized the late-Victorian veneer of *earnestness*. He found amusing some remarks by other critics that Wilde's play "could never have been written but for the opening up of entirely new paths in the drama last year by Arms and the Man."

The Importance of Being Earnest "amused me," Shaw confessed, ". . . but unless comedy touches me as well as amuses me, it leaves me with a sense of having wasted my evening. I go to the theatre to be moved to laughter, not to be tickled or bustled into it. . . ." He found little beyond the "rib-tickling: for instance, the lies, the deceptions, the cross-purposes, the sham mourning, the christening of two grown-up men, the muffin eating, and so forth. These could only have been raised from the farcical plane by making them occur to characters who had, like Don Quixote, convinced us of their reality and obtained some hold on our sympathy." Wilde's play, Shaw thought, not his own *Arms and the Man*, had lapsed into "Gilbertism." Still, although the play lacked a humanity he thought necessary to the best drama, he admitted to "the force and daintiness of its wit," which required "an exquisitely grave, natural, and unconscious execution on the part of the actors" that he found wanting.

If the play had been performed with the grave absurdity Shaw deemed necessary, he might have found more in it. Meeting Wilde soon after, he

understood that Oscar had read disloyalty in the review. But at that point
the question was not how long the farce could run—it looked as if it might
go on forever, unaffected by Shaw's unhappiness with it—but whether
homosexual scandal would close it down. The matter came up at one of the
Monday lunches that Frank Harris arranged for his writers at the Café
Royal. For a while Shaw had attended with some reluctance. ("These
lunches wasted my time and were rather apt to degenerate into bawdy talk,"
he noted in his 1895 diary.) "Oscar Wilde came, . . . immediately before
the Queensberry trial, with young Douglas. They left in some indignation
because Harris refused to appear as a witness—a literary expert witness—to
the high artistic character of Wilde's book *Dorian Gray*."

"On that occasion," Shaw told Harris in 1916, Wilde "was not too
preoccupied with his [legal] danger to be disgusted with me because I, who
had praised his first plays handsomely, had turned traitor over The Importance of Being Earnest. Clever as it was, it was his first really heartless play."
At the Café Royal he asked Wilde "calmly" whether the guess about the
play—that it had been an early work influenced by W. S. Gilbert, then
modernized—had been on the mark. "He indignantly repudiated my guess,
and said loftily (the only time he ever tried on me the attitude he took
toward . . . his more abject disciples) that he was disappointed in me. I
suppose I said, 'Then what on earth has happened to you?' but I recollect
nothing more . . . except that we did not quarrel over it."

Shaw offered to leave when Wilde and Harris began discussing what
moves might be made to evade Oscar's inevitable conviction. They insisted
that he stay. Harris's answer to Wilde had been, Shaw recalled, something
like,

> For God's sake man, put everything on that plane out of your head.
> You don't realize what is going to happen to you. It is not going to
> be a matter of clever talk about your books. [Your attorney, Sir
> Edward] Clarke will throw up his brief. He will carry the case to a
> certain point; and then, when he sees the avalanche coming, he will
> back out and leave you in the dock. What you have to do is to cross
> to France tonight. Leave a letter saying that you cannot face the
> squalor and horror of a law case; that you are an artist and unfitted
> for such things. Don't stay here clutching at straws like testimonials to
> Dorian Gray. *I tell you I know.* I know what is going to happen. . . . I
> know what evidence they have got. You must go.

Wilde made no claims of innocence, nor did he question the folly of his libel action against Douglas's father. "But he had an infatuate haughtiness as to the impossibility of his retreating. . . . Douglas sat in silence, a haughty indignant silence, copying Wilde's attitude as all Wilde's admirers did. . . . Oscar finally rose with a mixture of impatience and his grand air, and walked out with the remark that he had now found out who were his real friends; and Douglas followed him, absurdly smaller, and imitating his walk, like a curate imitating an archbishop."

Harris recalled, rather, that Douglas got up first and said, "Your telling him to run away shows that you are no friend of Oscar's." Then Oscar rose and said goodbye to Shaw, whom he had not asked to testify. A notorious socialist, Shaw could do little by expatiating to a jury on the salubrious morality of *Dorian Gray*.

"I hope you don't doubt my friendship," said Harris; "you have no reason to."

"I don't think this is friendly of you, Frank," said Wilde, walking out.

Shaw never again went to Harris's lunches, with their "brag and bawdry." They soon collapsed anyway when Wilde was arrested and went to trial. On 25 May 1895 he was sentenced to two years of hard labor. Many of Wilde's cronies fled across the Channel. Afterward Shaw thought that the "hateful" inhumanity revealed in Oscar's *Earnest* "represented a real degeneracy produced by his debaucheries," but this did not keep Shaw from trying to act in the imprisoned Wilde's interest. On a railway journey to the north, where he was to lecture, remembering the Chicago anarchists, Shaw drafted a petition to the Home Secretary for Wilde's release.

Returning to London, he discussed strategy with Oscar's brother, Willie, asking whether other efforts of the sort were in the works. While Shaw offered the petition, he warned that although he and Stewart Headlam would sign, it would be "of no use, as we were two notorious cranks, and our names alone would make the thing ridiculous and do Oscar more harm than good."

Willie agreed, adding "with maudlin pathos and an inconceivable want of tact" as they stood talking in St. Martin's Lane, outside the Duke of York's Theatre, that "Oscar was NOT a man of bad character: you could have trusted him with a woman anywhere." Willie also thought that useful signatures would be unobtainable and dropped the idea.

All that was left for Shaw was to mention Wilde's artistry wherever he could, to keep his reputation alive. In a review of a play by Jerome K.

Jerome on 26 October 1895, a few months later, he referred to "a remarkable scene" by Wilde in *An Ideal Husband* since Jerome had handled a similar one ponderously, "laboriously explaining Mr Oscar Wilde's point, . . . thereby very effectually reducing it to absurdity." A year later (17 October 1896), with Oscar still in prison, Shaw reviewed a play by Charles Hawtrey in which Charles Brookfield had a leading role. Both had procured perjured evidence against Wilde and had joined the Marquess of Queensberry for a victory dinner on the night the third and last trial had ended. Shaw wrote, intending that both playwright and player would understand, that the play "cannot be compared to the comedies of Mr Oscar Wilde, because Mr Wilde has creative imagination, philosophic humor, and original wit, besides being a master of language; whilst Mr Hawtrey observes, mimics, and derides quite thoughtlessly, . . . and otherwise keeps on the hither side of the boundary that separates the clever *flâneur* from the dramatist."

Late in 1897, with Wilde out of prison and in abject exile, Shaw entered into a correspondence in *The Academy*, which had published (6 November) a list of possible candidates for a British Academy of Letters, on the French model. In a rejoinder published on the thirteenth Shaw suggested, daringly since Wilde had become a nonperson in the English press, "The only dramatist, besides Mr Henry James, whose nomination could be justified, is Mr Oscar Wilde." (In the same issue, H. G. Wells even more bravely recommended Shaw as well as Wilde.) In March of the next year, Shaw referred to Wilde four times in a review and then, a few weeks later (2 April 1898), wrote of a minor effort by a minor playwright, "Will he ever handle a pen and play with an idea as . . . Mr Oscar Wilde can? Clearly never—not even were we to wrap him in blotting paper and boil him in ink for a week to make his literary faculty supple and tender." The remark was, in context, gratuitous, but Shaw was keeping Wilde's name before the serious reader while it was blotted off the stage and eliminated from the bookshops. Aside from any loyalty, Shaw had found in him something he did not want lost from the stage—a peculiarly Irish exasperation with English solemnity.

By then some suggestions of Wilde had begun echoing in Shaw's own plays, some echoes apparently intentional. As early as 19 November 1894 Shaw had warned Golding Bright, "You must give up detesting everything appertaining to Oscar Wilde. . . . The critic's first duty is to admit, with absolute respect, the right of every man to his own style. Wilde's wit and his fine literary workmanship are points of great value. There is always a vulgar cry both for and against every man or woman of distinction, and . . . you have heard it about Whistler, Sarah Grand, Ibsen, Wagner—everybody who has a touch of genius." When Shaw began writing his comedy *You Never Can Tell* in July 1895, he gave it the working title "The Terrestrial Twins," after Mrs. Grand's feminist novel *The Heavenly Twins*.[12] It also would have something of Wilde in it, emanating from the very heartless play that Shaw had disliked and responding to Shaw's own sense of the play's chilly mechanicalness.

You Never Can Tell would have a dentist as young lover, Valentine; a Gorgon of a dowager feminist, Mrs. Lanfrey Clandon; her twins, Dolly and Philip; her elder daughter, Gloria; the children's father and estranged husband of their mother, the cranky Fergus Crampton; a serenely comic waiter, William Boon; and his omniscient lawyer-son, Walter Bohun. Comic figures seemingly drawn at a level of deliberate unreality, as were Wilde's characters, Shaw's characters were as rational and outspoken as Wilde's, and their motives, as in Wilde's play, were clear and never in doubt. Wilde's characters remained stylized from beginning to end, almost to abstraction; Shaw's were more warmly conceived, for as he wrote in a review of some farces in 1896, perhaps still remembering *The Importance of Being Earnest*, "To laugh without sympathy is a ruinous abuse of a noble function, and the degradation of any race may be measured by the degree of their addiction to it." When barren of sympathy, he insisted, farce was "at bottom . . . the deliberate indulgence of that horrible, derisive joy in humiliation and suffering which is the beastliest element in human nature."

With Wilde out of the picture in the summer of 1895 (he was in prison) Shaw had been tempted to turn to "fashionable comedies for the West End theatres"—satirical fun on the order of his *Arms and the Man* but raised some social notches for fashionable audiences. Determining to humanize the genre of "imperturbably impudent comedies," and very likely recalling his cavils about Wilde's *Earnest*, he blended Oscar Wilde with Sarah Grand. In Wilde's play, Jack Worthing must find a father if he is to capture his society bride, Gwendolen Fairfax, ward of that apostle of propriety, Lady Bracknell. By the curtain, after some accidents and coincidences, he has located a father in the Army lists—a satisfactory general, safely deceased. In *You Never Can Tell*, the Clandon children are in search of a father, and they find one, under another name (their mother lives under her pen name), as a patient in a dentist's office.

The dentist, meanwhile, requires a father so that his suit for Gloria Clandon has credibility, citing to the twins an apparent echo of Lady Bracknell's injunction to Jack Worthing that he produce at least one parent before the end of the social season. "In a seaside resort," Valentine explains, "there's one thing you must have before anybody can be seen going about with you, and that's a father, alive or dead." Valentine's beloved, Gloria, the twins' elder sister, shares their need, redoubling Wilde's parental predicament. "A woman who does not know who her father was," she informs her emancipated mother, cannot accept a respectable offer of marriage.

Even the profession of dentistry—unusual in drama then and now—is found in both comedies, Shaw turning allusion into reality. "Come, old boy," says Algernon in Wilde's farce as he tries to extract the identity of the mysterious Cecily Cardew from Jack Worthing, "you had much better have the thing out at once."

"My dear Algy," retorts Jack, trying to evade the question, "you talk exactly as if you were a dentist."

Shaw's irrepressible lover, Valentine, is a "five-shilling dentist," new to his role and struggling to earn a living. Philip Clandon thinks that "dentist" is "an ugly word," but Valentine, who has tried and failed in other occupations, has a symbolic profession as well as a farcical one in Shaw's play. (His very name may be a deliberate echo from *Earnest*—of "the 14th of February last," Valentine's Day, when Cecily claims to have accepted Algernon, posing as Jack's wayward brother Ernest, "under this dear old tree here.") Old Crampton follows young Dolly in having the throbbing thing out, but he suffers from a pain beyond dentistry, he admits, upon seeing Dolly and Phil: "A twinge of memory, Miss Clandon, not of toothache."

"Have it out," Dolly advises, quoting from *Macbeth*, " 'Pluck from the memory a rooted sorrow.' With gas, five shillings extra."

Name changes—Algernon and Jack in Wilde's play schedule baptisms, in order to become "Ernest" to satisfy their brides-to-be—are significant in both comedies. Mrs. Clandon—formerly Crampton—has changed her daughter's name from the dowdy Victorian Sophronia to the more modern Gloria, while waiter William Boon, content with the English corruption of his name, finds that his son Walter, for professional respectability, has restored the Norman original, Bohun. The suggestively named young lover Valentine, who seems to have no parent, aptly has no other name, and whether Valentine is surname or Christian name is left in Shavian uncertainty.

Other elements of the play suggest a close study of *Earnest*.[13] The muffin-eating scene, more serious farce than Shaw realized, becomes a full, formal luncheon in *You Never Can Tell*, and Wilde's irreverent servant Lane, who serves bread and butter in lieu of cucumber sandwiches, becomes the deferential and even more shrewd waiter Boon. The haughty Gwendolen is metamorphosed into the even more haughty Gloria; the imperious but conventional Lady Bracknell becomes the even more imperious and emancipated Mrs. Clandon.

More significantly, the play is replete with earnestness, both purported and real. Mrs. Clandon, whose earnest and "scientific" tracts for the twentieth century demonstrate a love of humanity, is unable to show warmth for the individual human being, not even for her children. Even in the play the irrepressible twin, Dolly, makes fun of her mother's tracts on modern ethics, and Mrs. Clandon retorts that although her values are a joke to the younger generation, "It is such bitter earnest to me." And *earnestness* reappears literally throughout the comedy. When Mrs. Clandon interrogates Valentine about his intentions in Act III, as Lady Bracknell had done with Jack in *Earnest*, she inverts the conventional social premises for marriage, declaring that she cares little for money and that Valentine has a right to amuse himself with women as he pleases. "Amuse myself!" Valentine protests. "Oh, Mrs. Clandon!"

"On your honor," Gloria's mother asks skeptically, "Mr Valentine, are you in earnest?"

"On my honor," he claims (*"desperately,"* in Shaw's stage directions), "I am in earnest. Only," he confesses, "I have always been in earnest; and yet—! Well, here I am, you see."

The wordplay on *earnestness* is too pervasive to be coincidence. Later, Mrs. Clandon's old family friend, Finch M'Comas, warns the effervescent Dolly, who has interrupted him, "I insist on having earnest matters earnestly and reverently discussed." And Gloria rebukes Valentine for the levity in his personality ("lightness of heart," he labels it) that his infatuation with her cannot conceal: "If you were really in love, it would not make you foolish: it would give you dignity! earnestness!" "Ah," Valentine retorts, "you see you're not in earnest. Love can[']t give any man new gifts. It can only heighten the gifts he was born with."

In the last act, Valentine contends to Gloria that his brand of earnestness is driven by biology, the necessity to complete their mutual genetic fate. "Why was I tempted? Because Nature was in deadly earnest with me when I was in jest with her." It was not sensible, but as Bohun points out, "All matches are unwise. It's unwise to be born; it's unwise to be married; it's unwise to live; and it's wise to die." "So much the worse," says William, his father, "for wisdom!" The world of feeling, nonexistent in the heartless universe of *The Importance of Being Earnest*, is reborn in *You Never Can*

Tell, where biology is destiny. While Wilde's farce remains a masterpiece of artifice, Shaw's response has become a belatedly recognized masterwork itself.

After Shaw completed *You Never Can Tell* in 1896, he began his answer to Shakespeare, *Caesar and Cleopatra*, going for his facts to Theodor Mommsen's massive *History of Rome*, which he followed closely.[14] The subject and Shaw's source seem almost to have emanated from an implicit challenge in Wilde's *Soul of Man Under Socialism*, gestating through the decade as Shaw recoiled from late-Victorian interpretations of Shakespeare. "It is a question," Wilde had written, "whether we have ever seen the full expression of a personality, except on the imaginative plane of art. In action, we never have. Caesar, says Mommsen, was the complete and perfect man. But how tragically insecure was Caesar! . . . Caesar was very perfect, but his perfection travelled by too dangerous a road." It is the note on which Shaw ends his play. Caesar, warned about the knives being sharpened for him in Rome, responds with a stoic shrug and sets sail from Egypt anyway.

When Shaw turned again to drawing-room comedy for his next major stage work, *Man and Superman* (1901–2), the frame-play was Shavianized Wilde, and the epigrammatic nature of the dialogue suggested another work in the Hibernian School, complete with an Irish-American father and son among snobbish Londoners. When a character at the close offers the paradox, "There are two tragedies in life. One is to lose your heart's desire. The other is to gain it. Mine and yours, sir," Wilde, by then dead, seems resurrected. Dumby's remark in *Lady Windermere's Fan* had been, "In this world there are only two tragedies. One is not getting what one wants, and the other is getting it." And John Tanner's "Maxims for Revolutionists," an epigrammatic catalogue that Shaw's leading character has attached to his allegedly notorious handbook, reads like a political parallel to Wilde's "Phrases and Philosophies for the Use of the Young."

A second play that begins in the drawing room, written in 1905, also seems like Shavianized Wilde and echoes *The Importance of Being Earnest*. Lady Britomart, a champion of public form, again suggests Wilde's society Gorgon, Lady Bracknell, and *Major Barbara*'s outcome hinges on found-lings and fathers despite its dark philosophical dimensions. The drawing-room wit suggests that *Lady Windermere's Fan* also lingered in Shaw's memory, most vividly Lady Windermere's "*grave*" observation to Lord Darlington, chastising him, "Believe me, you are better than most other men, and I sometimes think you pretend to be worse." Lady Brit improves on this in her exasperated aspersions upon Andrew Undershaft's character, for her estranged husband goes about "saying that wrong things are true" and pretends to a wickedness that is closer to saintliness. Shaw was not paying debts but recognizing stageable devices that had passed the test of usage.

Shaw's last personal contact with Wilde had come via an inscribed copy of "The Ballad of Reading Gaol," sent from Paris in 1898. (Wilde died in 1900.) No acknowledgment survives, but Shaw, who would write an influential essay, *The Crime of Imprisonment*, could not have forgotten it. Yet Shaw told Harris that the long poem was not essential for Wilde's posthumous reputation. "Well," Shaw suggested,

> suppose Oscar . . . had . . . died the day before Queensberry had left that [accusing] card at the Club! Oscar would still have been remembered as a wit and a dandy, and would have had a niche beside Congreve in the drama. A volume of his aphorisms would have stood creditably on the library shelf with La Rochefoucauld's Maxims. We should have missed the Ballad of Reading Gaol and De Profundis; but he still would have cut a considerable figure in the Dictionary of National Biography and been read and quoted outside the British Museum reading room.

"We all dreaded to read De Profundis," Shaw observed of the posthumously published text of Wilde's long prison letter to Douglas: "Our instinct was to stop our ears, or run away from the wail of a broken, though by no means contrite, heart. But we were throwing away our pity. De Profundis was de profundis indeed. Wilde was too good a dramatist to throw away so powerful an effect; but none the less it was de profundis in excelsis. There was more laughter between the lines of that book than in a thousand farces by men of no genius. Wilde, like Richard III and Shakespeare, found in himself no pity for himself." Few read Wilde that way, but Shaw knew him.

To Lord Alfred Douglas, who first ranted at Shaw and then strove to become a Shavian parasite, G.B.S. was pointed. Realizing that Douglas lived for decades on his notorious relationship with Wilde, Shaw attempted to disabuse Douglas of his feeling that the past was his bread and butter. It meant diminishing Oscar's presence, and in Shaw's letters to Douglas, most of them from the 1930s, he downplayed the post-prison Wilde as a drunkard and swindler, yet excused him as a diseased and broken man.[15] Wilde, Shaw explained, had been reduced by circumstances to exile and beggary. "Let me again remind you that I am an Irishman. I know that there is no beggar on earth as shameless as an Irish beggar." He detested attempts by Wilde's former cronies to exploit their association, approving only of Frank Harris's efforts because Harris, he knew, had tried to save Oscar from himself.

Often asked for his opinions of Wilde, and even to write a screenplay of the Oscar Wilde catastrophe, Shaw resisted all pleas but Harris's, and his long letter to Harris (7 August 1916) remained his most extended recollection, reprinted with amendments to Harris's biography of Wilde. In life, Shaw had concluded for Harris, Wilde "was no doubt sluggish and weak because of his gigantism." Shaw could not reproach him for that. And for the "Ballad," Wilde's only post-prison work, Wilde received Shaw's blessing, despite the obvious borrowings from "The Ancient Mariner," because he showed "that he could pity others when he could not seriously pity himself." It was a gesture Shaw did not forget despite his feeling that Wilde would survive in the wit of his plays.

"When Oscar heard the child crying in prison," he recalled again to Harris (7 May 1918),

> his pity was certainly not for himself. There is a story that Jesus Christ once began to notice that some very shady people were getting into Heaven. At last he could stand it no longer, and went to the gate and accused Peter of neglecting his duties. Peter immediately became very sulky, and would neither deny nor explain. Jesus would not be put off; and at last Peter took him round outside the wall to one of the bastions, where they peeped round the corner and saw the Virgin Mary letting down her girdle from the parapet and helping up the poor devils whom Peter had turned away. Wilde might have half a chance there because he not only felt for the children but stuck to it and wrote about it when he got out.

Much of Shaw's respect for Wilde was due to Oscar's artistry, and some, it seems, to that belated humanity. Some, too, may acknowledge their early days in London as aspiring writers and the Haymarket petition. But Wilde paid Shaw the compliment of ranking their works together in the "great Celtic School" while Shaw was still a nobody in the theater with only two forgettable performances of a single play to his credit, which was encouragement above and beyond the sense of Hibernian duty. Few people who counted had taken Shaw seriously then. Wilde had.

Notes

1. Wilde's letters are quoted from the Rupert Hart-Davis edition of *The Letters of Oscar Wilde* (Oxford: Oxford University Press, 1962); Shaw's letters, except where noted otherwise, are quoted from Dan H. Laurence, *Bernard Shaw: Collected Letters, 1874–1897, 1898–1910,* and *1911–1925,* rev. eds. (New York: Viking, 1985).

2. Shaw's letters to Frank Harris, including the one later published, somewhat altered, by Harris as "My Memories of Oscar Wilde," are quoted from the originals as they appear in *The Playwright and the Pirate. Bernard Shaw and Frank Harris: A Correspondence,* ed. Stanley Weintraub (University Park: Pennsylvania State University Press, 1982).

3. Shaw's diary entries are quoted from *Bernard Shaw, The Diaries 1885–1897,* ed. Stanley Weintraub, 2 vols. (University Park: Pennsylvania State University Press, 1986).

4. *Court and Society Review,* 11, 18, and 25 May 1887. Wilde's letter to Heron Allen is postmarked 17 October 1887.

5. W. B. Yeats, *Autobiographies* (London: Macmillan, 1955), p. 283.

6. Shaw's complete *Pall Mall Gazette* reviews, most of them anonymously published, appear in *Bernard Shaw's Book Reviews Originally Published in the* Pall Mall Gazette *from 1885 to 1888,* ed. Brian Tyson (University Park: Pennsylvania State University Press, 1991).

7. Rossetti to Furnivall, 30 September 1887, letter 426 in *Selected Letters of William Michael Rossetti,* ed. Roger W. Peattie (University Park: Pennsylvania State University Press, 1990), pp. 510–11.

8. *The World,* 21 November 1888, unsigned, in *Bernard Shaw on the London Art Scene,* ed. Stanley Weintraub (University Park: Pennsylvania State University Press, 1989), pp. 249–50.

9. Quotations from "The Soul of Man under Socialism," *Fortnightly Review* (February 1891) are from *The Artist as Critic: Critical Writings of Oscar Wilde,* ed. Richard Ellmann (New York: Random House, 1969).

10. Shaw's recollections of his conversation with Lady Colin Campbell are recounted to Harris in the letter Harris published as "My Memories of Oscar Wilde."

11. *The Star* self-interview is reprinted in *The Bodley Head Bernard Shaw: Collected Plays with Their Prefaces,* ed. Dan H. Laurence (London: Max Reinhardt, 1970), 1:122–32, as "The Playwright on His First Play."

12. British Library Add. Ms. 50605A (December 1895).

13. Some of the parallels in artifice between the two plays are noted in Thomas R. Whitaker's "Playing in Earnest," *Omnium Gatherum,* ed. Susan Dick, Declan Kiberd, Dougald McMillan, and Joseph Ronsley (Gerrards Cross: Colin Smythe, 1989), pp. 416–17.

14. Stanley Weintraub, "Shaw's Mommsenite Caesar," in *The Unexpected Shaw* (New York: Frederick Ungar, 1982), pp. 111–23.

15. Shaw's letters to Douglas, which refer often to Wilde, are collected in *Bernard Shaw and Lord Alfred Douglas: A Correspondence,* ed. Mary Hyde (New York: Ticknor & Fields, 1982).

BERNARD SHAW IN DARKEST ENGLAND

G.B.S. and the Salvation Army's "General" William Booth

"What is the use of the gospel of thrift to a man who had nothing to eat yesterday and has not threepence today to pay for his lodging tonight?" So challenged "General" William Booth in *In Darkest England and The Way Out*, a manifesto written with W. T. Stead that declared that allegedly Christian England was in no condition to compare itself favorably with the horror and degradation of central Africa. (Earlier in its year of release, the intrepid Henry Morton Stanley had published an account of his explorations, *In Darkest Africa*.) The disgrace of a "submerged tenth" of unemployed and down-and-out, with its attendant spiritual degradation, the book charged, could be put down to their moral defects. Salvation was not going to come by prayer but by drastic alteration of the social fabric.

Given the London, 1890, place and date of publication, one might assume that it was the latest Fabian polemic, perhaps written, as were many of them then, by a musical critic and political activist named Bernard Shaw. In actuality he would not get around to reading it until February 1891, and its real author was the feisty "General" William Booth, founder of the Salvation Army. Shaw, however, seems to have never forgotten a line of it. As one-time Pre-Raphaelite painter Edward Burne-Jones remarked a few years later to his assistant, the Army began "at the right end. They begin with enthusiasm and they begin at the poorest [audience]. The very name I like; it's a good one. . . . One thing they did I didn't like; they put outside their meeting house in Hammersmith in big letters 'Blood and Fire'—what did they mean, whose blood and whose fire I should like to know? You can get anything out of mankind by appealing to its sense of beauty and its enthusiasm—but in people's sense of right I have not the least belief. The Socialists will never do anything with it."[1]

Coincidentally, one of the major Socialist headquarters was also in Hammersmith, presided over by another feisty, charismatic prophet, William Morris. Bernard Shaw, often at Hammersmith Terrace, must have also seen the "Blood and Fire" slogan more than once, and he wanted the Socialists to have some of the enthusiasm he saw among the Booth adherents. His *Major Barbara* (1905) seems an attempt to dramatize the possibility—a theatrical *Darkest England*.

Shaw's first acquaintance with Booth's Army was as a young walker of the streets, when he tried to find himself as a new Irish émigré in London. In his first novel, *Immaturity*, written in 1878–79 when he was twenty-two, Shaw includes an obviously autobiographical episode in which Smith, the young hero, new to London, wanders unfamiliar neighborhoods in the quiet of Christmas Day and happens upon an evangelical meeting that has the characteristics of early William Booth. Having broken with Methodism—as being too passive—in 1861, Booth and his wife, Catherine, had established an independent revivalist mission that only received the name of Salvation Army in 1878. At that early stage the Army was one without uniforms and ranks, but with a strong impetus to street meetings, vehement tracts and hymn–happy bands, banners, and the saving of souls. Shaw's acquaintance with chapels of this order emphasized the music and the tracts, Smith finding the tracts neither credible nor interesting, but the music "fairly sung." Although the congregation "either followed the tune or improvised a drone bass which only moved at the cadences, there was a tolerable attempt at part singing; and Smith found no fault in the performance."[2]

The last hymn, emphasizing "We will all be happy over there," with the antiphonal repeat of "over there," is infectious, and Smith joins his "feeble tenor"* to the harmony. "Then there arose a young man, earnest and proud of his oratory, who offered up a long prayer, in the course of which he suggested such modification of the laws of nature as would bring the arrangement of the universe into conformity with his own tenets. When he was done, several others delivered addresses; but they lacked variety, as the speakers were all very ignorant. The addresses of one or two men who related the atrocities committed by them before their conversion disgusted Smith; and he watched for an opportunity of retiring quietly."

---

*Manuscript of *Immaturity*; Shaw later changed that to the more autobiographical "colorless baritone."

Fig. 5. "General" William Booth as drawn by "Spy" for *Vanity Fair*, 25 November 1882, before his whitened hair and beard made him look like Michaelangelo's *Moses*.

In 1885 in one of his early music reviews, Shaw, anonymously, wrote approvingly in the *Dramatic Review* of the impetuous "war songs of the Salvation Army,"[3] and even a few years later, as "Corno di Bassetto" in *The Star*, he praised "the excellent music" of the "proletarian bands of the industrial North and of the Salvation Army."[4] He liked the way they performed Donizetti's choruses. "These, by the bye," he wrote, "have been discovered by the Salvation Army: I heard one of their bands playing *Per te d'immenso giubilo* [from *Lucia de Lammermoor*] capitally one Sunday morning." In *Major Barbara* he would have the band leave the West Ham shelter playing *immenso giubilo*, Adolphus Cusins giving the time with his drum and Barbara's father playing a borrowed trombone. It was only after the completion of *Major Barbara*, late in 1905, that he was asked, despite his reservations about the Army, to attend its music festival at Congress Hall in Clapton. Booth thought the play would be good publicity. Shaw was even asked, as a former music critic, to write a confidential report for the Army, not published until forty-five years later, after his death.[5]

In his report Shaw explained that there was no condescension on his part. He had listened to the Salvation Army performances just as he had done "to some of the best professional orchestras and bands in Europe" when he had been a music critic. And he had found "precision and snap" in the execution. There were no "incompetent conductors" on the Salvation Army's podium merely "because they had won a musical degree at a university." But he found their solo instrumental skill often florid, an excess he attributed to the emotional dimension of the Army, the talented amateur's desire to show off a musicianly virtuosity. What he found fault with was not the "joyous vivacity of style and clear jubilant tone" but the monotony of hymnal music. The Army needed, he suggested, more "marches and quick-steps." He understood, he said, that Salvation Army music

must not be over the heads of the people. At the Festival I sat next [to] a laborer who had probably worked half as long again that day as any man should work at heavy physical toil: at all events he was partly stupefied with mere fatigue. If the bands had played very refined music for him—say the Priest's march from Mozart's Magic Flute, the overture to Gluck's Alceste, the Elysian Fields music from Gluck's Orpheus, or the entry to the Castle of the Grail from Wagner's Parsifal—he would have been fast asleep in three minutes. And when the Chalk Farm Band played a piece of empty but exciting circus music for him in the most violently spirited way, he woke up and was pleased, as most of the audience were. But it woke him up at the cost of switching off the current of religious enthusiasm and switching on the current of circus excitement. It woke him up very much as a tablespoon of brandy would have woken him up. And with all its racket, which was powerfully reinforced by the low roof and the terrific clatter of the overtones set up by the instruments, it was not nearly as stirring as I'm climbing up the golden stairs to glory or When the roll is called up yonder. Music can be impetuous, triumphant, joyful, enrapturing, and very pretty into the bargain without being rowdy or empty. I know the difficulty of keeping up the necessary supply of good marches, and the danger of wearing out the best ones by too frequent repetition. But after making all allowances, I think it is a pity that the Salvation Army, which has produced a distinctive type of religious service and religious life, should not also produce a distinctive type of marching music.

Later Shaw wrote of a great Salvation Army meeting in memory of Mrs. Booth at the Albert Hall that "the massed Salvation bands played the Dead March from 'Saul' as I verily believe it has never been played in the world since Handel was alive to conduct it," and he resented publicly, in letters to the press, any suggestion that he was libeling Army bands in his play. General Booth himself had supplied Shaw with a seat "in the middle of the centre grand tier box, in the front row," from which he sang "When the roll-ll-ll is called up yonder," he wrote John Vedrenne (2 October 1905), "as it has never been sung before. The Times will announce my conversion tomorrow."[6] His relations with the Salvation Army had been good from the beginning, and he genuinely admired its work if not its theology.

"I took on myself," Shaw noted in a letter in the *Daily Citizen* (26 October 1912), "the duty of leading the singing in my box, being of opinion that hymn-singing, when the tune is a jolly one (and the Salvation Army has enough genuine religion in it to specialise in jolly hymn tunes), is a highly enjoyable, healthy, and recreative exercise. Now the art of leading a choir, or an orchestra, or anything else, consists, not in being 'carried away,' but in carrying other people away; and this I did with such success that a young lady in the Army bonnet took my hands as we left the box at the end of the meeting, and said, with moist eyes, 'We know, don't we?' And really I think we did."[7]

But after the hymns, Booth expected a "sobriety of the soul," Shaw thought, which is why the General refused to take a high moral tone with sinners, a worldly realism found in few pulpits. That perspective may have had an impact on *Mrs Warren's Profession*, which Shaw wrote only two years after Booth's book. "Terrible as the fact is," Booth had observed without prudery or theological polemics, ". . . there is no industrial career in which for a short time a beautiful girl can make as much money with as little trouble as in the profession of courtesan." In industry a penny an hour was possible; in a brothel a woman might surpass the earnings of a cabinet minister. Recalling her girlhood to Vivie, Mrs Warren explains that one of her two half-sisters "worked in a whitelead factory twelve hours a day for nine shillings a week until she died of lead poisoning. She only expected to get her hands a little paralyzed; but she died." Her full sister, Liz, after watching Vivie's mother wear herself out as a barmaid, exploded, "What are you doing there, you little fool? wearing out your health and your appearance for other people's profit!" And Liz would give Kitty Warren her start as prostitute and procuress.

"Why shouldn't I have done it?" she challenges her daughter. And Vivie can only reply, in terms General Booth would have understood, "You were certainly quite justified—from the business point of view."

"What's the use in . . . hypocrisy?" Mrs Warren agrees. "If people arrange the world that way for women, theres no good pretending it's arranged the other way. No: I never was a bit ashamed really."

And "Unashamed" would be the working motto of the most Boothian character that Shaw would create in *Major Barbara*, a play that owes much to General Booth.

Very likely even before Shaw had completed his first play—the manuscript fragment has the appearance of the 1880s—he had sketched an encounter that has in it all the makings of Snobby Price, Bill Walker, Jenny Hill, and Barbara Undershaft. The setting is a Salvation Army shelter.

> The solitary rough is not brave. He is restless and shamefaced until he meets with other roughs to keep him in countenance. He especially dreads that strange social reformer, the Hallelujah lass. At first sight of her quaint bonnet, jersey, and upturned eyes, he rushes to the conclusion that chance has provided him with a rare lark. He hastens to the outskirts of her circle, and after a few inarticulate howls, attempts to disconcert her by profane and often obscene interjections. In vain. He may as easily disconcert a swallow in its flight. He presently hears himself alluded to as "that loving fellow creature," and he is stricken with an uncomfortable feeling akin to that which prompted Paul Pry's protest, "Don't call me a phoenix: I'm not used to it." But the Hallelujah lass is not done with him yet. In another minute she is praying, with infectious emotion, for "his dear, precious soul." This finishes him. He slinks away with a faint affectation of having no more time to waste on such effeminate sentimentality, and thenceforth never ventures within earshot of the Army except when strongly reinforced by evil company or ardent spirits. A battalion of Hallelujah lasses is worth staying a minute to study. . . . As long as they speak strenuously, they consider them-

selves but little about lack of matter, which forces them to repetitions which, it must be confessed, soon become too tedious for anyone but a habitual Salvationist to endure.[8]

Later, when "the general" quoted some of Shaw's comments on the excellence of Salvation Army bands "again and again in public"—these are Shaw's recollections—Shaw "took advantage of the relations thus established to ask the Army staff why they did not develop the dramatic side of their ritual by performing plays." He "even offered to write a short play as a model of what might be done. The leaders of the Army . . . could not venture to offend the deep prejudices against the theatre that still form part of evangelism." Unless, Shaw was told, "I could assure them that all the incidents in the play had actually happened; otherwise the play would be considered a lie. To my mind, of course, a very curious misapprehension of the difference between truth and mere actuality." Finally, Booth's daughter-in-law, wife of his heir-apparent, Bramwell, told Shaw that the Army would prefer a large subscription rather than a model play.

The possibility "of using the wooing of a man's soul for his salvation as a substitute for the hackneyed wooing of a handsome young gentleman for the sake of marrying him," Shaw recalled, had occurred to him years before when, as a Radical lecturer in the 1890s, "he had often found himself on Sunday mornings addressing a Socialist meeting in the open air in London or in the provinces while the Salvation Army was at work on the same ground. He had frequently, at the conclusion of his own meeting, joined the crowd round the Salvation lasses and watched their work and studied their methods sympathetically." If the Army did not want to create its own model play, Shaw would write it himself, with the raw material that the Army had already provided him. Many of the Salvation lasses had sung, "with great effect," Shaw recalled,

> songs in which the drama of salvation was presented in the form of a series of scenes between a brutal and drunken husband and a saved wife, with a thrilling happy ending in which the audience, having been persuaded by the unconscious art of the singer to expect with horror a murderous attack on the woman as her husband's steps were heard on the stairs, were relieved and delighted to hear that when the villain entered the room and all seemed lost, his face was lighted with the light of Heaven; for he too had been saved. Bernard Shaw

was not at that time a playwright; but such scenes were not lost on him; the future dramatist was collecting his material everywhere.[9]

He was not merely collecting material; he would be using it all his life. After *Major Barbara* Shaw would dramatize another upper-middle-class daughter, Margaret Knox of posh and respectable Denmark Hill, in *Fanny's First Play* (1911), who is carried away by a prayer meeting that changes her life. One of the unforeseen results is that she assaults a policeman and lands in prison, but she finds her soul. "I can only say," Shaw observed in an interview in 1911, "that I myself have participated with enormous enjoyment in just such a prayer-meeting as that which carried Margaret off her feet, although my natural sphere of enjoyment is in the artistic world."[10] His Lavinia in *Androcles and the Lion* (1912) and his *Saint Joan* (1923) embody the power of faith and the struggle for reason when in the grip of religious ecstasy; and in *Too True to Be Good* (1931) Shaw creates a mesmerizing preacher (turned burglar) and evangelical army sergeant. Even as late as *Buoyant Billions*, completed in Shaw's ninetieth year, he would depict a self-styled World Betterer, who in a pre-atomic world might have followed Booth's course.

Booth's remedies for the regeneration of England had long before captured Shaw's attention. He had already noted in his diary (19 July 1889) the purchase of the Army's official gazette, *War Cry*.[11] When Booth's *In Darkest England* was published, Shaw was first alerted to it by fellow Fabian Graham Wallas, who took him into the library at the National Liberal Club to read Thomas Huxley's letter to *The Times* "on General Booth's scheme," which was one of many responses skeptical not only about the Army's demands for conversion and obedience but also about its statistics and its social strategies. That combination of a militaristic religious organization and social engineering had already made the newly published book a lively focus of controversy. The utopian projects required start-up funds, and one letter writer to *The Times* had offered £1,000 if ninety-nine others would subscribe similar amounts. None publicly did, but Booth went ahead with pennies and shillings from his broadest constituency, the poor.

One of Booth's schemes was a model farm at Benfleet, which Shaw planned to visit. He also noted in his diary plans to attend a lecture by a Mr. Reed on Booth's book. Yet he missed the lecture, and—a chronic oversleeper—he missed the train from Fenchurch Street Station. But it is clear that he read *In Darkest England* and that not long after he saw the farm at Benfleet. It would take a dozen years more, but Shaw would eventually incorporate both Booth's social engineering ends and his own sweeping reservations about the means into *Major Barbara*. Even the matching-funds idea went into the play when Shaw's Salvation Army leader—a woman commissioner, perhaps to deflect identification with Booth—asks for five wealthy businessmen to match a £5,000 donation from Lord Saxmundham, formerly Horace Bodger, the millionaire distiller. Referring to Booth's ends and his own skepticism about Booth's means, and the Thomas Huxley controversy in *The Times* when *In Darkest England* was first published, Shaw observed to Beatrice Webb (30 July 1901), "Nothing is more unpopular in England than hauling down a flag, even if it has become a flagrantly impossible flag. If General Booth were to declare tomorrow that he had given up the Bible & adopted the views of Huxley, he would obliterate himself from public life, because the Huxleyites would give him no credit for coming to his senses, & would never attach the least importance to a man who had compromised himself by salvationism; the pious people would be horrified; & everybody would regard him as an apostate." Conceding Booth the peg on which to hang his program, and long attracted to paternalistic but efficiently planned industrial communities, Shaw put into *Major Barbara*, as Undershaft's utopian Perivale St Andrews, Booth's scheme of "a series of Industrial Settlements or Suburban Villages, lying out in the country, within a reasonable distance of all our great cities," with cottages "of the best material and workmanship," and cooperative stores "supplying everything that was really necessary at the most economic prices." For, as Booth had explained, the gospel of thrift was of no consequence to a man who had nothing to eat nor threepence to pay for lodging. But Booth did not add, as Shaw would in *Major Barbara*, that the unemployed poor should not have to embrace any gospel in order to join the queue for economic salvation.

When St. John Ervine approached Shaw about writing his biography, Shaw assured the biographer of Booth (29 October 1932), "I like the little I heard from him (the story of Major Barbara will be the only interesting chapter in your book) and . . . I really believe what his Commissars said when I put it to them, that he would have fought just as hard for the poor and their salvation if there had been no other world for him than this." Booth, he felt, was a reformer who employed the tools of religion rather than a religious zealot who used the language of social reform. It was more in fun than truth when Shaw teased playwright Arthur Pinero (29 November 1909), "Nowadays when I contemplate your remarkable nose, I think of that other remarkable nose, the nose of General Booth—both noses out for soul saving."

When Shaw's Barbara vows a return to soul-saving on different premises than she has first assumed, her father tempts her to try her hand on his workmen, since their bellies were full and they could have no material motive. The fear of real-world hell had been removed. As Andrew Undershaft would, Booth described the underside of England—"the submerged tenth" of the population—as living in "Dante's Hell." Shaw had already used Booth's metaphor in *John Bull's Other Island* (1904), in which the unfrocked priest Father Keegan describes "this world of . . . torment and penance" as hell. "For me there are only two countries: heaven and hell," he adds; "[and] but two conditions of men: salvation and damnation." Keegan may be Irish and Catholic, but the conception might have been Booth's. Darkest England is given life in the shelter scene of *Major Barbara*, and in other comments by his munitions-czar hero, and when the demands of the drama require that some aspects of the problem—and solution—be relegated to the play's long preface, they reappear as the sardonically titled "Gospel of St Andrew Undershaft." (Unseen but oft-mentioned in the play is Undershaft's gentle Jewish partner Lazarus, a reasonable name to suggest a Jew, and suggestive in other ways as well. It is no surprise, then, to find early in Booth's book a reference to the biblical Lazarus—but only to suggest the ragged and starved unemployed. Still, the name may have lodged in Shaw's subconscious.)

A striking link is Booth's reference to the seven deadly sins "which of late years . . . have contrived to pass themselves off as virtues," a description which Undershaft turns to the "seven deadly sins" of "Food, clothing, firing, rent, taxes, respectability and children"—burdens that only money can relieve. To the startled Barbara, Undershaft claims to have saved her own soul from them through his generous allowance for her upkeep. Drink, too, is a major theme of Booth's—his certainty that the craving for it sprang from the need to blot out the pain of living, and that the inevitable addiction was the root of most social evils. But he saw no likelihood that poverty would be abolished by a Socialist Millennium. Dismissing two of the books most influential on Shaw's thinking in the 1880s and 1890s, Henry George's *Progress and Poverty*, which relied on a redistribution of wealth through a tax on land values, and Edward Bellamy's utopian—and secular—socialism in *Looking Backward*, as "religious cant," Booth sought immediate relief. "When the sky falls we shall catch larks. No doubt. But in the meantime?"

The utopian schemes of Socialism, he warned, required "a bloody and violent overturn of all existing institutions." Those who had something to lose by that possibility would be more prudent, he suggested, in financing his spiritual revolution, for the religious discipline guaranteed social change within social order. Booth's recipe for the regeneration of man has the ring of a Shavian preface, and Shaw would use the same catalogue approach:

> *The first essential that must be borne in mind as governing every Scheme that may be put forward is that it must change the man when it is his character and conduct which constitute the reasons for his failure in the battle of life.* No change in circumstances, no revolution in social conditions, can possibly transform the nature of man. Some of the worst men and women in the world, whose names are chronicled by history with a shudder of horror, were those who had all the advantages that wealth, education and station could confer or ambition could attain.
>
> The supreme test of any scheme for benefiting humanity lies in the answer to the question, What does it make of the individual? . . . You may clothe the drunkard, fill his purse with gold, establish him in a well–furnished home, and in three, or six, or twelve months he will once more be on the Embankment, haunted by delirium tremens, dirty, squalid, and ragged. Hence, in all cases where a man's own character and defects constitute the reasons for his fall, that character must be changed and that conduct altered if any permanent beneficial results are to be attained. If he is a drunkard, he must be made sober; if idle, he must be made industrious; if criminal, he must be made honest; if impure, he must be made clean; and if he be so deep down in vice, and has been there so long that he has lost all heart, and hope, and power to help himself, and absolutely refused to move, he must be inspired with hope and have created within him the ambition to rise. . . .
>
> Secondly: *The remedy, to be effectual, must change the circumstances of the individual when they are the cause of his wretched condition, and lie beyond his control.* Among those who have arrived at their present evil plight through faults of self-indulgence or some defect in their moral character, how many are there who would have been very differently placed to-day had their surroundings been otherwise? . . . Favourable circumstances will not change a man's heart or transform his nature, but unpropitious circumstances may

render it absolutely impossible for him to escape no matter how he may desire to extricate himself. The first step with these helpless, sunken creatures is to create the desire to escape, and then provide the means for doing so. In other words, give the man another chance.

Thirdly: *Any remedy worthy of consideration must be on a scale commensurate with the evil with which it proposes to deal.* It is no use trying to bail out the ocean with a pint pot. This evil is one whose victims are counted by the million. The army of the Lost in our midst exceeds the numbers of the multitudinous host which Xerxes led from Asia to attempt the conquest of Greece. Pass in parade those who make up the submerged tenth, count the paupers indoor and outdoor, the homeless, the starving, the criminals, the lunatics, the drunkards, and the harlots—and yet do not give way to despair! Even to attempt to save a tithe of this host requires that we should put much more force and fire into our work than has hitherto been exhibited by anyone. There must be no more philanthropic tinkering, as if this vast sea of human misery were contained in the limits of a garden pond.

Fourthly: *Not only must the Scheme be large enough, but it must be permanent.* That is to say, it must not be merely a spasmodic effort coping with the misery of to-day; it must be established on a durable footing, so as to go on dealing with the misery of to-morrow and the day after, so long as there is misery left in the world with which to grapple.

Fifthly: *But while it must be permanent, it must also be immediately practicable.* Any Scheme, to be of use, must be capable of being brought into instant operation with beneficial results.

Sixthly: *The indirect features of the Scheme must not be such as to produce injury to the persons whom we seek to benefit.* Mere charity, for instance, while relieving the pinch of hunger, demoralises the recipient; and whatever the remedy is that we employ, it must be of such a nature as to do good without doing evil at the same time. It is no use conferring sixpennyworth of benefit on a man if, at the same time, we do him a shilling's worth of harm.

Seventhly: *While assisting one class of the community, it must not seriously interfere with the interests of another.* In raising one section of the fallen, we must not thereby endanger the safety of those who with difficulty are keeping on their feet.

What Shaw perceived was that Booth's Victorian idealism about hard work and human renewal was slipping away as the Army succeeded in winning converts. There were too many branches, too many inexperienced officers. Spirituality excited more innocent fervor than economics, and the emphasis in any case was becoming one endemic to charitable organizations. It became more vital to save souls and to count the collection, to stir and restir the faithful to pay the increasing costs of maintenance of the growing network of Army personnel and rented chapel space. Booth's goal of social regeneration to eliminate the causes of poverty was giving way to the goal of building and buttressing the charity bureaucracy of Salvation Army colonels and majors and captains. Its chapels where the poor received bread-and-scrape, and a hymn book, and the promise of some kind of job, usually unrealized, was substituting for the farms and factories and new towns that had been the models for tomorrow.

That realization gives added meaning, and even poignancy, to Undershaft's challenge to Major Barbara and her fiancé, Dolly Cusins, "Dare you make war on war? Here are the means!" Booth had almost ceased to make war on the sources of poverty; rather, he was accepting what amounted to unacknowledged bribes from the whiskey distillers and from other entrepreneurs whose commodities were counterproductive to social change, to keep the West Ham shelter in East London, and others like it, alive to dispense soup and salvationism. The reorganization of work and the workplace about which William Booth wrote in his *In Darkest England* was left to Shaw, who drew upon Booth and Barbara's other spiritual fathers to challenge charity to furnish more than a Band-Aid and thus eliminate the need for its own existence. That bureaucratic instinct to survive, and then to prosper on the pennies of the faithful, is seen now with a melodramatic glare in the soap-opera saga of the "electric church" of television evangelism.

"What is the use of preaching the Gospel," Booth asked in *In Darkest England*, "to men whose whole attention is concentrated upon a mad, desperate struggle to keep themselves alive? . . . The first thing to do is to get him at least a footing on firm ground, and to give him room to live. Then you may have a chance." More bluntly, but in the same terms, Shaw's Undershaft would challenge Barbara, "It is cheap work converting starving men with a Bible in one hand and a slice of bread in the other. . . . Try your hand on my men; their souls are hungry because their bellies are full."

Booth's description of a typical afternoon and evening at a Salvation Army shelter could be the scenario for Act II of *Major Barbara*. A wash and a meal are followed by "a rousing Salvation meeting," during which "there are addresses, some delivered by the leaders of the meeting, but most of them [are] the testimonies of those who have been saved at previous meetings, and who, rising in their seats, tell their companions of their experiences. Strange experiences they often are of those who have been down in the very bottomless depths of sin and misery." But Shaw remains skeptical about confessions for bread. As Rummy Mitchens complains to Snobby Price in Shaw's depiction of the shelter, "Thats whats so unfair to us women. Your confessions is just as big lies as ours; you dont tell what you really done no more than us; but you men can tell your lies right out at the meetins and be made much of for it; while the sort of confessions we az to make az to be whispered to one lady at a time. It aint right." But Barbara's true-believer reaction, in her ecstasy of worldly innocence, impresses Snobby: "Ive hardly ever seen them so much moved as they were by your confession, Mr Price. . . . If you had given your mother just one more kick, we should have got the whole five shillings!" Undershaft offers to contribute the odd tuppence, but Barbara refuses her father's offer: his money is tainted, as she thinks her pitiful collection is not.

Undershaft's allegedly suspect millions are made in munitions manufacture, supplying one of the necessities of modern civilization. However tainted, and however threatening they seem to the very civilization that the jobs he creates sustain, their impact is much like that of Booth's ideal— utopian "self-sustaining communities, each a kind of co-operative society, or patriarchal family, governed and disciplined on the principles which have already proved so effective in the Salvation Army." Its motto, Undershaft has already explained, might be his own: "Blood and Fire."

"But not your sort of blood and fire, you know," counters his future son-in-law, Charles Lomax.

"My sort of blood cleanses: my sort of fire purifies," Undershaft explains, and Major Barbara says "So do ours." And in his preface to the play Shaw suggested "that when General Booth chose Blood and Fire for the emblem of Salvation instead of the Cross, he was perhaps better inspired than he knew: such knowledge, for the daughter of Andrew Undershaft, will clearly lead to something hopefuller than distributing bread and treacle."

Bread and treacle without an ideal left an emptiness of soul, something that Shaw had recognized years before he put down a word of *Major Barbara*. One of the positive elements of Booth's Army, he found, was the replacement of Christian gloom by Christian vitality:

> Joyousness, a sacred gift long dethroned by the hellish laughter of derision and obscenity, rises like a flood miraculously out of the fetid dust and mud of the slums; rousing marches and impetuous

dithyrambs rise to the heavens from people among whom the depressing noise called "sacred music" is a standing joke: a flag with Blood and Fire on it is unfurled, not in murderous rancor, but because fire is beautiful and blood a vital and splendid red; Fear, which we flatter by calling Self, vanishes; and transfigured men and women carry their gospel through a transfigured world, calling their leader General, themselves captains and brigadiers, and their whole body an Army: praying, but praying only for refreshment, for strength to fight, and for needful MONEY (a notable sign, that); preaching, but not preaching submission; daring ill-usage and abuse, but not putting up with more of it than is inevitable; and practising what the world will let them practise, including soap and water, color and music. There is danger in such activity; and where there is danger there is hope.

The danger, he saw, was still money. The Salvation Army was

building up a business organization which will compel it eventually to see that its present staff of enthusiast-commanders shall be succeeded by a bureaucracy of men of business who will be no better than bishops, and perhaps a good deal more unscrupulous. That has always happened sooner or later to great orders founded by saints; and the order founded by St William Booth is not exempt from the same danger. It is even more dependent than the Church on rich people who would cut off supplies at once if it began to preach that indispensable revolt against poverty which must also be a revolt against riches.[12]

"Where does all the money go to?" Snobby Price charged in words deleted from the manuscript of the play. "Why old Booth gets millions." Shaw knew better than to suggest misappropriation of Army donations, even when spoken by the sly but ignorant Snobby Price, and dropped the line.[13] Yet Shaw was concerned about the evangelical distortion of Christ's "Blessed are the poor in spirit" into "Blessed are the poor." One Salvationist who had seen the play in December 1905 came away shaken and drafted a fourteen-page typewritten report to an Army Commissioner, Alex M. Nicol. "You come away feeling not very sure of yourself," the writer confessed. "Human nature is shewn as such a rotten sort of thing, that you even wonder if you aren't a bit of a humbug yourself."[14] Humbugging, one assumes, to extract money from the poor as well as for the poor.

The *War Cry* of 4 November 1905 had been more cautious. "A leading dramatist," the official voice of the Army reported, "has written a new play, 'Major Barbara,' which concerns the love affair of a Salvation Army officer, and is woven more or less around the General's slum work. The second act is laid in a Salvation 'doss-house,' and the dialogue is largely the expression of views on General Booth's religious campaign. 'I greatly admire his rescue work,' said the dramatist."[15]

Not a mention of Bernard Shaw!

Notes

1. Entry for 30 April 1897 in *Burne-Jones Talking: His Conversations as Preserved by His Studio Assistant, Thomas Rooke*, ed. Mary Lago (Columbia: University of Missouri Press, 1981), p. 144.

2. Shaw, *Immaturity* (1878–79), published in the *Collected Edition* as vol. 1; the manuscript is in the National Library of Ireland.

3. Shaw, *Dramatic Review*, 26 September 1885, reprinted in *Shaw's Music*, ed. Dan H. Laurence (New York: Dodd, Mead, 1981), p. 364.

4. Shaw, *The Star*, 13 May 1889, reprinted in *Shaw's Music*, p. 627.

5. Report to the Salvation Army, 31 March 1906, published as "'The Bands of the Salvation Army" in *Shaw's Music*, pp. 588–94.

6. *Collected Letters 1898–1910*, ed. Dan H. Laurence (London: Max Reinhardt, 1972), p. 564. All extracts from Shaw's letters are from *CL* unless otherwise identified.

7. Letter to the *Daily Citizen*, 26 October 1912, reprinted in *Agitations*, ed. Dan H. Laurence and James Rambeau (New York: Frederick Ungar, 1985), p. 150.

8. "Open Air Meetings," autograph manuscript, p. 6, c. 1879–80, in the Harry Ransom Humanities Research Center, University of Texas at Austin, Reproduced with the permission of the HRHRC and published with the authorization of the Society of Authors on behalf of the Bernard Shaw Estate. Copyright © 1990 by the Estate of Bernard Shaw.

9. "Facts about Major Barbara," a press release drafted by Shaw for *The Sun*, New York, 26 December 1915, reprinted in *The Bodley Head Bernard Shaw Collected Plays with Their Prefaces* 3:193–97.

10. Press cutting from the Ivo Currall collection, Royal Academy of Dramatic Art, London, identified as from *The Standard* (London), September 1911.

11. Diary entry for 19 July 1889, in *Bernard Shaw, The Diaries 1885–1897*, ed. Stanley Weintraub (University Park: Pennsylvania State University Press, 1986), p. 523. Other diary references are from this edition.

12. Preface to *Major Barbara, Bodley Head Bernard Shaw*.

13. Garland facsimile edition of the *Major Barbara* manuscript, ed. Bernard F. Dukore (New York: Garland, 1981), leaf 69.

14. Alex M. Nicol, Commissioner of the Salvation Army, TLS, 18 December 1905, accompanying a fourteen-page typewritten criticism of the play by an unidentified Salvationist who had attended the 15 December 1905 matinee of *Major Barbara*. HRHRC Austin, #315 in the catalogue,

Shaw: An Exhibit, ed. Dan H. Laurence (Austin: Humanities Research Center, The University of Texas, 1977).

15. Quoted from the *War Cry* in Arch R. Wiggins, *History of the Salvation Army* (London: Nelson, 1968), 4:251–52.

APOSTATE APOSTLE

H. L. Mencken as Shavophile and Shavophobe

It is ironic that we owe to the self-publicizing paradox purveyor Henry Louis Mencken, more than to any other American critic, the popular misconception of Bernard Shaw as self-advertising clown and coiner of cheap paradoxes. Although once a Shavophile, in middle age Mencken was wont to look back upon his discipleship as a youthful indiscretion, fostering the impression that *George Bernard Shaw: His Plays*, his first major publication, was more biological necessity than pioneering work. One of his earliest biographers even wrote, "Mr. Mencken had his attack of Shavianitis at the appropriate age, when there was some merit in 'discovering' Shaw, and before it was too late to recover from the generous illusions of one's critical nonage."[1]

Bernard Shaw had to wait until his fiftieth year before a book on his work appeared, and even then the modest claim it made for Shaw's reputation was rendered suspect by its appearance not in the Ireland of his birth or the England of his residence, but in intellectually suspect America. Worse still, the author was a young American newspaperman, and the work was his first book.

What time Mencken had been able to spare from his duties on the *Baltimore Sun* in 1904 had been devoted to reading Ibsen, Conrad, and Thomas Huxley. During that year, Will A. Page of the *Washington Post* added Bernard Shaw to the young journalist's reading list, and before long Mencken had determined to do for Shaw what Shaw himself had done for Ibsen. That summer he spent his spare time outlining a critical study of Shaw's plays—a "Quintessence of Shavianism." The obvious potential publisher was Brentano, publisher in the U.S. of *The Quintessence of Ibsenism*, but Mencken met with a polite lack of enthusiasm there and turned prudently to John W. Luce, a small Boston firm that had published—unauthorized—a slender volume of Shaw's, the *Savoy* essay "On Going to Church."

Mencken worked on the manuscript for Luce through the early part of 1905, afterwards exchanging long letters with the publisher about revisions that had been recommended. By autumn the slender volume was in production, and in the first days of December the author's own copies arrived at 1524 Hollins Street, Baltimore. Inscribing his initial presentation copy to his subject, Mencken apologized above his signature for his youthful zest and inexperience and added the hope that he would have the pleasure of meeting Shaw some day.[2] But to insure that G.B.S. would open the package in which the book was shipped, its author simultaneously mailed a letter announcing the book. It was even more modest than his inscription, offering no hint of the curmudgeonly qualities around which Mencken later developed his self-publicized persona:

My dear sir:

I am sending to you today, under another wrapper, a copy of a little book I have just published. It is called "George Bernard Shaw: His Plays," and as the title indicates, it is an attempt to get between covers some sort of connected review of your dramas. That you will find it lacking in errors, both of fact and of judgment, is more than I may hope, but I sincerely trust you may see some evidence of the painstaking* and honesty and admiration and good intention that went into it.

Appearances to the contrary notwithstanding, this book was not thrown together in a hurry to wring a toll from the recent outbreak of Shawophobia in the United States. It was begun, in truth, early last spring, and was in type before Mrs. Warren outraged the virtue of New York. As you no doubt know, the mere fact of its publication is of some value to a young man in the writing trade, whatever its demerits. I should be much grieved if this gain of mine were obtained at the cost of annoyance to you.

In case you come to the United States shortly I shall give myself

---

*Mencken used *painstaking* as a noun here (taking pains).

the pleasure of calling upon you—to make my apologies. Meanwhile I have the honor to be, with great respect,

Yours very sincerely,
H. L. Mencken[3]

Except that he claimed erroneously that Shaw was a Darwinist, there was little in the unpretentious book to create any need for the apologies Mencken offered in advance, although even Shaw, who concealed from the reading public none of his immodest feelings about his talents, might not have ended the preface—as Mencken did—with the declaration, "Even the worst of Shaw is well worth study." Perhaps Shaw did wonder—if he read the book through—why the examination of *Major Barbara* promised in the table of contents was nowhere to be found in the text, but the reason would have been more apparent to G.B.S. than to Mencken's other readers. The book had been rushed into print without waiting for publication of the play, which had had its first performance only a week before Mencken had mailed his Shaw book to London. In an excess of enthusiasm, he had very likely listed the title in his book on hearing of its existence and its imminent production at the Court Theatre.[4] *Major Barbara* was still unpublished, and another ten years would pass before the play would be produced in America.

George Bernard Shaw: His Plays had a less-than-respectable sale, but respectful treatment from the critics. Mencken made no money from it. Whether or not it was "of some value to a young man in the writing trade," Mencken's stock rose thereafter, ascending even more dizzyingly after the writer disowned, in effect, that first youthful enthusiasm via irreverent, anti-Shavian polemics announcing his discovery that Shaw's playwriting practice really consisted of the routing of platitudes with "super-platitudes." But whether Mencken's turnabout regarding Shaw was a matter of style or a matter of faith, he apparently still longed for the opportunity of calling on the first hero of his prose, who had never come to America to give him that opportunity he asked for in his letter of 1905.

In 1922, a bushel of anti-Shavian tirades later, a now-famous Mencken journeyed to England and walked the streets of London near Shaw's flat in Adelphi Terrace. Although Shaw would shortly tell one visitor that Mencken was "an amusing dog, and a valuable critic, because he thinks it more important to write as he feels than to be liked as a good-hearted, gentlemanly creature,"[5] someone else—possibly the never trustworthy Frank Harris—had told Mencken that G.B.S. was angry with him. The two never met.

They would not have enjoyed each other's company. To the ascetic Shaw the obscenity-prone, heavy-smoking, beer-swilling Mencken represented almost everything he disliked about Americans. Dismissing Mencken's being taken for a "gentlemanly creature" suggests that Shaw knew that. Meanwhile, Mencken wrote to his friend Estelle Bloom not that he was too timid to try to meet his former hero, but that Shaw was the wrong sort himself. "He is a teetotaller and I detest them."[6]

Shaw seldom remained angry at anyone for very long, but in Mencken's case he had good reason. On 22 September 1930 the American newspapermen John Haslup Adams and Paul Patterson called on him in London, and Adams, editor of the paper for which Mencken wrote, the *Baltimore Sun*, mentioned his irascible star. Mencken, said Shaw, "makes delightful reading. I even recall that he once wrote a book about me."[7]

At the time the book had appeared in 1905, American reviews of Shaw's work were often lengthy and emotional but seldom flattering. To the young critic, Ibsen then paled beside Shaw, whom Mencken saw as more than a "mere imitator." "In some things," he wrote, then, "indeed—such, for instance, as in fertility of wit and invention—he very greatly exceeds the Norwegian." Furthermore, he thought that no other contemporary dramatist, with the possible exception of Ibsen, had so stimulated the public's thinking:

> Pick up any of the literary monthlies and you will find a disquisition upon his technique, glance through the dramatic column of your favorite newspaper and you will find some reference to his plays. Go to your woman's club, O gentle reader! and you will hear your neighbor, Mrs. McGinnis, deliver her views upon "Candida." Pass among any collection of human beings accustomed to even rudimentary mental activity—and you will hear some mention, direct or indirect, and some opinion, original or cribbed, of or about the wild Irishman. . . . And so we may take it for granted that Shaw tries to make us think and that he succeeds.

At this early stage in Mencken's Shavolatry it was possible that a play by Shaw could have some serious faults, but each flaw was vastly overshadowed by its preponderant merit. *Captain Brassbound's Conversion*, for example, was "decidedly inferior" to most of Shaw, chiefly because the exposition in the first act required "an immense amount of talk without action." Yet the piece was "a melodrama of the true Shaw brand, in which the play of mind upon mind overshadows the play of club upon skull." Even *Caesar and*

Cleopatra, which Mencken described as "sweeping" and "spectacular" as well as "more human and more logical" than Shakespeare's Caesar play, admittedly had a serious flaw—Caesar himself, who was "scarcely a Roman." But Mencken's innate iconoclasm was whetted most by the gargantuan *Man and Superman*, which he described with pre-Hollywoodian fireworks: it was "the most entertaining play of its generation" as well as "a tract cast in an encyclopedic and epic mold—a stupendous, magnificent colossal effort to make a dent in the cosmos with a slapstick."

When Mencken became literary critic for *Smart Set* several years later (and particularly when he rose to co-editor in 1914), a different approach to Shaw became inevitable. The early apostolic enthusiasm had not quite worn off, but Shavian drama no longer needed a Paul; it had already been noisily received on American shores and was now more than a curiosity peddled by crackpots. Amateur and professional groups were successfully presenting *You Never Can Tell, Candida, Arms and the Man, The Devil's Disciple, Man and Superman*—and New York police had successfully blocked presentation of *Mrs Warren's Profession*, causing Mencken to boast in 1914, "To see

Fig. 6. Henry Louis Mencken at work in 1912. Contemporary photo.

Shaw's 'Mrs Warren,' I had to go to Germany."[8] However, Mencken's position as literary critic and editor demanded more objectivity than hero worship, and the tone of *Smart Set* demanded as much irreverence as reverence. Furthermore, his emotions seem to have become affected by messianic impulses. The older generation—Nietzsche, Ibsen, Shaw—had served its function by clearing away much of the Victorian rubbish; it was now time for Mencken's generation, with Mencken as its spokesman, to impose its freshly jaundiced view of the times.

Mencken's strategy was the announcement—actually an elaboration of the obvious—that Shaw (now nearly sixty) was slowing down and becoming more repetitious. Reviewing *Misalliance, Fanny's First Play* and *The Dark Lady of the Sonnets* for *Smart Set*, he raised himself to Shaw's level through the leverage of his pen and condescendingly referred to "our loud and bold friend, George Bernard Shaw," adding further, "Is it time to add 'tiresome?' For one, I protest against it. . . . The long preface to 'Misalliance' (Brentano)—it runs to 121 closely printed pages, perhaps 45,000 words, a good sized book in itself—is one of the best things, indeed, he has ever done. . . . You will be constantly chuckling and glowing, and murmuring, 'How true! How true!' This is the special function of Shaw, the steady business of his life: to say the things that everybody knows and nobody says, to expose the everyday hypocrisies, to rout platitudes with super-platitudes. . . ."[9]

Although Mencken scoffed, his heart was obviously not in it, for nowhere yet had Shaw torn into so many human foibles so dear to Mencken's own iconoclastic heart as in *Misalliance* and its preface. The Brobdingnagian preface, with seventy-five such topics as "Wanted, a Child's Magna Charta," "How Little We Know about Our Parents," "Children's Rights and Duties," and "Natural Selection as a Religion," Mencken had to admit was one of the best things Shaw had done. Still he felt obliged to add, "No, these new plays will not lift Shaw nearer Shakespeare—he has yet to do anything better than the earliest fruits of his fancy—'Mrs Warren,' 'Candida,' and 'Arms and the Man.' But though he thus stands still as a dramatist, he yet remains a surpassing entertainer."[10]

By August 1916, Mencken was, as Irvin S. Cobb once remarked, "drunk with the power which he has found in his pen." Certainly it was a different Mencken than had written *Bernard Shaw: His Plays* a scant decade before. His new theme had appeared in milder terms in the review of *Misalliance* two years earlier—the accusation that G.B.S. was guilty of announcing the obvious in terms of the scandalous. Now Shaw—a Dubliner—had become the "Ulster Polonius," who in *Androcles and the Lion* had fooled the world with a "veritable debauch of platitudes" and "embalmed ideas." Moreover, Mencken announced, Shaw was "not at all the heretic his fascinated victims see him, but an orthodox Scotch Presbyterian of the most cock-sure and bilious sort." He took little stock in the "theory" that Shaw was Irish, demonstrating to his own satisfaction that Shaw's name and background were Scotch. The playwright's "ethical obsession," he railed, had founded in England "the superstition that Ibsen was no more than a tinpot evangelist."[11]

With more leisure, Mencken expanded the review of *Androcles* into an article-length diatribe, also entitled "The Ulster Polonius." Here Mencken's claim to authority was that he had written the first book about Shaw's works and still read and enjoyed them. But the earlier praise was hedged, *ex post facto:* "Yet so far as I know, I have never found an original idea in them. . . . What is seriously stated in them is quite beyond logical dispute. . . . As well try to controvert Copernican astronomy." Why then, asked Mencken, is the Ulster Polonius regarded as an arch-heretic? "Because he practices with great zest and skill the fine art of exhibiting the obvious in obvious and terrifying lights."[12] The "most searching and illuminating observations" that Mencken had praised in *Man and Superman* in 1905 were, in a reappraisal of the play, exposed as platitudes: evidence, perhaps, of Shaw's success in gaining wide intellectual acceptance. Also, by proclaiming Shaw now to be merely an entertaining windbag, a sham, Mencken was (it seems implied) setting himself up to be Shaw's successor as arch-heretic of the English-speaking world. Mencken had the need, "like so many of his fellow-critics since," as Louis Kronenberger put it, "in raising one thing up, to pull another down."[13] Thus to Mencken, Shaw became now "almost the arche-type of the blue-nose," a "Scotch Puritan" to whom "Beauty is a lewdness, redeemable only in the service of morality." In conclusion he sniped, "and this is Shaw the revolutionist, the heretic! Next, perhaps, we shall be hearing of Benedict XV, the atheist. . . ."[14] To Mencken's satisfaction, at least, G.B.S. was unmasked.

When necessary, Mencken (to use his own terms) even "dredged" reasons to deflate Shaw's reputation from the works of naive and specious Shavolators whose panegyrics could only have served to embarrass their subject. In 1918 the unlucky offender was Robert Blatchford, an English socialist, who wrote, "Shaw is something much better than a wit, much better than a politician or a dramatist; he is a moralist, a teacher of ethics, austere, relentless, fiercely earnest."[15] "What could be more idiotic," Mencken commented. "Then Cotton Mather was a greater man than Johann Sebastian

Bach. . . ."[16] Blatchford was merely a convenient soapbox from which to
blast Shaw's didacticism. Mencken had no quibble with Shaw's playwriting,
steadfastly praising his dexterity in the theater while insisting that Shaw
"smothers his dramaturgy in a pifflish iconoclasm that is no more than a
disguise for Puritanism."[17] The Sage of Baltimore obviously had designs
elsewhere than on Shaw's playwriting reputation.

Before Shaw's warmly admiring comment of 1922 appeared in print—
Archibald Henderson had published the Master's "Table-Talk" in the *Fortnightly Review*—Mencken had published more abuse, this time somewhat
at odds with his own earlier apostasy. Shaw was still a "Scotch bluenose
disguised as an Irish patriot and English soothsayer" who attempted "heroic
but vain struggles to throw off Presbyterianism." But now Mencken found
that the "discussion plays" such as *Misalliance* and *Getting Married*, which
he had condemned earlier as theatrical platitudes, were the only Shavian
plays "which contain actual ideas," although they "failed dismally on the
stage."[18] Many of his aphorisms were now inversions of his earlier convic-
tions: Ibsen and Shaw had served their purpose; there were no ideas in the
so-called "drama of ideas." A decade earlier, the Baltimore soothsayer,
already by then an apostate, had still been praising such plays as *Candida*,
Arms and the Man, and *Man and Superman*. Now he lumped them with
Androcles as barren of ideas:

> The successful plays contain no ideas; they contain only platitudes,
> balderdash, buncombe. . . . Shaw has given all these pieces a
> specious air of profundity by publishing them hooked to long and
> garrulous prefaces and by filling them with stage directions which
> describe and discuss the characters at great length. But as stage plays
> they are almost as empty as "Hedda Gabler." One searches them
> vainly for even the slightest novel contribution to the current theories
> of life. . . . Shaw's prefaces, of course, have vastly more ideational
> force and respectability than his plays. If he fails to get any ideas of
> genuine savor into them it is not because the preface form bars them
> out but because he hasn't any to get in.[19]

The middle 1920s found Mencken firmly atop his *American Mercury*
platform at the zenith of his fame and influence. Perhaps it seemed to him
no longer necessary to work at deflating Shaw in order to inflate Mencken.
After Shaw's philosophic excursions in *Heartbreak House*, *Saint Joan*, and
Methuselah, Mencken sounded almost orthodox when he mourned that

G.B.S., "once so agile and diverting, becomes a seer and a prophet."[20]
Writing on Mark Twain in the *Chicago Tribune*, he compared the American
with such literary giants as Wagner, Tolstoy—and Shaw. Like them,
Mencken thought, "he was a great artist, but also a great mountebank."[21]

In his last years, wheezy with heart trouble and unable to do more than
reach within for material, Mencken began his never-to-be-finished *My Life
as Author and Editor*. By November 1948—when he had to put it down—he
had only reached the 1920s, his heyday. "As I began to gather an audience,"
he confessed with possibly dubious innocence, "I discovered, somewhat to
my surprise and consternation, that I was becoming known principally as a
killer: the truth was that I was far more eager to discover and proclaim merit,
however modest, than to inflict blame and punishment." He carried on, he
claimed, "what amounted almost to crusades" for Shaw, Conrad, Galsworthy, Wells, and Bennett—even for James Huneker. He had even got in
"many a lick" for Nietzsche and Twain. "But all these were established
men, and of the eight, six were foreigners and two were dead. What
I needed was some American, preferably young, to mass my artillery
behind. . . ."[22]

What he neglected to add is that he preferred someone unpopular, even
controversial, so that the Mencken artillery could be seen as the deciding
factor. When several other candidates failed him, Mencken adopted the
ponderous but powerful Theodore Dreiser. He would even publish, in
Smart Set, the first Mencken magazine platform, plays that proved the
admittedly "dour" Dreiser no playwright, but the flaming reviews ceased,
and then the friendship, early in the early 1920s. (Dreiser would be recast as
"essentially a German peasant, oafish. . . .") Mencken had been better, after
all, he recognized, at puncturing balloons than at inflating them—as he
even boasted in the title of a 1918 collection, *Damn! A Book of Calumny*.

By 1930 Mencken was sufficiently settled in the pattern of his life to be
more objective about his first literary master. A quarter-century had passed
since he was a young man in a hurry, and he no longer had magazines—or
even himself—in need of promotion. According to a Mencken biographer
he could acknowledge that Shaw was both the most accomplished stylist and
the most successful of contemporary intellectual demagogues. Shaw and he,
Mencken admitted, were "working the same side of the street"—that is,
"stating the obvious in terms of the scandalous."[23] Yet Mencken had
been denouncing Shaw for doing that during the twenty previous years
of apostatehood.

To the Depression generation of the 1930s, Mencken, no longer editor of the now-declining *Mercury,* was also no longer hero and cause.[24] Still as reactionary as ever in his politics, he may have seen common ground between himself and the Shaw of the political plays, such as *On the Rocks* and *The Apple Cart,* who, without rejecting his Fabianism, had become disillusioned with the waste and stupidity he thought inherent in democratic processes. While sneering about G.B.S.'s socialism to associate editor Charles Angoff,[25] Mencken was writing in one of his last reviews for the *Mercury* that Shaw's socialism was only "a blackjack for clubbing the heads of the orthodox." Although both—admittedly here—*were* working the same side of the street, almost by reflex action, it seems, Mencken repeated his well-worn Scotch Puritan epithets. Even some lukewarm and condescending praise was in order now, however, as, in one of his interviews, he defended Shaw's comic style:

> Is there anything discreditable about being a really first-rate clown? Is it a sin against the Holy Ghost to go through life pricking bubbles? I incline to think not. What Shaw has to say is almost always what has been said before, and often it has been better said. Sometimes it is sense and sometimes it is nonsense. . . . He has not made life better for anyone, but he has made it more amusing, more exciting, and hence more endurable. It is thus idle to sneer at him, and silly to denounce him. He is a lightweight, true enough, but he has a long reach and knows how to use his feet, and he has brought many a heavyweight clattering to the floor.[26]

Here again was evidence that Mencken had not changed much. Through a quarter of a century—whether apostle or apostate—he had continued to demonstrate his inability to understand Shaw's religion and philosophy. Although he had done much to cause the thinking minority of the public to take Shaw seriously, his admiration was generally limited to surface aspects of Shaw. It is for this reason, perhaps, that it is to Mencken more than to any other American critic that we owe the popular notion of Shaw. Mencken consistently treated G.B.S. as primarily a satirist with a slapstick, a modernized and better-humored Swift or Voltaire. This was a confusion of ends and means, for although Shaw used satire and irony freely, it was not merely to expose hollow idols, sham ideals and feet of clay, but to expound his confessedly derivative "original morality"—which Mencken looked on as nonsense. Furthermore, Mencken the individualist could not understand Shaw the socialist, who considered his socialism not as an end but as a first faltering step in the grand design of Creative Evolution. Mencken's journalistic and superficial individualism was undirected and ego-satisfying, but essentially negative.

Following his retirement from the *American Mercury* at the end of 1933, Mencken undertook a complete rewriting of his major exhibit in evidence that scholarship can be entertaining—*The American Language*. First published in 1919, it had three revisions thereafter. For his fourth and final version, he had some business correspondence with another sage fascinated by language study—Bernard Shaw. In one exchange of notes regarding permission to insert a Shavian quotation in *The American Language*, Shaw replied warmly, "Yes, and you may go the limit."[27] But that was also the limit to which familiarity ever went between the old warriors.

In the 1936 edition were several graceful nods to G.B.S. in his role as innovator and conservator of the English language. Mencken praised Shaw's activities as the dissenting member of the B.B.C.'s Advisory Committee on Spoken English and his reasonable approach toward accepting change in the language. As Mencken mellowed, he burrowed even deeper into philological researches, emerging regularly to issue blasts against the New Deal and Franklin Roosevelt, F.D.R. having replaced G.B.S. as radical villain. When *Supplement One*—a work almost as large as the final version of the original work—was published in 1945, again Shaw was present—as contributor of *Comstockery* to the American language.[28] Here Shaw's cause was one particularly dear to Mencken's heart, and the Sage of Baltimore spent a long footnote detailing the Shavian term's exposure of America's moral provinciality. Another contribution from G.B.S. was the lessening of the horror to Englishmen of *bloody* (already quite innocuous to Americans) after its use by "Mrs. Pat" Campbell in *Pygmalion*. Again Mencken's pleased reference was to Shaw's part in accelerating the decline of prudery.[29] Yet only a dozen years earlier Mencken had still been repeating in print his assertion that G.B.S. was a "Scotch blue-nose."

Nostalgic as the old faith might have seemed to the mellowing Mencken, recantation was impossible. We may infer from Mencken's last publications that he preferred to let his writings on Shaw be forgotten out of neglect. In *A Mencken Chrestomathy* (1953), "a collection of choice passages" edited and annotated by the author, he explained his selections by prefacing, "I have occasionally allowed partiality to corrupt judgment."[30] None of his many past references to Shaw, pro or con, appear in the hundreds of closely printed pages, not even in the section on "Literati," although names several degrees lesser in literary magnitude wither again or are re-enobled under the

Mencken pen. In *Minority Report* (1956), the jottings from his notebooks published in the year of his death, the ailing curmudgeon would only admit about his Shavolatrous landmark of a half-century before, "I succumbed to more sophisticated and tortured devices, and there was a good deal of empty ornament in my first prose book, 'George Bernard Shaw: His Plays.' "[31] So Shaw—once prophet and cause to Mencken—appeared and disappeared in the wan light of Mencken's last years.

Notes

1. Ernest Boyd, *H. L. Mencken* (New York: R. M. McBride, 1925), p. 23.

2. From the copy of the book in the Hanley Collection, HRHRC, University of Texas at Austin.

3. Edgar Kemler, *The Irreverent Mr. Mencken* (Boston: Peter Smith, 1950), p. 115.

4. H. L. Mencken, *George Bernard Shaw: His Plays* (Boston: J. W. Luce, 1905), p. xix.

5. Archibald Henderson, "Literature and Science. A Dialogue between Bernard Shaw and Archibald Henderson," *Fortnightly Review* (October 1, 1924), p. 512.

6. Fred Hobson, *Mencken: A Life* (New York: Random House, 1993), p. 322.

7. Charles A. Fecher, ed., *The Diary of H. L. Mencken* (New York: Knopf, 1989), p. 95.

8. Mencken, "Thirty-Five Printed Plays," *Smart Set*, 44 (September 1914): 154.

9. "Thirty-Five Printed Plays," p. 160.

10. Ibid.

11. "The Ulster Polonius," *Smart Set* 46 (August 1916): 140.

12. *Prejudices, First Series* (New York: Knopf, 1929), p. 182.

13. "An Ill-Will Tour of the American Mind," *Saturday Review of Literature*, August 6, 1949, p. 42.

14. Prejudices, *First Series*, p. 190.

15. Quoted in Mencken, *Damn! A Book of Calumny* (New York: Philip Goodman Co., 1918), p. 39.

16. Ibid.

17. *A Book of Prefaces*, Second (revised) Edition (New York: Knopf, 1918), p. 26.

18. *Prejudices, Third Series* (New York: Knopf, 1922), pp. 304–5.

19. Ibid.

20. "The American Novel," reprinted in *Prejudices, Fourth Series* (New York: Knopf, 1924), p. 281.

21. *The Bathtub Hoax and other Blasts and Bravos*, ed. Robert McHugh (New York: Knopf, 1958), p. 86.

22. Mencken, *My Life as Author and Editor* (New York: Knopf, 1992), p. 128.

23. Kemler, p. 115.

24. As Mencken's Shavophobia lessened it was still to breed such embarrassing phenomena as Benjamin de Casseres' near-libelous volume of fulminations in praise of Mencken and in scorn of Shaw, *Mencken and Shaw* (New York, 1930).

25. Letter to the author from Mr. Angoff, July 3, 1958.

26. "Harris on Shaw," *American Mercury* 25 (February 1932): 255.

27. Kemler, p. 116.

28. *The American Language. Supplement One* (New York: Knopf, 1945), p. 350 fn. Anthony

Comstock had led the Society for the Suppression of Vice when *Mrs Warren's Profession* was closed by the New York Police Department at Comstock's behest in 1905. The *Oxford English Dictionary* credits Shaw for the first coinage, in *The New York Times*, 26 September 1905, of *Comstockery* as the overzealous suppression of allegedly immoral art.

29. *Supplement One*, pp. 678–79.

30. *A Mencken Chrestomathy* (New York: Knopf, 1953), p. vi.

31. *Minority Report* (New York: Knopf, 1956), p. 292.

A JENNIFER FROM AUSTRALIA

Edith Adams, Her Husband, and *The Doctor's Dilemma*

During Easter weekend in 1893 Shaw picnicked with friends in Surrey and noted for the first time in his diary the names of Francis William Lauderdale Adams, a poet, and his strikingly attractive Australian second wife, Edith Goldstone Adams, a former actress who had also taken up nursing, a role she continued in caring for her ailing husband.[1] The laconic reference suggested that Shaw had met the Adamses before, and he had, through Henry and Kate Salt, who lived near Tilford and with whom he was holidaying in the country. A novelist and poet best known for his politically radical *Songs of the Army of the Night*, Adams had returned from Australia (where he had gone in 1884) to publish in London in hopes of being more widely known before the coffin lid closed over him. He was suffering from tuberculosis, which was now so far advanced that there was little expectation of a cure.

Francis Adams, Frank Harris recalled in *My Life and Loves*, had been "really my first good English friend." Galway-born, Harris had gone to America but had returned to London to take up journalism and politics. In Hyde Park, where Harris spoke on "introducing some Socialist measures in English life," Adams had come up to the speaker's area afterwards and introduced himself, and they became friends. Then Adams went to Australia, returning five years later when Harris was editor of the *Fortnightly Review*. Harris offered him some work, but was distressed at his condition and unimpressed by his pretty wife. (The editor of the *Fortnightly* had a yen for teenage girls.) "I managed to help him to go to Egypt. I told him he should live in the desert above Assouan, or in some high place such as Davos. . . ."

Adams returned from Egypt in 1893 with his health having further deteriorated. He could not afford to live abroad any longer and had no hope. He had even tried to kill himself, he confided to Harris, but his courage had failed him. He would go back to Margate with Edith. Harris preached courage, and gave him a short story he had written on the subject.

Shaw heard, and thought, nothing of the Adamses for months after their meetings at picnics and vegetarian restaurants. While Adams declined further at the seaside, G.B.S. returned to music reviewing and to writing his first plays. For one music column in *The World* he went for the first time to the Star and Garter in Richmond, where the Richmond Orchestral Society was performing. The terrace of the Star and Garter would later be the setting of the second act of his *Doctor's Dilemma,* in which he would place, it seems, the Adamses as prospective patient and adoring spouse among a covey of admiring physicians. He would dine at the Star and Garter again the next month with James Brown, the orchestra's director, the setting somehow remaining in his subconscious along with the tubercular poet and his devoted wife.

Early in September it was all over for Adams. Although the tubercular Louis Dubedat in Shaw's play, pushed onstage *"in an invalid's chair,"* would expire in the presence of his spouse, who was nursing him, and several doctors, dying with a challenge for posterity on his lips, the end for Adams was even more theatrical (although unstageable) and far more trying for his wife than for the drama's Mrs. Dubedat. On 4 September 1893, Francis Adams was about to go for an outing in the restorative sea air at Margate, pushed by Edith in a bath-chair, when at the gate of their lodgings he began coughing violently, and one of the hemorrhages he feared flooded his throat. He had already been told by his doctor that he had less than three weeks to live. "I'm choking: it's finished," he struggled to say to his wife. He was suffocating and motioned that she should tear his collar loose. She lifted him—he was badly emaciated—and carried him back to their bedroom, where she sat him on the edge of the bed. When more blood spurted, he managed to get to his feet and staggered to an adjoining sitting room where he reached for his gun, gasping, "It's all over, darling!"

At the inquest Edith claimed that she pleaded with him, "Not that, dearie!" But he cocked the pistol and gasped, one word at a time, "If—you—love—me—you'll—let—me—do—it!" As she crouched at his knees he tried three times to force the barrel into his mouth before he managed to fire it. The bullet passed through his head and lodged in the ceiling. She caught him in her arms.

Asked by Coroner Boys whether she could have prevented the suicide, the widow replied, "Of course I could, but I should have considered myself a contemptible coward if I had done so when things were as they were." Following her, one of Adams's doctors gave evidence that he had already lost so much blood that he could not have lived more than another few minutes. "It was proved that the deceased and his wife were a devoted couple. A verdict of suicide whilst in a state of temporary insanity, and expressing regret that the wife had not prevented the fatal act, was returned. Deceased was at work on a book about Egypt . . . as late as Saturday night."[2]

Edith returned from Margate to stay once more in Oxted, Surrey, with Kate and Henry Salt. There, Shaw saw her again. Twenty-eight, radiant, and proud, she appeared to him to see herself as a heroine. "After dinner," Shaw noted on 2 October, "took a walk with Mrs. Francis Adams, who told me a good deal about herself." Shaw was fascinated by her but could not decide how much to believe. On the sixteenth in London he saw—at different times—both Frank Harris and Edith Adams, and noted, "In the morning I had been delayed in getting to work by having to answer a letter from Walter [Gurly] about her." The inference must be that he had been seeing so much of her (however unrecorded) that his physician uncle was curious about the new lady in his life. On the twenty-fifth he noted, "Leave Ms. of F. Adams' *Tiberius* at the Democratic Club for Mrs. Adams." She was seeking someone to edit for publication her late husband's verse drama, and although Shaw had little interest in it, he retained considerable interest in her.

Eventually the editing would be undertaken by sixtyish widower William Michael Rossetti, whose interest, possibly, was entirely in the flaming radicalism of Adams's verses. Yet the exotic Edith must have stirred other fires, too, in the grizzled Rossetti, who later described her as "tall and stately, and not far from being decidedly handsome. . . . She talks with liveliness and plenty of sense; spent half a year or more in a Syrian harem—was not an 'Odalisque' but a governess there."[3]

Where Rossetti got his history other than from Edith is unclear, but she and her next husband lived (as she had with Adams) for several years in Egypt, where they seem to have met, and the Sudan, where he would paint his colorful Orientalist canvases, Edith having left England to find herself—or to find work.

One letter from Edith to Shaw—on mourning notepaper—survives, from late in 1893, in which she chaffs him as a "delightful wind bag of a genius"—and then teases him a bit more. "So you don't believe I've been to Egypt, or in fact anything! Now, my dearie, who ever asked you to?!!" Her next line becomes a bit more provocative. "No, it wasn't my handkerchief I forgot: it was simply the buckle of my garter!"

"I am glad, O cynic," she continued, "you do not take me seriously; all the men I know do and to tell the truth (for once!) it's a paralyzing nuisance. So you thought I was a good study for you?! Beloved of my soul you haven't got to the bottom of your study by any means. Sometimes I only *fancy* (only fancy) you're a bit of a liar yourself. Yours tenderly. . . ."

As a postscript she penned, "Don't be angry; this is a mild shake of the left leg after a trying day in town." And she conceded that Shaw was "a brick."[4]

Early in 1894 he was still magnetized by her, but there were other complications in his love life. On 23 January he noted in his diary that he had discussed Edith on a visit to William Morris's daughter May, with whom he often exchanged confidences. May herself was in love with Shaw, but knew that he was still amorously involved with Florence Farr, the fiery Louka of his *Arms and the Man* production to be mounted that spring. She may not have known that his first mistress, the tempestuous and aging Jenny Patterson, was still pursuing him.

While May understood that she had no chance—she had even married, lovelessly, Henry Halliday Sparling in 1890 when G.B.S. refused to be tied down—it seems possible that had his intimacy with Florence, then at its peak, not thwarted his possibilities with the young widow, his biography might have taken a different turn. As it was, he was not at all sure that Edith was really a widow. She claimed that Adams burned their Australian marriage certificate,[5] but Shaw, in filing the letters he preserved, noted next to her E.H.A. signature—the H. was for Helen—"Mrs Adams, widow (?) of Francis." That had made her all the more perplexing. Nevertheless, there would be a matrimonial future for Edith Adams. In a church in Hampstead in 1896, she married London landscape painter Frank Dean. William Michael Rossetti gave the bride away. (Unable to resist embroidering her past, she identified, on the marriage application, her father, Richard Goldstone, as a medical doctor. *His* father had been a doctor; the younger Richard Goldstone was a builder.)

By the time of the first performance of *The Doctor's Dilemma* late in 1906, Edith Adams Dean was long out of Shaw's life, and her second

Fig. 7. Vivien Leigh as Jennifer Dubedat in *The Doctor's Dilemma*, Haymarket Theatre, London, March 1942. With permission of the Raymond Mander & Joe Mitchenson Theatre Collection, Beckenham, England.

husband may never have been in it, yet even in the second marriage Shaw's play had anticipated reality. In the Epilogue to the play, the beautiful widow remarries, but remains an enigmatically difficult woman. Shaw may never have seen her again after the middle 1890s, but she remained in memory something of a vixen, much as was his Jennifer of *The Doctor's Dilemma* to Shaw's protagonist in the play, the smitten Colenso Ridgeon. The playwright would characterize her, as he would few women, as a "vulgar liar and rapscallion."[6] By the time of Shaw's play she was showing signs of the mental instability that would contribute to the breakup of her second marriage[7] and to a troubled stint as a journalist in Cape Town, South Africa.[8] By 1913, toward the end, she was in the County Asylum in Devon.[9]

Had she already become, as Shaw suggested she might, "a good study" for her "wind bag of a genius"? Is there anything of Edith in the stately, beautiful—and deceitful—Jennifer Dubedat whom Shaw drew, the devoted nurse to her dying artist husband who captivated men eagerly awaiting her widowhood? "I know I helped him live his true life, [even] if I didn't do all I might have done at his death," she insisted about Adams to W. M. Rossetti in 1906.[10] It was a position that she might have taken with Shaw, since it parallels Jennifer's claim, "I gave him myself and all that I had that he might grow to his full height. . . ."

Shaw often combined living originals in a character, but no one else hints at the heroine of *The Doctor's Dilemma*. Deflecting identification, he makes Jennifer a Cornishwoman, suggesting exotic origin less remote than Australia—a Guinevere rather than a Helen.[11] Later, reflecting on the noble attitudes his leading lady had struck, Shaw wrote to Cathleen Nesbitt, who was playing Jennifer in a 1923 London production, "Jennifer is a sort of woman whom, I, personally, cannot stand, enormously conceited, morally patronizing to everyone, setting herself always in some noble, devoted, beautiful attitude, never looking facts in the face or telling herself or anyone else the truth about them for a moment, and making even her husband's death a splendid opportunity for taking the centre of the stage."[12]

Much like the mysterious Edith Adams, whom Shaw could not forget, his Jennifer is also a splendid poseur. "I suppose you heard of the birth and death of our babies?" she wrote, dramatically, to a friend in Australia after her husband's death.[13] Were there any babies? Were these miscarriages? And was there a legal marriage? In *The Doctor's Dilemma*, the dying artist is accused of bigamy, but it turns out that his marriage to a pretty chambermaid was invalid and his marriage to Jennifer, perhaps like Francis Adams's with Edith, only passed as one. "Lots of people do it," Louis Dubedat tells the astonished doctors, playing with their shocked propriety. ". . . I only asked you whether you had seen Jennifer's marriage lines; and you concluded straight away that she hadnt got any. You don't know a lady when you see one." Jennifer, he declares, carries her marriage certificate "in her face and in her character."

No other woman out of Shaw's life so suggests Jennifer, while Louis Dubedat's disease (and profession) may have come not only from Francis Adams—an artist of a different sort—but from Aubrey Beardsley, whom he knew, or from Dante Gabriel Rossetti, whose amoral charm with artistic patrons was notorious and parallels that of Dubedat. Shaw's characters were often an amalgam of real life and imagination, and it is remarkable that in the years of his encountering the fascinating Adamses—both of whom may reappear in the Dubedats—he would also be introduced to the setting in which part of his play occurs. The creative process is a complex one.

Notes

1. *Bernard Shaw, The Diaries 1885–1897* (University Park: Pennsylvania State University Press, 1986), ed. Stanley Weintraub, is the major source on the dates noted. Frank Harris's *My Life and Loves* (1926) and William Michael Rossetti's *Some Reminiscences* (1906) furnish further background.

2. "Death of Mr. Francis Adams. A Pathetic Story," Melbourne *Argus* (10 October 1893). (The Australian sources in this study are indebted to Megan Tasker of Ballarat University.)

3. William Michael Rossetti to Richard Curle, 24 September 1896, in Roger W. Peattie, ed., *Selected Letters of William Michael Rossetti* (University Park: Pennsylvania State University Press, 1990), p. 667.

4. British Library Add. MS. 50513, f. 29; Edith Adams to Shaw, 21 December 1893.

5. Information from Megan Tasker, Ballarat University, Australia, 7 March 1995.

6. At ninety-four, in 1950, writing a preface to a biography of Henry and Kate Salt (Stephen Winsten, *Salt and His Circle* [London: Hutchinson, 1951]), Shaw used the term in recalling Edith as "a romancer," but failing to remember through the haze of years that an inquest had dealt with Edith's role in her husband's suicide, which was real yet in the circumstances not culpable.

7. Rossetti refers to Edith's mental instability in a letter to Richard Curle, 18 November 1909 (University of Indiana). The text implies her separation from Frank Dean.

8. Edith Adams Dean to W. M. Rossetti, letters from Cape Town, 1910, Angeli-Dennis collection, University of British Columbia.

9. Edith wrote to Rossetti from the Asylum in 1913 (Angeli-Dennis collection, UBC).

10. Edith Adams Dean to Rossetti, ca. 1906 (Angeli-Dennis collection, UBC).

11. Perhaps it added to Edith Adams's exoticism that she was not only Australian, but Jewish. At the inquest in Margate it was reported (*Keble's Margate and Ramsgate Gazette*, 9 September 1893) that, presumably at her request, the widow "was sworn in the Jewish form." (Information from Megan Tasker.)

12. Shaw to Cathleen Nesbitt, 28 April 1923, in *Collected Letters 1911–1925*, ed. Dan H. Laurence (New York: Viking, 1985), pp. 823–24.

13. Edith Adams to Sydney Jephcott, Tintaldra, Australia, 12 November 1893, for a general letter to Australian friends of Francis Adams. National Library of Australia MS. 3271, Brunton Stephens Collection.

UNEASY FRIENDSHIP

Shaw and Yeats

For W. B. Yeats, who despite British law had arranged for a censored-in-England play by Bernard Shaw, *The Shewing-up of Blanco Posnet*, to be performed to full houses in Dublin, that 1909 coup might well have been considered the apex of an uneasy friendship. Nevertheless, Yeats's curious relationship with his fellow townsman would have far to go.

It had begun accidentally in the converted coach house on William Morris's property on the Mall in Hammersmith where, usually on Sundays, he convened socialist meetings attended largely by young London intellectuals. Sometimes there were amateur entertainments as well, Shaw once appearing as "I. Roscius Garrick" in a dramatic sketch, *The Appointment*, by his friend Dolly Radford. Shaw noted laconically in his diary for 12 February 1888 only that he had been to Morris's and remained for supper, where he "met an Irishman named Yeats."[1] An impressionable twenty-two (Shaw was thirty-one), Yeats wrote a cautious letter to Katharine Tynan about meeting Shaw—"who is certainly very witty. But, like most people who have wit rather than humour, his mind is maybe somewhat wanting in depth. However, his stories are good, they say" (L 59).

Shaw was even less impressed. Yeats affected poetic garb and other poetic mannerisms that Shaw may have later borrowed for his unworldly young poet Eugene Marchbanks in *Candida* (1894). In the first years in which they encountered each other, it was with Yeats as an intrusive nuisance, hanging about Shaw's current lover Florence Farr, an actress five years older than Yeats, whom she would meet regularly at occultist gatherings. Florence, whom Shaw was trying to coach into an Ibsenite actress, and with whom he was passionately in love, could keep neither her emotions nor her intellectual interests well focused. "She set no bounds to her relations with men whom she liked, and already had a sort of Leporello list of a dozen adventures. . . . She was in violent reaction against Victorian morals, especially sexual and domestic morals. . . ."[2] Separated from her actor-husband John Emery, she was Shaw's romance of the moment, although he had not completely disentangled himself from the possessive Jenny Patterson, who would be Grace Tranfield to Florence's Julia Craven in the autobiographical *The Philanderer* (1893).

Seeing theatrical promise in Florence Farr, and also wanting her available for him, Shaw resented her wasting time and energy at sessions of the "Golden Dawn," her excursions into Theosophy and Egyptology, and especially Yeats's mooning about. It would soon become necessary to out-stay the still-virginal young poet at Florence's Brook Green flat, in Hammersmith, out of concern that "FE" (as Shaw referred to her in his diary) might decide to initiate Yeats sexually—something Shaw's Candida would threaten to do for timid Eugene Marchbanks just a year after the 13 July 1893 diary reference about an evening at Florence's in Dalling Road, "Willy Yeats came in about 21 [9:00 P.M.] and stayed a long time chatting." Later, Shaw would identify her as "the heroine in my first play [*Widowers' Houses*] in 1892."[3] She may very well have had something in her of the "wilful, violent" Blanche Sartorious, who introduces her diffident admirer, Harry Trench, to some of the seamier facts of life.

Writing poetic plays because he wanted to, and literary journalism because he needed the money, Yeats in his journalism managed a few digs at the somewhat older Irishman he may have looked upon as a domineering rival. In an essay on Wilde, he referred waspishly to "a certain notorious and clever, but coldblooded Socialist" (UP1 204), yet Yeats appeared clever enough himself, for when Florence was backed for the rental of a theater by Annie Horniman, who had inherited part of the Colman's Mustard fortune and began to produce a season of drama, it was his play written at her request rather than one by Shaw that was first on a double-bill with John Todhunter's play *A Comedy of Sighs*. Although the Avenue Theatre was a London location, 29 March 1894 was in effect the beginning of the Irish National Theatre since both new plays were Irish; but the modest success of Yeats's brief *The Land of Heart's Desire* ("an exquisite curtain raiser," Shaw recalled)[4] was obscured by the failure of Todhunter's play. To rescue Florence, Shaw rushed to completion his *Arms and the Man*. The playhouse was closed for a week while the new work was rehearsed, with Florence as the sexy, strong-willed maid Louka, a role probably written with her in mind. Yeats's modest play would be overshadowed by the flashy new work.

To his friend John O'Leary on 15 April, Yeats wrote with disappointment that Todhunter's jettisoned play "was really a brilliant piece of work," yet Shaw's, if successful, he realized, might make it possible for a more ambitious Yeatsian play to be staged. He was sure of only one thing, that Shaw's would be controversial, since "chuckers out"—bouncers—had been hired for the opening night of Arms and the Man. "They are to be distributed over the theatre and are to put out all people who make a row. The whole venture will be history anyway for it is the first contest between the old commercial school of theatrical folk and the new artistic school" (L 231).

No one had to be ejected. When the play opened on 21 April, Yeats wrote years later in The Trembling of the Veil, the opening that Shaw had planned "to confound his enemies" worked:

> For the first few minutes Arms and the Man is crude melodrama and then just when the audience are thinking how crude it is, it turns into excellent farce. . . .
>
> On the first night the whole pit and gallery, except certain members of the Fabian Society, started to laugh at the author and then, discovering that they themselves were being laughed at, sat there not converted—their hatred was too bitter for that—but dumb-founded, while the rest of the house cheered and laughed. In the silence that greeted the author after the cry for a speech one man did indeed get his courage and boo loudly. "I assure the gentleman in the gallery," was Shaw's answer, "that he and I are of exactly the same opinion, but what can we do against a whole house who are of the contrary opinion?"[5] And from that moment Bernard Shaw became the most formidable man in modern letters, and even the most drunken of medical students knew it. (Au 281–82)

His own play, Yeats recalled, had a quieter reception, and enough mild critical approval to warrant keeping it on with Arms and the Man, which meant that he felt drawn to the theater almost nightly for the weeks of its run. That the play worked so well exasperated him. It seemed too contrived, and indeed Shaw had used chessboard pieces to move characters about before he wrote out his stage directions. To Yeats there was a clockwork quality that he viewed "with admiration and hatred. It seemed to me inorganic, logical straightness and not the crooked road of life, yet I stood aghast before its energy as to-day before that of the *Stone Drill* by Mr. Epstein or of some design by Mr. Wyndham Lewis. . . . Presently I had a nightmare that I was haunted by a sewing-machine, that clicked and shone, but the incredible thing was that the machine smiled, smiled perpetually. Yet I delighted in Shaw, the formidable man. He could hit my enemies and the enemies of all I loved, as I could never hit, as no living author that was dear to me could ever hit" (Au 283).

For part of the way home, some evenings, he would walk and talk with Florence Farr. Often the topic was Shaw, and although she seemed to share his "hesitations," Yeats wondered when they discussed G.B.S. "whether the cock crowed for my blame or for my praise" (Au 284).

It has been noted by a number of critics[6] that Yeats's part of the double-bill at the Avenue may have contributed to Shaw's next play: in fact, so may have Yeats himself as a personality. The likelihood is that he never knew it and that in *Candida* Shaw had his quiet fun in making at least a side of his emotional young poet, Eugene Marchbanks, a parody of Yeats's poetic affectations. *

Although Marchbanks also reflects some of the characteristics of Shelley and De Quincey, and even of the author of the play, who had his own involvements in domestic triangles, the Yeatsian dimension, however real, also suggests some of the dangers of biographical criticism. It is easy to turn coincidence into cause-and-effect logic, as one critic does by noting that there is a Marchbanks Road near what had been a Yeats family residence in London. Shaw's young poet was originally named *Marjoribanks*, pronounced *Marchbanks*, and why or how Shaw would have known early Yeatsian geography is unknown.

Ten years after *Candida*, Yeats would confide to his friend George W. Russell (the poet "AE") that in *The Land of Heart's Desire* and some of his lyric verse of that time "there is an exaggeration of sentiment and sentimental beauty which I have come to think unmanly" (L 434). The poet's mannerisms and speech in *Candida* suggest that. Even some of the dialogue seems to echo Yeats's play, for in *The Land of Heart's Desire* the young wife rebels against such domestic drudgery as cleaning pots and pans—something Shaw's poet objects to on Candida's part although she makes no fuss about

---

*Ellmann notes (*Identity of Yeats* [New York: Oxford, 1964], p. 130) that Yeats would, by the end of the 1890s, begin "to generate more activity in his verbs, throwing out most of those, which, like 'sighing,' 'waning,' 'brooding,' 'weeping,' were liable to Shaw's criticism that while he had worked to alleviate human distress, his Irish contemporaries had [only] sung sad songs about it."

Fig. 8. W. B. Yeats in the 1890s. The portrait photo suggests why Shaw may have imagined Yeats as Marchbanks.

the indelicacy. And in Yeats's play, too, she escapes through death to a happier existence in a fairyland where "nobody gets old and godly and grave" (VPL 184), something Shaw seems to satirize at the close of *Candida*, in the poet's conceit, rebuking Candida's reference to their difference in ages, that in a hundred years they would be the same age. Marchbanks—and Shaw—may have been thinking about lines in Andrew Marvell's "To His Coy Mistress," but the dialogue in *Candida* was written only a few months after Shaw had sat through many evenings of Yeats's curtain raiser.

One can imagine an unpublished dialogue of Yeats's, attributed to 1915, as his looking back at the play with Florence Farr, both of them now older and wiser:

THE ACTRESS. I saw Mr. Shaw's *Candida* last night. There was a poet there who shudders to the depths of his soul because he sees his sweetheart is cutting onions. I had always thought a poet was like that, that everything moved him. . . .

THE POET. Do you know any great poet or great writer who is easily moved?
THE ACTRESS. Well, when I come to think of it, I have found all poets, great
or small, exceedingly blasé. It has done more for my chastity even than my
knowledge of their unfaithfulness. When they have paid me compliments, I
have wondered if they were laughing at me.[7]

Sometime in 1896 the Farr-Shaw love affair cooled. Shaw was developing
other interests, one of which would lead to his marriage in 1898. He had
failed to win Florence over to the New Drama as her hermetic studies
consumed her enthusiasms. And although in 1894 Shaw had pressed her to
divorce her absent husband, he did not suggest himself as substitute. She
turned briefly to Yeats, who had finally been initiated by someone else, but
their letters of the period, Yeats's wife of later years has written, do not reveal
the intimacy of that friendship. "WBY once said to me," she recalled,
"[Florence Farr] 'was the only person to whom I could tell *everything.*'"
But, George Yeats added, "Their brief love affair came to an end because
'she got bored.'"[8] Nevertheless, Florence remained close to him through
their continuing occultist interests, as well as through Yeats's aspirations for
her as a reader of his dramatic verse. Despite her strong acting as the wilful
Louka in *Arms and the Man*, Shaw had been unsuccessful in his ambitions
for her as a comedienne in his later plays. Yeats visualized her plucking a
psaltery and chanting—"cantilating," Florence described it to Shaw[9]—the
poetry. "Speaking to the Psaltery," Yeats called it (L 401).

On the rebound from Shaw, she cantilated. At least it provoked him. She
was wasting herself, he insisted (6 June 1902), seeing "no new art" in the
business at all. "Yeats thinks so only because he does not go to church. . . .
It is no use for Yeats to try to make a distinction: there is no distinction, no
novelty, no nothing but nonsense. . . . The psaltery amuses people; and
there is no reason why they should not use a string or a pipe to remind them
of the normal pitch of their voices . . . take care of the consonants and the
vowels will take care of themselves." Only emotional and intellectual
conviction, he warned, makes speech effective. "Without it cantilation can
do nothing except intensify ordinary twaddling into a nerve destroying
crooning like the maunderings of an idiot-banshee. Remember that even in
singing, it is an Irish defect to lose grip and interest by neglecting the words
& thinking only of the music. . . . Yeats is heaping fresh artificialities &
irrelevances & distractions & impertinences on you. . . ." (CL 1898–1910,
pp. 274–75).

The effort to remake Florence Farr would fail, just as the cantilating would lose its appeal. Florence drifted to new interests. Shaw would turn his Pygmalion energies toward others, never losing his impatience with Yeats although retaining respect for Yeats's abilities and vision. When he and Lady Gregory had got their experimental Irish theater going, Shaw even promised them a play. He had not yet begun *Man and Superman*, which would be his next big work. But, wrote Yeats to Lady Gregory early in 1900, "I saw Shaw to-day. He talks of a play on the contrast between English and Irish character which sounds amusing. He came to the 'Three Kings' on Saturday. I replied to a speech of his . . . by proving that Shaw's point of view belonged to a bygone generation—to the scientific epoch—and was now 'reactionary.' He had never been called reactionary before. I think I beat him. He was not in very good form however" (L 335). To Yeats the relationship with Shaw was always a sort of rivalry.

In October 1901, to prod Shaw to make good his offer of a play appropriate for Irish production, Yeats wrote to him encouragingly to "come and see our 'Theatre,' "[10] and late in 1902, with *Man and Superman* now completed, the idea of a play for Dublin again came up. "Bernard Shaw talks again of writing a play for us," Yeats confided to Lady Gregory. "Certainly it would be a great thing for our Company if he will do us an Irish play" (L 387). The next year, with the writing under way, Yeats was emboldened to write in *Samhain*, the Irish Literary Theatre's organ, "A play Mr. Bernard Shaw has promised us may be ready to open the summer session. His play will, I imagine, unlike the plays we write for ourselves, be long enough to fill an evening, and it will, I know, deal with Irish public life and character. Mr. Shaw, more than anybody else, has the love of mischief that is so near the core of Irish intellect, and should have an immense popularity among us. I have seen a crowd of many thousands in possession of his spirit, and keeping the possession to the small hours" (Ex 103).

In the meantime Shaw offered to let the company do *Arms and the Man*, *Widowers' Houses*, or *The Devil's Disciple* (although not *The Man of Destiny*, which Yeats wanted but which Shaw felt they could not handle), and Yeats would wangle from Shaw, for the inaugural number of an Irish miscellany, *The Shanachie* (1906), reprint rights to an 1885 Shavian short story with an Irish setting, "The Miraculous Revenge." Yeats would tell Michael Roberts, who was assisting the editor, Joseph Hone (an inexperienced pair that could keep the quarterly going for only six issues), that Shaw had given the story to him for the Dun Emer Press, founded by Yeats's sister Elizabeth. "Shaw does not care about money," he explained to Stephen Gwynn, then a director of the Dublin publishing firm of Maunsel & Co., "but . . . I rather think that my argument to him about this little story . . . was that he would be encouraging the first Irish publication of its kind to pay contributors" (L 473–74). Whatever Yeats's persuasiveness, Shaw was willing to be helpful, whether or not it was a theatrical matter.

Fibbing slightly, Shaw postcarded Yeats good-humoredly on 20 June 1904, "Not a word of the play yet on paper." Then, sketching a recognizably Shavian head erupting with smoke like a pipe-bowl, Shaw added, "Seething in the brain."[11] Actually he had written the first dialogue three days earlier, and the long play would go quickly.

Finishing on 17 August, he toyed with stage business a bit longer, and then, assuming from the enthusiasm that had echoed from Dublin that the Irish Literary Theatre would stage the play, Shaw queried Yeats on 31 August about technical matters. Changes of scene in the second and fourth acts were best handled mechanically. "I am greatly touched," Shaw added, "by learning that history is repeating itself in the matter of our backer. It was revealed to me in a dream (this is literally true) that Miss Horniman backed Arms and the Man & The Land of Heart's Desire, and now I see that she is the benefactress of the I.L.T. also" (CL 1898–1910, 452). Via a prompt copy, a text was soon enroute to Yeats, who asked W. G. Fay, the company manager, to explore the production possibilities.

Fay quickly confessed his reservations. While it was "full of good things," he was worried that "the difficulty of getting a cast for it would be considerable."[12] Thomas Broadbent, the repellently hearty Englishman, would be particularly difficult; besides, the cast was a large one for a small stage. J. M. Synge, who also looked at the script for the cautious management, had equally mixed opinions, but Yeats only quoted him to Shaw as predicting that the play "will hold a Dublin audience, and at times move them." In a singularly imperceptive opinion for a shrewd comic playwright, Synge also told Fay and Yeats that the saintly Father Keegan's scene with the grasshopper, in which Shaw reaches toward the future theater of the absurd, and the hilarious episode of transporting a pig in the recently invented automobile ("The Handy Andy like scene about carrying the goose") should be cut.[13]

Yeats began venturing his own suggestions as he carefully distanced himself from his earlier eagerness for production. The first act and the beginning of the second, he began, disappointed him. "The stage Irishman who wasn't an Irishman" (because of long residence in England) amused him, but then, he said, he asked himself, "What the devil did Shaw mean by all this [sentimental] Union of Hearts–like conversation? What do we care here if this country, which despite the Act of Union [with England] is still an island, about the English Liberal party and the Tariff, and the difference between English and Irish character, or whatever else it was all about. Being raw people, I said, we [Irish] do care about human nature in action, and that he's not giving us." Then, he assured Shaw, his interest began to pick up,

> That young woman who persuaded that Englishman, full of the impulsiveness that comes from a good banking account, that he was drunk on nothing more serious than poteen, was altogether a delight. The motor car too, the choosing the member of Parliament, and so on right to the end, often exciting and mostly to the point. I thought in reading the first act that you had forgotten Ireland, but I found in the other acts that is the only subject on which you are entirely serious. In fact you are so serious that sometimes your seriousness leaps upon the stage, knocks the characters over, and insists on having all the conversation to himself. However the inevitable cutting (the play is as you say immensely too long) is certain to send your seriousness back to the front row of the stalls. You have said things in this play which are entirely true about Ireland, things which nobody has ever said before, and these are the very things that are most part of the action. It astonishes me that you should have been so long in London and yet have remembered so much. To some extent this play is unlike anything you have done before. Hitherto you have taken your situations from melodrama, and called up logic to make them ridiculous. Your process here seems to be quite different, you are taking your situations more from life, you are for the first time trying to get the atmosphere of a place, you have for the first time a geographical conscience. . . .[14]

To his own surprise, Yeats then confessed tactlessly, "I do not consider the play dangerous. There may be a phrase, but I cannot think of one at this moment. Here again, you show your wonderful knowledge of the country. You have laughed at all the things that are ripe for laughter. . . . I don't mean to say that there won't be indignation about one thing or another, and a great deal of talk about it all, but I mean that we can play it, and survive to play something else" (CL 1898–1910, p. 453; S 174).

Reading between the lines, Shaw understood that Yeats did not mean that at all. The play, Shaw realized—as he would explain in the preface to *John*

Bull—"was uncongenial to the whole spirit of the neo-Gaelic movement, which is bent on creating a new Ireland after its own ideal, whereas my play is a very uncompromising presentment of the real old Ireland."[15] The play was also big and difficult to cast; it did need cuts, and was too long in the draft that Yeats saw. The insuperable problem, however, was that Shaw was seeing past the Ireland of poets and dreamers (the play's Larry Doyle) to a reality in conflict with sentimental Celticism, a reality that Synge himself would soon dramatize in *The Playboy of the Western World*. Yeats almost certainly recognized an allusion to his own 1902 play in Doyle's scoffing first-act line, "If you want to interest him"—the average Irishman—"in Ireland youve got to call the unfortunate island Kathleen ni Hoolihan and pretend she's a little old woman."

Shaw's Irish peasant, unlike the folkloric one, was the play's Matt Haffigan, whose tragedy, bluntly explained by Larry Doyle in the play, "is the tragedy of his wasted youth, his stunted mind, his drudging over his clods and pigs until he has become a clod and a pig himself—until the soul within him has smouldered into nothing but a dull temper that hurts himself and all around him. I say let him die, and let us have no more of his like. . . ."[16] Ironically, W. G. Fay, although then afraid of the play, would eventually be cast as Matt Haffigan in an English production, and *John Bull's Other Ireland* would establish Shaw's reputation in England, only afterward becoming one of the Abbey Theatre's perennial box-office successes. But Yeats did not want public turmoil, even over a major play by Ireland's best playwright, to cloud the future of his infant Irish theater.

After some months of negotiations, during which *John Bull* was mounted to great acclaim in London, Yeats agreed to drop any plans for the play and free Louis Calvert of the Royal Court Theatre production to tour it in Ireland. "All right," Yeats wrote Shaw as if with reluctance, "give that queer elephant to Calvert. We all admire it but don't feel we could do the English man at all." (Since there was only one significant English character, Shaw recognized a lame excuse when he saw one.) "We might be able to play it but it is all uncertain and the great thing is to get it done here. Calvert will do it far better than we could."[17] By then Yeats had seen a London performance, about which he wrote Lady Gregory in November 1904 that it acted "very much better than one could have foreseen. . . . I don't really like it. It is fundamentally ugly and shapeless, but certainly keeps everybody amused" (L 442).

Few more derogatory criticisms could be lodged at Shaw than that his plays were amusing. Yeats would write jesting plays himself, but when he

did, he looked on them as minor affairs despite the success of his friend
Synge in satiric modes. To Yeats it was more important to show Ireland
onstage as "not the home of buffoonery and easy sentiment, as it has been
represented, but the home of an ancient idealism." Comedy was only "a
display of energy," while there was a "sorrowful calm" at the core of
tragedy.[18] To Yeats that was closer to the real Ireland.

Somehow the strains of the *John Bull's Other Island* affair did not fracture
the tenuous relationship. Shaw had every right to be angry with what he
could have considered Yeats's timidity and obtuseness. Yet he found things
he liked about Yeats and saw how much Yeatsian energies were needed in
Ireland. Shaw was not a great admirer of Yeats's own plays, which may have
appeared to him languid and suffused with pallid pathos and stale romance,
but he had even helped, in the frustrating year of John Bull, to get a Yeats
play produced in London. Shaw had read and admired *Where There is
Nothing,* and he arranged for three performances just prior to the Vedrenne-
Barker repertory seasons at the Royal Court Theatre which he was backing
financially and which would have *John Bull* as its first smash success.

A realistic play, unobtrusive in its verse and almost in the Ibsen manner,
with the last two acts set in or near the Irish monastery to which Paul
Ruttledge retires as a protest against conventional life, *Where There is
Nothing* apparently appealed to Shaw because he recognized in the hero the
elderly (and by then dead) William Morris, whom both Yeats and Shaw had
known and revered as younger men. (The Vedrenne-Barker productions
would also include, late in 1904, Yeats's one-act folk-drama *The Pot of
Broth*, a slight fable about a tramp who tricks a West-of-Ireland couple out
of their food. It was not in the vein in which Yeats felt comfortable, and he
returned to legends with more allegorical possibilities, producing such verse-
plays as *The Shadowy Waters*—1905—and *Deirdre*—1906.) To New York
attorney and collector John Quinn, who was already purchasing Yeats's
manuscripts, he had written in 1903 about *Where There is Nothing*, "I have
tried to show Paul [Ruttledge]'s magnetic quality, his power of making
people love him and of carrying them away. I don't think he himself would
have been in the ordinary senses sympathetic. I think he was a man like
William Morris, who was too absorbed and busy to give much of himself to
persons. . . . People love Paul because they find in him a certain strength, a
certain abundance" (VP1 1167).

What Shaw almost certainly saw in the work also was a drama of unusual
and nearly unique style for Yeats, a protest play with a difficult idealist-hero
on the order of Ibsen's driven minister, Brand. Later, with Lady Gregory's

assistance, Yeats revised that out of the play. The new version, *The Unicorn from the Stars*, thinned the plot and emphasized the mystical qualities.

Shaw liked Lady Gregory enormously; although he was not a fan of her plays, he admired her efforts on behalf of Irish theater. They would visit each other, in England and in Ireland, as long as she lived, a Shavian female link with Yeats beyond Florence Farr. Both men still saw Florence occasionally after Yeats's cantilating enthusiasm faded, Shaw helping her with London journalism. And Yeats apparently felt a continuing need to put Shaw in a Yeatsian perspective for her. Perhaps because critics had begun to refer to his plays in the same breath as those of Shaw's, he was quite willing to see merits in G.B.S. that had previously escaped him, writing to Florence in 1905 that in one notice of *The King's Threshold*, in which she had performed, "Synge and myself and Shaw are enumerated with Ibsen and Maeterlinck as great dramatists" (L 453). Two years later he observed to her, about a G.B.S. letter to *The Times*, that it was

> logical, audacious and convincing, a really wonderful letter, at once violent and persuasive. He knew his opponent's case as well as his own, and that is just what men of his kind usually do not know. I saw *Caesar and Cleopatra* with Forbes-Robertson in it twice this week and have been really delighted and what I never thought [to] be with a work of his, moved. There is vulgarity, plenty of it, but such gay heroic delight in the serviceable man. Ah if he had but style, distinction, and was not such a barbarian of the barricades. I am quite convinced by the by that the whole play is chaff of you in your Egyptian period, and that you were the Cleopatra who offered that libation of wine to the table-rapping sphinx. (L 500)

The real-life Cleopatra whom Shaw had in mind was almost certainly the sultry Mrs. Patrick Campbell, for whom he would later write *Pygmalion* when she was much too old to play the role (but did so anyway). Yet there *is* something to Yeats's observation. Shaw puts a number of occult practices into Cleopatra's court, from table-rapping to more esoteric Egyptology. Perhaps some of Florence's obstinate independence is there too. Yeats had also experienced both.

While his own plays, he thought, were organic and poetic, Shaw's were formulaic, but Shaw, he told Lady Gregory, "takes as much pains to hide [the formula] as a dog burying a bone."[19] Although he would write in his journal (March 1909) that Shaw seemed to dislike "all crooked illogical things," with his plays reminiscent of "buildings made by science in an architect's office, and erected by joyless hands" (MEM 195), Yeats was enthusiastic when Lady Gregory visited Shaw at Ayot St. Lawrence and returned with the offer of another play for Dublin. In 1909, having been inspired, so he said, by Tolstoy's old soldier in *The Power of Darkness*, Shaw had written, in a Bret Harte vein, his Wild West religious farce *The Shewing-up of Blanco Posnet*. The play was immediately refused a license by the Lord Chamberlain's office on grounds of blasphemy. Ireland, by a technicality, did not come under the jurisdiction of the Royal censorship. Sensing a coup, Yeats met Lady Gregory and decided to accept the play for the Abbey, scheduling it for the big tourist week of the Dublin Horse Show at the end of August.

Despite protests from the Lord Lieutenant in Dublin Castle, as well as threats that the Abbey's patent might be revoked, rehearsals began, and Yeats and Lady Gregory issued a statement under both their names, refusing to concede that English censorship could legally intrude into Ireland and declaring "that so far from containing offence for any sincere and honest mind, Mr. Shaw's play is a high and weighty argument upon the working of the Spirit of God in man's heart." Besides, they insisted, it was "a befitting thing for us to set upon our stage the work of an Irishman, who is also the most famous of living dramatists, after that work had been silenced in London. . . ." The statement was published in *The Arrow*, the Abbey's house organ, on 25 August, the day of the opening (UP2 377). Appended was Yeats's exegesis of the play for Abbey audiences:

THE RELIGION OF BLANCO POSNET

The meaning of Mr. Shaw's play, as I understand it, is the natural man, driven on by passion and vain glory, who attempts to live as his fancy bids him but is awakened to the knowledge of God by finding himself stopped, perhaps suddenly, by something within himself. This something which is God's care for man, does not temper the wind to the shorn lamb, as a false and sentimental piety would have it, but is a terrible love that awakens the soul amidst catastrophes and trains it by conquest and labour.

The essential incidents of the play are Blanco's giving up the horse, the harlot's refusal to name the thief, and the child's death of the croup. Without the last of these Mr. Shaw's special meaning would be lost, for he wants us to understand that God's love will not do the work of the Doctor, or any work that man can do, for it acts by awakening the intellect and the soul whether in some man of science or philosopher or in violent Posnet. (UP2 380)

The play was performed without protest, and but for James Joyce, to critical approval. Yet the play had more than theatrical significance: as Yeats and Lady Gregory realized, it was a symbolic Irish break from English dictation. Getting away with the production would embolden seekers after more solid evidences of independence. "The theatre made a good deal of money," Yeats wrote to his father, "and is supported now even by Sinn Fein" (L 535).

Even the matter of expurgations that a wary Abbey management intended to make was settled satisfactorily, Shaw (while holidaying in Kerry) writing to Yeats that he would accept use of two substitute passages accompanying the letter, but no bowdlerization. He had understood from a message from Lady Gregory that "a certain speech was open to misconstruction," and he had rewritten it, he told Yeats, "more strongly and clearly." However to oblige the Lord Lieutenant he had withdrawn the word *immoral* "as applied to the relations between a woman of bad character and her accomplices. . . . I am quite content to leave the relations to the unprompted judgment of the Irish people." He also agreed to withdraw Blanco Posnet's opening words of his impromptu sermon, "Dearly beloved brethren," since "the Castle fears they may shock the nation." Wryly he added that much of the theology might have been written by the Catholic Archbishop of Dublin, "and in point of consideration for the religious beliefs of the Irish people the play compares very favorably with the Coronation Oath" (CL *1898–1910*, pp. 860–61).

Happy with the outcome on every level, Shaw arranged for the Abbey Company to give two technically private performances of *Blanco Posnet* for the Stage Society on 5 and 6 December 1909. The visit brought Yeats back to London, where Shaw saw him and talked about expanding the audiences abroad for Yeats's plays, even recommending his own agent in Germany for locating German and Austro-Hungarian markets. A few months later he took Yeats to the London production of his new comedy, *Misalliance*, writing afterwards (11 March 1910) to Lena Ashwell, who played the formidable Polish acrobat and aviatrix Lina Szczepanowska, "I indulged in the luxury of a peep at you at the matinée yesterday. I had in my box W. B. Yeats who, being a poet, occasionally says the right thing. At the end of the 2nd Act he said 'That is what is so extremely rare: *Beautiful gaiety.*' So you see it is not quite completely a secret between you and me" (CL *1898–1910*,

p. 905). Yeats and his sister Lily were also invited to lunch with the Shaws, the new warmth not resulting in the conversion of either by the other, but in a renewed consideration.

The day after, Shaw introduced Yeats at a benefit lecture (ticket: 1 guinea) for the Abbey Theatre at the Adelphi Club, Yeats commenting in the course of it that he had been "delighted . . . by a character of Mr. Bernard Shaw's—his girl acrobat who read her Bible while tossing her balls in the air. I remember some student of Eastern magic, I think an Oriental, who said, 'Imagine in front of you a flame, and if you can keep your thoughts for two minutes fixed entirely on that flame you will obtain Nirvana.' But no one can do so. . . . The mind wanders off in endless irrelevancies."[20] The talk was on contemporary Irish drama, largely on Synge, recently dead, and it left Shaw, who was in the chair, little to say, especially when Yeats ended with a paradox of a peroration in which he declared that "Life is the only theme of the arts," but also that "to do great literature" the writer "must be a solitary, unsocial creature . . ." (YT 56).

Yeats, Shaw concluded, was able to speak with "great extravagance and great remoteness," yet with "great exactitude," someone who understood that "poetry is only an attempt to try and get at the profoundest object of your life . . ." (YT 57). Shaw added, "If you meet an artist you always find he is a monomaniac. He is born with it and must go through with it . . ." (YT 58). In this instance Yeats almost certainly would have agreed, but he would soon be writing T. Sturge Moore, perversely, "When a man is so outrageously in the wrong as Shaw, he is indispensable" (LTSM 19).

Their letters suggest that Shaw and Yeats saw each other with some regularity when Yeats was in London. For the play's publicity potential more than its theatrical values, Yeats was even willing to see *Blanco Posnet* performed in America by the Abbey company in 1911–12 (he even went along for the first part of the tour); and there is no indication that he was disturbed by such notices as one in Philadelphia that declared that Shaw "had no conception of an American mining camp, and the Western atmosphere is as strange to the Irish Players as to Shaw himself."[21] Later in 1912, in a long interview in the London magazine *Hearth and Home*, Yeats paradoxically told Hugh Lunn ("Hugh Kingsmill") that Shaw was "irreverent, headlong, fantastic," with a "feminine logic" and "an extraordinary sense of moral responsibility."[22] Whether or not Shaw reconciled in his life or his work such incompatibilities, Yeats was calling attention in their recital to his own ambivalence toward his fellow Dubliner. Yet the language, but for the inoffensively meant sexual suggestion, was wholly positive. Yeats was not in any sense implying homosexuality: in his critical terminology, there were masculine and feminine casts of mind, and Yeats predictably saw his own as powerfully masculine. When he really wanted to be negative about Shaw he would downgrade him from "feminine" to "sexless" (LDW 128).

During the 1914–18 war, as events transformed both Yeats and Shaw into outspoken Irish patriots, Yeats at first wrote little about the war itself. Seeing no monopoly of righteousness on either side, Shaw wrote compulsively, penning pamphlets of Swiftian urgency and abrasiveness and urging that arbitration replace wholesale killing. Then, that failing, he wrote several playlets unsubtly satirizing superpatriotism. One of them, a look at the effort to recruit Irishmen to fight on the English side, *O'Flaherty, V.C.*, unlikely to be performed in England and in actuality meant for the Irish, was offered, in October 1915, to Yeats for another Hibernian evasion of the censorship. Although Yeats responded that no Dublin theater would object to what Shaw had ironically subtitled his "recruiting pamphlet" and even suggested "a private performance inviting all Dublin notables & taking up a collection" (S 175–76), no performance came off. Shaw had tried to press the authorities in Dublin by suggesting—he told Yeats—"the hardship to the starving theatre" and the "mischievous scandal" that would ensue if the public were to assume that the play had been suppressed as "anti-English."[23] But Dublin Castle would not be budged. It was far more incautious in wartime to satirize patriotism than to spoof religion.

Insisting that the war was a stupid blunder for both sides, Shaw interceded with officialdom whenever he could to rescue the unorthodox soldier and the less-than-patriotic civilian. Both Bertrand Russell and Yeats wrote to him to ask his help in the case of Eric Chappelow, who had been exempted as a conscientious objector, then reclaimed for army noncombatant service, which he refused. Shaw vainly pressed the case with a Labour member of the Cabinet, Arthur Henderson. When Henderson declined to take any action, Shaw took the matter to the press in the pages of the hospitable *Nation* (27 May 1916), using Chappelow as symbol of the futility of resistance and the equal futility of compliance.

It was not a Yeatsian cause. He preferred that Shaw, who enjoyed controversy, take up the cudgels. At the start, in "On Being Asked for a War Poem," Yeats even declared cautiously that it was better in such times that "A poet's mouth be silent" (VP 359), although after the Easter Rebellion in Dublin failed he changed his mind. He was not silent, either, when Major Robert Gregory, son of his friend and patron, was killed in action in January

1918. In the months soon after, Yeats wrote three poems on the subject of the flier's death. The best-known of them is almost certainly indebted to Shaw.

A reputation for voicing unpopular truths about the war had dogged Shaw through the first years of the slaughter, but by early 1917, when it became evident that he was listened to at home, the high brass offered to send him to France to have a look at the war and send back some newspaper accounts. At one airbase Shaw met Robert Gregory, whom he had known for years. As Yeats recalled in an article in *The Observer* three weeks after Gregory's death, "Major Gregory told Mr. Bernard Shaw, who visited him in France, that the months since he joined the Army had been the happiest of his life. I think they brought him peace of mind . . ." (UP2 431). What Yeats learned from Shaw seems to emerge in his elegiac "An Irish Airman Foresees His Death," where the unnamed Irish flier explains that he was not risking his life for his countrymen: neither law, nor duty, nor politicians, nor cheering crowds bade him fight. Rather,

> A lonely impulse of delight
> Drove to this tumult in the clouds;
> I balanced all, brought all to mind,
> The years to come seemed waste of breath,
> A waste of breath the years behind
> In balance with this life, this death.
>
> (VP 328)

As late as 1937 Yeats was acknowledging what he had discovered from Shaw, that Robert Gregory, a writer and artist who had lived in the shadow of his mother's reputation, "was never happy until he began to fight."[24] It is likely that all three—Lady Gregory, Shaw, and Yeats—never knew that the Major had been shot down in error by an Italian pilot, one of his own side.

Early in the 1920s, working on his memoir *The Trembling of the Veil*, Yeats penned his half-hostile, half-admiring remembrance of Shaw during the Florence Farr–*Arms and the Man* period. Once only a rationalist (in Yeats's view), Shaw had become, to Yeats, more and more the mystic, especially in his newest plays, *Heartbreak House* and *Back to Methuselah*. To George Russell, known in print as "AE," Yeats wrote perceptively in July 1921, "I agree about Shaw—he is haunted by the mystery he flouts. He is an atheist who trembles in the haunted corridor" (L 671). Russell, for whom G.B.S. had great affection, wrote back,

I think Shaw is coming back to Zion which is the natural home of the Irish. He has been out slaying the Philistine and as all conflicts result in an exchange of characteristics he had become a little of a Philistine himself but now he is returning to his natural spiritual resting place as you will see if you read through "Back to Methuselah" where his meditation on life comes back from external things to the soul itself & its powers & while he expresses himself in a phantasy I think the change is real. He was never afraid of anything in his life except himself & that fear he is now overcoming. He expresses perhaps in the last speech of Lilith more of his spiritual faith than he has yet done. You or I would say the same things in different language as the ultimate hope. I think we may say Shaw is coming back to Zion. Wells could not get to Zion if he tried in spite of his late much advertised discovery of "God the Invisible King" (LTWBY 389).

Aware of the ambivalence in Yeats's attitude toward Shaw, St. John Ervine early in 1920 had written in the *North American Review* that "in spite of his sincere regard and admiration for Mr. Shaw, Mr. Yeats seems to be totally incapable of comprehending his work. He is able to communicate with ghosts, but he cannot communicate with Mr. Shaw. He can understand astrologers and necromancers and spiritualists . . . but he cannot understand Mr. Shaw." On one of Yeats's Monday evening at-homes in Dublin when no one else came, Ervine listened at length to Yeats on the acquaintances of his London prentice years, including Shaw, who Yeats confided in puzzlement was "that strange man of genius." Ervine told him of attending a Shaw debate with Hilaire Belloc, where Shaw, explaining his role in life, had said, "I am a servant." Yeats was pleased—"moved by the humility of it."[25] But not long after the exchange with George Russell, when the twenty-two-year-old Victor Pritchett called at Merrion Square, he evoked only one Yeatsian retort he would remember. Pritchett had brought up the subject of Shaw and said something about Shaw's socialist principles. The effect on Yeats was "splendid." A teapot in his hands, Yeats rose to his feet to deny that Shaw had principles. "He was a destroyer." But the reaction was a flash of lightning that quickly flamed out. The subject was closed.[26]

Although to Yeats Shaw's genius did not extend to his "destructive" socialist principles, politics as expounded by Shaw was not that easy to categorize. Yeats found himself in November 1926 at the Chelsea Palace, at a performance of *Major Barbara*, with G.B.S. and visiting Swedish sculptor

Carl Milles, and discovered in Plato-quoting industrialist Andrew Under-shaft a Shavian businessman hero utterly at odds with Yeatsian preconceptions, more Right than Left, and soon in *The Apple Cart* he would discover a monarchist Shaw. Yeats had already seen *Heartbreak House*, which ended with the opening of the 1914 war, and recognized that the Shaw of "public meetings and committee meetings" also had his contemplative side, a need for solitude that Yeats felt was peculiarly Anglo-Irish.

In 1923 the Nobel Prize for Literature went to Yeats, and the 1925 Prize (*Saint Joan* having worked its miracle) to Shaw. The sudden literary visibility of newly independent Ireland suggested to Yeats in the year of Shaw's recognition that an Irish Academy of Letters be founded on the model of the French Institute. At the beginning of a new nation, Yeats wrote, "where conditions are unsettled, it is important to have an authoritative body . . . in creative literature" (L 717). His letter to the Royal Irish Academy (an offshoot of the Royal Academy in London) got nowhere. He was assured that the matter was being carefully studied, but after a year and a half of silence when he was certain that the proposal had been carefully buried, he sent his resignation to the Secretary of the Academy (L 732).

The idea lay dormant until Yeats discussed it, in the winter of 1931–32, with the dying Augusta Gregory. Again he began formulating an Irish Academy of Letters, using fifty pounds Shaw furnished for secretarial expenses (S 177). Between the two they developed a plan for a body of twenty-five members who had written creatively "with Ireland as the subject matter" (L 800), plus, as associates, ten Irishmen whose work was distinguished but who did not fall within the definition. The letter of invitation sent to prospective members under both their names (although written entirely by Shaw, Yeats told Lady Gregory)[27] made it clear that censorship was an enemy of literature that both had experienced and that the Academy would battle.

According to the invitation, Shaw and Yeats were proposing with the authority of their collective reputations "an instrument" for action on behalf of Irish authors, to make it more possible for writers "to live by distinctive Irish literature." The intellectual and poetic qualities of their work might furnish them an influence disproportionate to their numbers if they banded together as an Academy. "In making this claim on you," the pair concluded, "we have no authority or mandate beyond the fact that the initiative has to be taken by somebody, and our age and the publicity which attaches to our names makes it easier for us than for younger writers." Nominees were to reply to George Russell in Dublin (L 801–802).

All the prospective members but one or two suggest Yeats's preferences, none of them unpalatable to Shaw. Two "Associates" suggest Shaw's hand— the American playwright Eugene O'Neill—whose work Shaw admired—and Welsh-born "Lawrence of Arabia," who by then had legally changed his name to Shaw. T.E. Lawrence, a surrogate son to Charlotte and G.B.S., was of illegitimate but Irish parentage, his father a County Meath baronet named Chapman. Few besides the Shaws—and now Yeats—even knew T.E.'s secret. Yeats had not known Lawrence's writings until Shaw introduced him to *Revolt in the Desert*, the 1926 abridgment of *Seven Pillars of Wisdom*, which "startled and excited" Yeats by its "sense of a hardship borne and chosen out of pride and joy."[28]

Although a few stubborn individualists, such as Lord Dunsany, James Joyce, and Sean O'Casey, refused nomination, the Academy was formally launched at a hurried meeting Yeats called in Dublin for 14 September 1932. The only absent member was Shaw. Yeats had apparently failed to check with G.B.S. on the date, for the evening before, Shaw's new play, *Too True To Be Good* (with the leading character a parody of T. E. Lawrence), was to open in London. The usual rule prevailed: the absent G.B.S. was unanimously elected president (S 177–78), with Yeats as vice-president and George Russell secretary and treasurer.

"I am against myself as President," Shaw protested (20 September 1932) to Yeats. "The President should also be Resident, and should be a man . . . who loves gassing at public banquets, state unveilings and foundation stone layings" (*CL 1926–1950*, p. 308). He accepted nevertheless, serving until Yeats succeeded him in 1935, and on the death of Yeats in 1939 he agreed to a further interim year as President.

Not asked to be among the founding members was the novelist Thomas MacGreevy, who had carped to Yeats, "An Academy which included Shaw would probably only sanction such literature as English suffragette spinsters like, the sort of [thing] that pours from the printing presses of England to-day and not a page of which is worth reading" (LTWBY 538).

Curiously, Shaw's opinion of the state of fiction was the same. When, early in 1934, the Irish Academy was asked to adjudicate the 1933 Harms-worth Award, Yeats asked Shaw to judge the fiction. Declining with his usual contempt for literary awards, he told Yeats (14 January 1934), "The prize should be for the worst English novel. That would at least amuse the public. Donkey races are always popular" (*CL 1926–1950*, p. 351). Unwilling himself, Yeats recruited someone else.

By 1932 Yeats was already in ill health, and in April 1934 he underwent the controversial Steinach sexual rejuvenation operation, for which he would claim at least temporary benefits. Like his earlier compatriot Swift, Yeats had long been torn by sexual stirrings as well as by an equally powerful sense of disgust at both the itch and the act. "Love has pitched his mansion in / The place of excrement" (VP 513), Yeats would put it in "Crazy Jane Talks with the Bishop" (1933). He had also, as he grew old, and had married late (at fifty-two) a young wife, brooded over physical as well as mere sexual decay, writing, as in "The Tower" (1927), of "Decrepit age . . . tied to me / As to a dog's tail . . ." (VP 409) and of the dream of an ecstasy beyond fleshly existence. Yeats's ideas had come from Blake and Swift and others, perhaps Shaw as well. Don Juan in *Man and Superman* (1903) had railed against "this tyranny of the flesh" that made men "slaves of reality" (CP2 650). Shaw had written often of the bondage of sex and of the possibility that man might someday shed all his physical limitations. As his He-Ancient in the futuristic last segment of *Back to Methuselah* (1921) observes, "Whilst we are tied to this tyrannous body we are subject to its death, and our destiny is not achieved." Agreeing, the She-Ancient adds, "The day will come when there will be no people, only thought," while the sculptor Martellus confirms, "Nothing remains beautiful and interesting except thought, because the thought is the life" (CP5 622). It is unlikely that such lines were lost on Yeats, who knew the play, although it would be too much to claim that he would have written on the subject very differently without the example of Shaw. If nothing else, Shaw had ventured to make such indelicate ideas public. *

Except in Ireland, G.B.S. was rarely accused of indelicacy. It was no surprise to him that his picaresque religious fable *The Adventures of the Black Girl in Her Search for God* became the first major rallying cause for the fledgling Academy of Letters after the best-selling little book was suppressed as "indecent and obscene." A deputation from the Academy called on the Minister for Justice, Patrick J. Ruttledge, who expressed doubts about the censorship, then reversed himself. Encouraging the protest at first, Shaw warned Yeats (18 May 1933) that the clever illustrations by John Farleigh were likely to be more objectionable to "the reverend censors," who "probably regard a nude negress as the last extremity of obscenity."

*Another biological idea that Yeats would pick up, at least in part, from Shaw was that of the need for eugenic considerations in breeding. By the time of Yeats's last long essay, *On the Boiler* (1939), his interest in the subject had become obsessive. Quoting Shaw and several others, Yeats observed with dismay that since the turn of the century "the better stocks have not been replacing their numbers, while the stupider and less healthy have been more than replacing theirs" (Ex 423).

Offering a perverse line of defense, Shaw suggested in *Saint Joan* fashion that "the book completely justifies the Church in its objection to throwing the Bible into the hands of ignorant persons to be interpreted by their private judgment" (*CL 1926–1950*, p. 340).

Yeats urged a lawsuit by the Academy and Shaw responded (4 September 1933) to Yeats's innocence, "You can't prosecute a Government: the King can do no wrong." All that can be done, if editors and publishers cared to print them, was to hurl "Miltonic essays" at the Government. "And even that will be a waste of time. I shall not protest: if the Churchmen think my book is subversive they are quite right from their point of view. Only as the word obscene can hardly apply to my text, I wish some member of the Dail would ask Mr. Ruttledge whether, if I issue a special edition for Ireland with the negress depicted in long skirts, the ban will be withdrawn" (*CL 1926–1950*, pp. 352–53).

A lover of tailcoats and testimonial dinners, Yeats was further perplexed by Shaw's refusal to adjudicate and preside, for the Academy, over the 1934 Harmsworth Award. "Failing a schoolmaster," he responded to Yeats (14 January 1934), "get a boxing referee, accustomed to declare winners 'on points.' Anyhow you won't get *me*" (*CL 1926–1950*, p. 361).

It was the jeering side of G.B.S. that Yeats had particularly disliked over the decades. It was also a disappointment since everything that Shaw did or said had publicity potential. He was news, unlike Yeats, as he had confessed wryly to Lady Gregory in 1929, when his play *Fighting the Waves* and Shaw's *Apple Cart* (which would be his longest opening run since 1911–12—258 performances) premiered close upon each other. The *Irish Times* had reported that the plays had been "produced amid such stir of attention as seldom gratified the most notable of dramatists." It was, Yeats scoffed, "nonsense so far as my play is concerned" (L 767). Some months later he went to see *The Apple Cart*, which was still playing to enthusiastic London audiences. "I hated the play," he again confided to Lady Gregory, adding "It was the Shaw who writes letters to the papers and gives interviews, not the man who creates" (L 770–71). He preferred Shaw the mystic, whom he and AE had seen emerging from the public Shaw, yet even the public man would have his attractive side, as Yeats would soon recognize.

Public and private controversies failed to dent the somewhat uneasy respect each continued to have for the other. Shaw's assistance on the Academy project so dear to Yeats's heart had come soon after the Abbey Theatre controversy over rejecting Sean O'Casey's play *The Silver Tassie*, in which Yeats had played a prominent part and in which Shaw lobbied vainly

for O'Casey. A few years later—in 1930—Yeats would note in his diary that
the admiration for the play shown by Shaw and Augustus John (who
designed the London sets) "suggests that it was at least better than we thought
it, and yet I am certain that if any of our other dramatists sent us a similar
play we would reject it" (Ex 339).

Nobel Prizes and other affinities notwithstanding, Yeats's ambivalence
toward his most famous fellow townsman would persist, most notably in the
cranky astrological geometry of A Vision (1925), a mystical work in which
twenty-eight alleged phases of human life were classified according to phases
of the moon. Shaw was assigned (with the disliked H. G. Wells and the
even more offensive George Moore) to the twenty-first phase (remote from
Yeats's own), dominated by "freakish or grotesque, mind-created passions,
simulated emotions" (AV-A 88–90). Shaw, so Yeats had written in the
Autobiographies, "has no quarrel with his time, its moon and his almost
exactly coincide. He is quite content to exchange Narcissus and his Pool for
a signal-box at a railway junction, where goods and travelers pass perpetually
upon their logical glittering road" (Au 294). The observations were overly
rigid in both directions, for Yeats had already acknowledged a vein of
mysticism in Shaw, and had been finding himself drawn into mundane
matters despite his inclinations.

Yeats would emphasize Shaw's balance of the mundane and the mystical
in his preface to Oliver St. John Gogarty's Wild Apples (1930), writing,
"Even Shaw, who has toiled at public meetings and committee meetings
that he might grow into an effective superficial man of the streets, has made
the wastrels of Heartbreak House cry when they hear the whirr of a Zeppelin
overhead, 'Turn on all the lights.' Unlike those Fabian friends of his he
desires and doubtless dreads inexplicable useless adventure."[29]

Despite Yeats's rush to rigid categorizing and his impatience with politics,
he was finding himself enmeshed in the real world. He was even an Irish
senator, although he accepted the title more as an accolade than as an
agenda. While Shaw was putting playwriting aside to write a long political
treatise, Yeats stubbornly worked at reforming minds in his own cranky way.
Reviewing A Vision, AE wondered whether it was "insight or impishness"
that impelled Yeats to link Shaw to Wells and Moore, to link Galsworthy
with Queen Victoria, and to link AE himself, in phase twenty-five, to John
Calvin, Martin Luther, and Cardinal Newman (although he welcomed
George Herbert). Edmund Wilson found it interesting to compare A Vision
"with that other compendious treatise on human nature and destiny by
that other great writer from Dublin"—Shaw's then-recent The Intelligent

Woman's Guide to Socialism and Capitalism. Coming to London from Ireland as young men, they had followed "diametrically opposite courses":

> Shaw shouldered the whole unwieldy load of contemporary sociology, politics, economics, biology, medicine and journalism, while Yeats, convinced that the world of science and politics was somewhat fatal to the poet's vision, as resolutely turned away. Shaw accepted the scientific technique and set himself to master the problems of an industrialized democratic society, while Yeats rejected the methods of Naturalism and applied himself to the introspective plumbing of the mysteries of the individual mind. While Yeats was editing Blake, Shaw was grappling with Marx; and Yeats was appalled by Shaw's hardness and efficiency.[30]

In Yeats's "Great Wheel" of twenty-eight segments, Wilson noted, Yeats had "situated" G.B.S.

> at a phase considerably removed from his own, and where the individual is headed straight for the deformity of seeking, not the soul, but the world. And their respective literary testaments—the "Vision" and the "Guide"—published almost at the same time, mark the extreme points of their divergence: Shaw bases all human hope and happiness on an equal distribution of income, which he believes will finally make impossible even the pessimism of a Swift or a Voltaire; while Yeats, like Shaw a Protestant for whom the Catholic's mysticism was impossible, has in "A Vision" made the life of humanity contingent on the movements of the stars. "The day is far off," he concludes, "when the two halves of man can divine each its own unity in the other as in a mirror, Sun in Moon, Moon in Sun, and so escape out of the Wheel."
>
> Yet, in the meantime, the poet Yeats has passed into a sort of third phase, in which he is closer to the common world than at any previous period.[31]

Wilson's comments in *Axel's Castle* (1931) were a reconsidered version of a *New Republic* review (16 January 1929) in which he had also observed that there appeared to be some real symbolism in the fact that while Shaw lived in the middle of London, Yeats had "secluded himself in a tower on the farthest Irish coast." Still, Wilson was right the second time around—that

Yeats was closer to immediate human concerns than at any previous time in
his life, preoccupied not only with sexuality and with the aging process, but
with political matters, both as an Irish senator and as an observer of a violent
world once more hurtling out of control.

A 1931 commentary on his "A Parnellite at Parnell's Funeral" seemed to
insist upon the personalization of A Vision even while Yeats was accommo-
dating himself to other aspects of Shaw. There G.B.S. was one of "three
men too conscious of intellectual power to belong to party," with Wilde and
George Moore—"the most complete individualists in the history of literature, abstract, isolated minds, without a memory or a landscape. It is this
very isolation, this defect, as it seems to me, which has given Bernard Shaw
an equal welcome in all countries, the greatest fame in his own lifetime any
writer has known. Without it, his wit would have waited for acceptance
upon studious exposition and commendation" (VP 834). How the lines
applied collectively to Moore, Anglo-Irish in text and subtext, or to Wilde,
self-consciously artificial and mannered, as well as to Shaw (whom Yeats
clearly admired far more than the other two), is difficult to see, but none
had Yeats's vision of Ireland. Still the artist as political man was becoming
more acceptable to Yeats in his scheme of things, and although he would
publish a new edition of A Vision in 1937, without significant alteration, by
1933 Shaw loomed to him as the only Irish figure of world class since the
eighteenth-century trio of Swift, Berkeley, and Burke.[32] But he claimed that
it was Shaw who had changed, observing to an American patron, Patrick
McCarten, that G.B.S. had "grown amiable in his old age."[33]

Mellowing further, he would write to Margaret Ruddock, in criticizing a
play she had sent to him, that while her script would not work, "Shaw can
write a play where everybody is his mouthpiece because he takes the popular
thought upon the stage, plays with it, and reverses it. You and I can only
put our own thought there." And Shaw's method, he concluded, had the
most potential. "I do not think a play where everyone speaks my thought
can be the greatest kind of play no matter how written."[34] To Dorothy
Wellesley he would write in 1936 of the indignation over alleged injustice
in his two Roger Casement poems, "I am fighting in those ballads for what
I have been fighting all my life, it is our Irish fight though it has nothing to
do with this or that country. Bernard Shaw fights with the same object"
(L 876).

Frank O'Connor remembered visiting Merrion Square in the 1930s and
in the boldness of youth passing "some disparaging remark on Shaw's style."
In a low voice Yeats, although dressed pointedly in a blue shirt to demon-

strate his identification with General Gavan O'Duffy's Rightist militia, reminded him, "And yet if ever an angel of God walked upon this earth in the form of a man, his name was Bernard Shaw."[35] Nevertheless, when Shaw failed to be on the same side, Yeats's admiration could slip a little. A Shavian comment in the newspapers that he did not like he characterized to Lady Dorothy in 1937 as "a long, rambling, vegetarian, sexless letter" (L 884). Even so, in his collection of essays, *On the Boiler*, he found himself remembering Shaw's most mystical and poetic character, "the spoilt priest in *John Bull's Other Island*" (Ex 411). And he recalled Father Keegan again the next year, in the *Irish Independent* (13 August 1938), thinking of the unfrocked priest's remark, "There is only one place of horror and torment known to my religion; and that place is hell. Therefore it is plain to me that this earth of ours must be hell. . . . " In the character of Keegan, more than a generation before, Yeats observed, Shaw had captured the character of Ireland "as it appears to the Irish novelists and dramatists of today, and summed up what might be their final thought." Four years earlier, he recalled, when he had been ill in Italy (after his surgery) "and not sure I would know active life again," he had recorded in his diary "the events of life and art that had most [moved] me." The only one he revealed was that unearthly figure out of Shaw, from the play he had been too timid, then, to produce.[36] In 1904 it had been a difficult truth to stage. In July 1938, in perhaps his last words on the subject, he wrote, "The Irish mind has still, in country rapscallion or in Bernard Shaw, an ancient, cold, explosive, detonating impartiality" (Ex 443).

After Yeats died in January 1939, critic Stephen Gwynn set about collecting a volume of "Essays in Tribute," and wrote to Shaw. When Shaw failed to respond and the volume went to press without him, Gwynn had every reason to think that Shaw's assumed lack of harmony with things Yeatsian was responsible. (The final essay, by L. A. G. Strong, even made the point that Yeats "never loved Shaw.")[37] Then, late in August 1940, nearly a year after the letter of invitation had been mailed to Shaw, Gwynn received an answer. At his age, Shaw wrote—he was 84—his memory was becoming unreliable, and the letter had been put aside and forgotten. He had little to contribute to a book, he felt, since he had not been on close literary terms with Yeats, although they had always retained a personal rapport. Further, while he felt that Yeats often tinkered too much with his language in an effort to be "supersubtle," Shaw insisted (28 August 1940) that he had no business trying to be a critic of Yeats's verse. He thought of him as a penetrating critic and conversationalist, and in their own relationship he encountered little of the mannered early Yeats (visible nevertheless, in the Marchbanks of *Candida*) who, to other people, Shaw recalled, suggested Gilbert and Sullivan's aesthetically affected poet Algernon Bunthorne in *Patience* come to life. "Bunthorne was not a bit like Wilde, but he presently came to life in the person of W.B.Y., who outBunthorned [Oscar Wilde] enough to make him seem commonplace."

Rather, Shaw preferred to think of his old friend as he once saw him on a "pitchblack" London night in Chancery Lane when into the pool of illumination made by a street lamp stepped the tall, elegant Maud Gonne, dazzling in white silk, with Yeats in evening clothes matching the lock of black hair that arched across his forehead. Unseen in the dark, Shaw did not intrude upon the pair, and it was the only time he ever saw the beautiful Irishwoman who for years was the cause of frustration as well as inspiration for the poet. The striking image he preferred as his memory of Yeats suggested an admiration belying allegations and innuendoes of hostility (*CL 1926–1950*, pp. 576–77).

Even later, well into his nineties, Shaw admired the man more than the work. "Unlike Wilde," he told his neighbor Stephen Winsten, "Yeats could not spell and had no sense of number. That is why his poetry went wrong." But Shaw got along with Yeats because he never disparaged Yeats's writing while his colleague lived, and Yeats never posed as anything but himself when with G.B.S. "Yeats thought he combined both the West and the East, and so did Annie Besant, of course. I got on very well with Yeats, because he shed all his Eastern affectations when we two got together."[38] Whatever Shaw's private reservations, he recognized that Yeats had style, and even as a "hardened professional in the theatre" Shaw remembered being "touched" by *Kathleen ni Houlihan* (Charlotte wept)[39] and moved by *Where There is Nothing*. To Yeats, Shaw had not only been his century's only equivalent to Swift and Burke, but the creator of the inimitable Father Keegan, who possessed in him more of the real Ireland than Yeats had succeeded in endowing in Kathleen ni Houlihan herself. It had been an uneasy friendship, but rewarding, and true.

Notes

Shaw's letters are quoted from the *Collected Letters 1898–1910* (New York: Dodd, Mead, 1972) and *Collected Letters 1926–1950* (New York: Viking, 1988), ed. Dan H. Laurence. Citation abbreviations to Yeats studies in the text represent the following publications:

Au   *Autobiographies.* London: Macmillan, 1955.
AV-A   *A Critical Edition of Yeats's "A Vision"* (1925). Ed. George Mills Harper and Walter Kelly Hood. London: Macmillan, 1978.
Ex   *Explorations.* Sel. Mrs. W. B. Yeats. London: Macmillan, 1962; New York: Macmillan, 1963.
L   *The Letters of W. B. Yeats.* Ed. Allan Wade. London: Rupert Hart-Davis, 1954; New York: Macmillan, 1955.
LDW   *Letters on Poetry from W. B. Yeats to Dorothy Wellesley.* Intro. Kathleen Raine. London & New York: Oxford University Press, 1964.
LTSM   *W. B. Yeats and T. Sturge Moore: Their Correspondence, 1901–1937.* Ed. Ursula Bridge. London: Routledge & Kegan Paul; New York: Oxford University Press, 1953.
LTWBY   *Letters to W. B. Yeats.* Ed. Richard J. Finneran, George Mills Harper, and William M. Murphy. London: Macmillan; New York: Columbia University Press, 1977.
MEM   *Memoirs.* Transcribed and edited by Denis Donoghue. New York: Macmillan, 1973.
S   "Hic and Ille: Shaw and Yeats." Michael J. Sidnell. *Theatre and Twentieth-Century Ireland.* Ed. Robert O'Driscoll. Toronto: University of Toronto Press, 1971.
UP2   *Uncollected Prose by W. B. Yeats.* Vol. 2. Ed. John P. Frayne and Colton Johnson. London: Macmillan, 1975; New York: Columbia University Press, 1976.
VP   *The Variorum Edition of the Poems of W. B. Yeats.* Ed. Peter Allt and Russell K. Alspach. New York: Macmillan, 1957.
VP1   *The Variorum Edition of the Plays of W. B. Yeats.* Ed. Russell K. Alspach. London & New York: Macmillan, 1966.
YT   "Yeats on Personality: Three Unpublished Lectures." Robert O'Driscoll and Lorna Reynolds. Toronto: University of Toronto Press, 1975.

1. References to Shaw's 1885–97 shorthand diaries are from *Bernard Shaw, The Diaries 1885–1897,* ed. Stanley Weintraub (University Park: Pennsylvania State University Press, 1986).
2. *Shaw: An Autobiography 1856–1898,* ed. Stanley Weintraub (New York: Weybright & Talley, 1969), pp. 165–66.
3. Shaw, "An Explanatory Word" to *Florence Farr/Bernard Shaw/W. B. Yeats: Letters,* ed. Clifford Bax (London: Hone & Van Thal, 1946), p. ix.
4. Ibid.
5. G.B.S. would not have spoken so awkwardly. "I quite agree with you, Sir," he has been quoted elsewhere as saying, "but who are we among so many?"
6. Notably Louis Crompton in *Shaw the Dramatist* (Lincoln: University of Nebraska Press, 1969), p. 30.
7. "The Poet and the Actress," dated 1915 by Richard Ellmann in *The Identity of Yeats* (New York: Oxford, 1964), pp. 98–99.
8. George Yeats (she was christened with the masculine name) recalls her husband's description of the liaison in "A Foreword to the Letters of W. B. Yeats," in Bax, pp. 33–34. According to Josephine Johnson, in *Florence Farr, Bernard Shaw's New Woman* (New York: Rowman and Littlefield, 1975), p. 42, Yeats later complained to Florence's sister Henrietta that he had known Florence for years and that "never once had they made love." Henrietta allegedly repeated the confession to Florence, who laughed, "But I'm years older than he is." It is far more likely that Yeats would have shared such an intimate confidence with his wife than with an acquaintance, and Henrietta's recollection, unattributed to any source, is suspect.
9. "An Explanatory Word," p. 10.
10. Yeats to Shaw, October 1901, in Michael J. Sidnell, "Hic and Ille: Shaw and Yeats," *Theatre and Nationalism in Twentieth-Century Ireland,* ed. Robert O'Driscoll (Toronto: University of Toronto Press, 1971), p. 171 (hereafter S). The Sidnell essay is the fullest examination of the Yeats-

Shaw relationship; however, like the others it focuses almost entirely on the *John Bull's Other Island* affair. Sidnell sees their persisting mutual admiration and respect despite contrary views as resulting from Shaw's recognizing "the enduring poet" in Yeats and Yeats's recognizing in Shaw "a great Public man" whose wit was a "scourge." Other articles on Shaw, Yeats, and *John Bull* include Norma Jenckes, "The Rejection of Shaw's Irish Play," *Eire-Ireland* 10:1 (Spring 1975): 38–53; and Harold Ferrar, "The Caterpillar and the Gracehoper: Bernard Shaw's *John Bull's Other Island*," *Eire-Ireland* 15:1 (Spring 1980): 25–45. The *Blanco Posnet* affair is chronicled in Dan Laurence, "The *Blanco Posnet* Controversy," *Shaw Bulletin* 1:7 (January 1955): 1–9, but much additional documentation has since emerged.

11. Shaw to Yeats, APC signed G.B.S.; item 200 in Sotheby (London) catalogue of the 15 December 1982 sale.

12. Quoted in Bernard Shaw, *Collected Letters 1898–1910*, p. 452.

13. Quoted in Bernard Shaw, *Collected Letters 1898–1910*, p. 453.

14. Quoted in Bernard Shaw, *Collected Letters 1898–1910*, pp. 452–53; S, pp. 172–73.

15. "Preface for Politicians" (to the first edition in 1906), *John Bull's Other Island, The Bodley Head Bernard Shaw: Collected Plays with Their Prefaces* (New York: Dodd, Mead, 1975), 2:808.

16. *John Bull's Other Island*, Act IV, CP 2:1014. *Collected Plays* hereafter CP in text.

17. Quoted in Bernard Shaw, *Collected Letters 1898–1910*, p. 453.

18. Yeats, *Autobiographies* (New York: Doubleday, 1958), pp. 318–19.

19. Lady Gregory, *Seventy Years* (New York: Macmillan, 1970), p. 313.

20. Yeats, "Contemporary Irish Theatre," a lecture at the Adelphi Club, 11 March 1910, with concluding remarks by Bernard Shaw, in "Yeats on Personality: Three Unpublished Lectures," *Yeats and the Theatre*, ed. O'Driscoll and Lorna Reynolds (Toronto: University of Toronto Press, 1975), p. 42. Hereafter in the text as YT.

21. Quoted from the *Philadelphia Evening Bulletin*, 9 January 1912, in Robert Hogan, Richard Burnham and Daniel P. Poteet, *The Modern Irish Drama, IV: The Rise of the Realists, 1910–1915* (Dublin: Dolmen Press, 1979), 421.

22. 28 November 1912, in E. G. Mikhail, ed., *W. B. Yeats: Interviews and Recollections* (London: Macmillan, 1977), p. 88.

23. Hogan, Burnham, and Poteet, p. 386 (12 November 1915).

24. "My Own Poetry," B.B.C. broadcast from Yeats's typescript read by V. C. Clinton-Baddeley and Margot Ruddock, 3 July 1937, in Donald Torchiana, *W. B. Yeats and Georgian Ireland* (Evanston: Northwestern University Press, 1966), p. 68.

25. St. John Ervine, "Some Impressions of My Elders: W. B. Yeats," *North American Review* (February 1920), reprinted in Mikhail, pp. 100–101, 107.

26. V. S. Pritchett, "Encounters with Yeats," *New Statesman* (4 June 1965), reprinted in Mikhail, p. 347.

27. 18 April 1932, quoted in Maurice F. Neville, Santa Barbara, Calif., *Literary Autographs: Letters and Manuscripts*, catalog no. 6, item 509.

28. Yeats, Preface (1929) to Oliver St. John Gogarty's *Wild Apples* (1930), in *Prefaces and Introductions*, ed. William H. O'Donnell (New York: Macmillan, 1989), p. 172.

29. Ibid., p. 173.

30. Edmund Wilson, *Axel's Castle*, as quoted in *W. B. Yeats: The Critical Heritage*, ed. A. N. Jeffares (London: Routledge & Kegan Paul, 1977), p. 303.

31. Ibid., p. 302.

32. "Modern Irish Literature," *Irish Times* (18 February 1933); also a review of a lecture by Yeats, "The Creation of Modern Ireland," September 1932, under the title "The New Reading," *United Irishman* (24 September 1932); both quoted in Torchiana, pp. 102, 162.

33. Yeats to Patrick MacCarten, 16 March 1935, quoted as item 195 in Paul Richards sale catalogue 207, 1986.

34. Yeats to Margaret Ruddock, 2 April 1936, in Roger McHugh, ed., *Ah, Sweet Dancer: W. B. Yeats to Margaret Ruddock* (New York: Macmillan, 1970), p. 80.

35. Frank O'Connor, "Two Friends: Yeats and A.E.," *Yale Review* (September 1939), reprinted in Mikhail, p. 264.

36. "Modern Ireland: An Address to American Audiences, 1932–1933," ed. Curtis Bradford, *Irish Renaissance: A Gathering of Essays, Memoirs and Letters from The Massachusetts Review*, ed. Robin Skelton and David R. Clark (Dublin: Dolmen, 1965), p. 25.

37. L.A.G. Strong, "William Butler Yeats," in Stephen Gwynn, ed., *Scattering Branches: Tributes to the Memory of William Butler Yeats* (London: Macmillan, 1940), pp. 204–5.

38. Stephen Winsten, *Days with Bernard Shaw* (New York: Vanguard Press, 1949), pp. 302–3.

39. The Shaws saw the Abbey production on a London triple bill with Lady Gregory's *Workhouse Ward* and G.B.S.'s own *Blanco Posnet* on 5 December 1909.

A RESPECTFUL DISTANCE

James Joyce and His Dublin Townsman Bernard Shaw

"Kick in the arse for the following," James Joyce wrote to his brother Stanislaus from Rome in 1906. "G.K.C.: G.B.S.: S.L.: H.J.: G.R. Kicks in the arse all round, in fact."[1] Gilbert Chesterton, critic Sidney Lee, Henry James, publisher Grant Richards were the others. It was Joyce's first fulmination at Bernard Shaw, then fifty and famous. Joyce was twenty-four. Shaw had never heard of him.

Earlier—as early as 1900, when Joyce was eighteen—he had referred to Shaw only as "a certain English critic" in an article that indicated in such language as "muck-ferreting dog," from Shaw's list of abusive epithets applied to Ibsen, that he had read, and admired, *The Quintessence of Ibsenism*.[2] A little later (15 October 1903), reviewing several novels of A.E.W. Mason in the Dublin *Daily Express*, Joyce observed that Mason's novel *The Philanderers* used "a title which Mr. Mason has to share with Mr. George Bernard Shaw." A likely candidate for banning by the Censor of Plays and published only in a small edition, G.B.S.'s comedy was little known, but Joyce was already following Shaw's career "attentively," as the editors of his collected *Critical Writings*, Ellsworth Mason and Richard Ellmann (1959), note. Shaw probably saw neither piece, but he would have been amused had he known that Joyce's interest in the *Quintessence* persisted into *Finnegans Wake*. There, "Shaw and Shea are lorning obsen." Also, in the *Wake* is "a Norwegian and his mate of the Sheawolving class," and Shaw's extract from William Archer's catalogue of invectives levied against *Ghosts* is transmuted (585. 15–21) into

The spiking Duyvil! First liar in Londsend! Wulv! . . . Such ratshause bugsmess so I cannot barely conceive of! Lowest basemeant in hystry! Inbscenest nansence! Noksagt! . . . The brokerheartened shugon! Hole affair is rotten muckswinish pokupig's draft. Enouch!

When the Shavian religious farce *The Shewing-up of Blanco Posnet*, subtitled with merciless accuracy "A Sermon in Crude Melodrama," was performed in Dublin in August 1909 to evade the stage censorship in London, Joyce was still unknown to Shaw. But Joyce was reading G.B.S. assiduously—the A.E.W. Mason reference had been to *The Philanderer* (1893)—and later he would pull puns out of Shaw's first Irish play, *John Bull's Other Island* (1904).

Countering criticism that it was vulgar to build his literary edifices upon puns, Joyce would remind Frank Budgen (20 August 1939), "The Holy Roman Catholic Apostolic Church was built on a pun. It ought to be good enough for me." Joyce knew his Shaw, who had remarked in the preface to *John Bull* that Ireland was "no bad rock to build a church on," and two years later, introducing his *Dramatic Opinions and Essays* (1906), added that the "Christian Church" was "founded gaily with a pun." Jesus, he was reminding his readers, had conferred upon his disciple Simon the surname *Peter*, the Aramaic word (afterward turned into Greek) for *stone*, to emphasize his steadfastness, and Peter had built the early Church. In 1933 Shaw had dramatized the pun in a bestselling novella, *The Adventures of the Black Girl in Her Search for God*, in which the Black Girl confronts "an ancient fisherman carrying an enormous cathedral on his shoulders" and warns him to take care, since it might break his back.

"Not it," he replies cheerfully, "I am the rock on which this Church is built."

"But you are not a rock," she says, anxiously—and literally.

"No fear," Peter assures her. "It is made entirely of paper."

Which of Shaw's punning references did Joyce know? Very likely all three; unquestionably the first two.

The play itself appears to have evoked another pun. The second act opens in Rosscullen upon "a hillside of granite rock and heather" where, near "a huge stone [which] stands in a nearly impossible place," is a white-haired man of fifty, "with the face of a young saint." A defrocked priest, Father Keegan is addressing a grasshopper, inquiring whether "ould Ireland" is Heaven, Hell, or Purgatory. Joyce got it right in the *Wake* when he humanized the unseen but not unheard creature into "gracehoper."

The gentle faith of Keegan is nothing like the melodramatic but intuitive theology of defrocked cowboy Blanco Posnet. By its opening performance Joyce was a resident of Trieste—a poorly paid language teacher and occasional journalist trying to find time for serious writing. Back, briefly, in Dublin, he had arranged to get into the Abbey theatre premiere of Shaw's play by claiming he was literary critic for *Il Piccolo della Sera* of Trieste. And critic he was, writing (in Italian) the only unfavorable review of the opening, which appeared on 5 September 1909 as *"La Battaglia Fra Bernard Shaw e la Censura: Blanco Posnet Smascherato."*[3]

After recording the sold-out house and thunderous applause, Joyce went on to describe Shaw's dramatization of the conversion of a horse thief in an improbable Wild West. Blanco Posnet's impulsive sermon was theological in subject, said Joyce, but "not very churchy in diction." The play ended happily, he observed, but

> Nothing more flimsy can be imagined and the playgoer asks himself in wonder why on earth the play was interdicted by the censor. Shaw is right: it is a sermon. Shaw is a born preacher. His lively and talkative spirit cannot stand to be subjected to the noble and bare style appropriate to modern playwriting. Indulging himself in wandering prefaces and extravagant rules of drama, he creates for himself a dramatic form which is much like a dialogue novel. He has a sense of situation . . . [and] in this case he has dug up the central incident of his "Devil's Disciple" and transformed it into a sermon. The transformation is too abrupt to be convincing as a sermon, and the art is too poor to make it convincing as drama.

Joyce asked George Roberts to send the Dublin *Evening Telegraph* condensation of his review, which appeared on 8 September, to various friends, and—typical bit of Joycean arrogance—to send one as well to Shaw, "with a request that he do what he could to help promote the fortunes of the same author's coming book, *Dubliners*."[4] There was nothing in Joyce's review to inspire Shaw to go out of his way to promote the critic, and he may never have been sent the notice.

Joyce's visits to the *Telegraph*'s offices, in part to solicit the review and then to deliver it, would be recalled in the "Aeolus" episode of *Ulysses*, which utilizes the *Telegraph*'s atmosphere and many of its physical details. As for Shaw himself, he did not remember having seen the Dublin version of the review when he was shown a translation of the Trieste piece in 1949, five days before his ninety-third birthday.[5]

An ironic commentary on Joyce's carping about Shaw's play is a bookseller's bill in Trieste a few years after the *Posnet* affair for six months of purchases totaling twenty books. It includes two Shaw plays, *The Devil's Disciple* and *Major Barbara*. Joyce had indicated that he knew *Devil's Disciple* well enough—perhaps from performance—to relate it to the farce he reviewed. Now he was even going to own a copy.

In 1918, during the war years Joyce spent in the safety of Zurich, he was briefly involved in an English Players Company in the city, which performed *The Importance of Being Earnest, the Heather Field* (of Edward Martyn), *Hindle Wakes* (of Stanley Houghton)—and *Mrs Warren's Profession.** The company also did Shaw's *Dark Lady of the Sonnets*, which gave Joyce occasion to write program notes critical of Shaw's view of Shakespeare, which he accepted literally rather than as the springboard for an appeal for a National Theatre:

> Mr. Shaw here presents three orthodox figures—a virgin queen, a Shakespeare sober at midnight and a free giver of gold, and the dark-haired maid of honour, Mary Fitton, discovered in the eighties by Thomas Tyler and Mr. [Frank] Harris. Shakespeare comes to White-hall to meet her and learns from a well-languaged beef-eater that Mr. W. H. has forestalled him. The poet vents his spleen on the first woman who passes. It is the queen and she seems not loth to be accosted. She orders the maid of honour out of the way. When Shakespeare, however, begs her to endow his theatre she refers him with fine cruelty to her lord treasurer and leaves him. The most regicide of playwrights prays God to save her and goes home weighing against a lightened purse, love's treason, an old queen's leer and the evil eye of a government official, a horror still to come.[6]

Shaw may not have known of the implicit criticism, but he did discover that his plays had been performed without permission or payment of royalty. Joyce afterwards explained innocently to Herbert Thring of the Society of Authors, Shaw's agents—at least with respect to *Mrs Warren's Profession*—that no rights could exist for a play the production of which was in England an indictable offense. It was Joyce's second brush with a censored Shaw play.

---

*Joyce's production of Wilde's play would be the basis of Tom Stoppard's comedy *Travesties* (1974).

During the war Joyce had completed his Ibsenite play *Exiles*, sending it
to the Stage Society in London through agent J. B. Pinker early in 1916. It
was rejected, then recalled for another review, during which Joyce withdrew
it in frustration. He thought that Shaw was behind the negative vote. So too
did Joyce's biographer,* Richard Ellmann, who hinted strongly that it was
G.B.S. who described the play in the balloting as "Filth and Disease." In
actuality it was a little-known committee member, H. A. Hertz, who wrote
on the ballot "Reminiscent of Strindberg at his worst. Putrid!" Shaw, not on
the committee at the time, nevertheless went out of his way to praise the
work, commenting on the ballot sheet (a privilege of any Stage Society
member, but exercised by few), "Just the thing for the S.S. G.B.S." In his
ninety-fourth year he would recall to the B.B.C., "I at once spotted a
considerable youthful talent; but as it contained a few words that were then
tabooed [by official censorship] as unmentionable, and still are, . . . I

Fig. 9. James Joyce in 1921; drawing by Wyndham Lewis. Courtesy
National Portrait Gallery.

*The allegation was finally dropped in the 1982 revision of the biography.

reported that the unmentionable passages must be blue pencilled. I never said that the whole play was obscene."[7]

Eventually Joyce went along with the minor deletions, for in 1926 the Stage Society relented and produced the play at the Regent Theatre in London. As part of his Stage Society annual subscription Shaw attended the 15 February performance, and at the public debate on the production two days later he allegedly spoke favorably about the play, although the press had savaged it.[8]

While Shaw would be in the paying audience for *Exiles*, he drew the line at buying a three-guinea subscription edition of *Ulysses*. Joyce had guessed differently, writing Sylvia Beach that he thought Shaw would subscribe anonymously, but the old curmudgeon was tight-fisted about paying for what he did not want. Shaw had already read extracts in the *Little Review* and explained that to Miss Beach:

> I have read several fragments of *Ulysses* in its serial form. It is a revolting record of a disgusting phase of civilisation; but it is a truthful one. . . . To you, possibly, it may appear as art: . . . to me it is all hideously real: I have walked those streets and known those shops and have heard and taken part in those conversations. I escaped from them to England at the age of twenty; and forty years later have learnt from the books of Mr. Joyce that Dublin is still what it was. . . . It is, however, some consolation to find that at last somebody has felt deeply enough about it to face the horror of writing it all down and using his literary genius to force people to face it. In Ireland they try to make a cat cleanly by rubbing its nose in its own filth. Mr. Joyce has tried the same treatment on the human subject. I hope it may prove successful.
>
> I am aware that there are other qualities and other passages in *Ulysses*: but they do not call for any special comment from me.
>
> I must add, as the prospectus implies an invitation to purchase, that I am an elderly Irish gentleman, and that if you imagine that any Irishman, much less an elderly one, would pay 150 francs for a book, you little know my countrymen.[9]

That Shaw had already read portions of *Ulysses* is evident from the preface to his autobiographical first novel *Immaturity* (1879), which he had been preparing for publication in the summer of 1921 as part of his collected edition. Refused by dozens of publishers in the 1880s, *Immaturity* evokes the young self-exile from Ireland, and Shaw in his preface noted that by 1876 he had "had enough of Dublin. James Joyce in his *Ulysses* has described, with a fidelity so ruthless that the book is hardly bearable, the life that Dublin offers its young men, or, if you prefer to put it the other way, that its young men offer to Dublin." But as Shaw's response to Miss Beach early the next year indicated, his reference to a book did not mean that he had even seen a copy. To Harriet Weaver, Joyce would write on 30 September 1924, having seen Shaw's letter, "As you see, he has not bought a copy—or rather pretends he has not. His remarks are seriously meant. He ought to be informed that there is now a special cheap edition 565,423 words $= 8 \times 70,877 \ 7/8 = 8$ novel lengths, slightly shopsoiled, a genuine bargain going for 60 francs $= 60/68 = 30/43 =$ about $3/4 \times 20/- = 15/- \div 8$ about $1/11\frac{1}{4}$ per normal novel suitlength real continental style— you can't beat it for the money. A few days ago he told a reporter he had made £10,000 out of *Saint Joan* or was it out of old saint Mumpledum?"[10]

The "Saint Mumpledum" allusion to the soldier's ditty sung in the play's Epilogue by the rough English soldier, now a saint for one day a year because he had given Joan her crude cross of sticks as she was bound to the stake, suggests again that Joyce had been keeping up with Shaw—as, in *his* fashion, Shaw had been keeping up with Joyce. And Joyce was pleased with Shaw's indirect praise. "As it is in a private letter," he suggested to Robert McAlmon, "no use should be made of it in print, I suppose. Still I think it ought to be made known otherwise. I think I can read clearly (with the one good eye I have) between the lines. I would also take on a small bet . . . that the writer has subscribed anonymously for a copy of *Ulysses* through some bookseller."

Much more outraged than Joyce was his managerial-minded friend Ezra Pound, who wrote letters of cranky rebuke to Shaw, whom elsewhere (in *The Dial*, June 1922) Pound would call "a ninth-rate coward" for being unwilling to face the seamy side of Dublin that Joyce had exposed. The exchange began when Pound took it upon himself to upbraid Shaw for not subscribing. "What aileth thee, Ezra?" Shaw replied on a postcard. "Am I bound to think in everything even as you do?" The cost of the one book, he objected, was "about fifty times what Mr Joyce could buy my entire works for. . . ." Pound responded even more insistently, and a week later came another card from Shaw with "Come: you are getting on." Joyce, he added, had "to please *me* and not you before he can succeed [in selling G.B.S.], because I am through with my wild oats, whilst you are still larking with life. I take care of the pence because the pounds will not take care of themselves."

A third letter in three weeks followed, and Shaw mailed Pound a further rejoinder, this time a picture postcard reproducing José de Ribera's painting *The Dead Christ*, with the mourning Mary standing over the corpse. Alongside the picture Shaw wrote, "Miss Shakespear consoling James Joyce, who has fainted on hearing of the refusal of his countryman to subscribe for Ulysses. Isnt it like him?" On the correspondence side, Shaw added, "Desto besser,* my boy; and bully for that heroic American lady who has done the trick, and whom you have tried to palm off on me as that soulless thing, a publisher." Following the paean to Sylvia Beach came a final line: "Five pounds be blowed! You can sell this postcard for ten."

Pound kept the card, and tried again. This time—on another postcard—Shaw put a stop to the farce, although observing seriously that private press publication was counterproductive for a writer like Joyce with "trade" potential: "I shall not do anything that may encourage him to be a coterie author: Irish talent, when it is serious, belongs to the big world and must behave itself accordingly." But enough was enough: "We must now chuck it, as it is getting too like Wilde & Whistler in the old days when no number of The World . . . was complete without some labored exchange between My Dear Jimmy and My Dear Oscar."[11]

To his biographer Archibald Henderson, Shaw added, a few years later, that although he would not pay more than the traditional seven shillings and sixpence for a novel, he was attracted to what he had read of *Ulysses* in magazine extracts without knowing that "they all belonged to the history of a single day in Dublin." He confessed to seeing a "classic quality" in Joyce's prose and to being too prudish to write some of the words Joyce used, but Shaw saw no reason why there should be any limit in literature to "black-guardly language." It depended only, he thought, "on what people will stand. If Dickens or Thackeray had been told that a respectable author like myself would use the expletive 'bloody' in a play . . . he could not have believed it. Yet I am . . . old-fashioned and squeamish. . . ." The important fact to Shaw about the texture of *Ulysses* was that its exposure of the underside of Dublin life had moral value: "You cannot carry out moral sanitation, any more than physical sanitation, without indecent exposures."[12]

---

*so much the better . . .

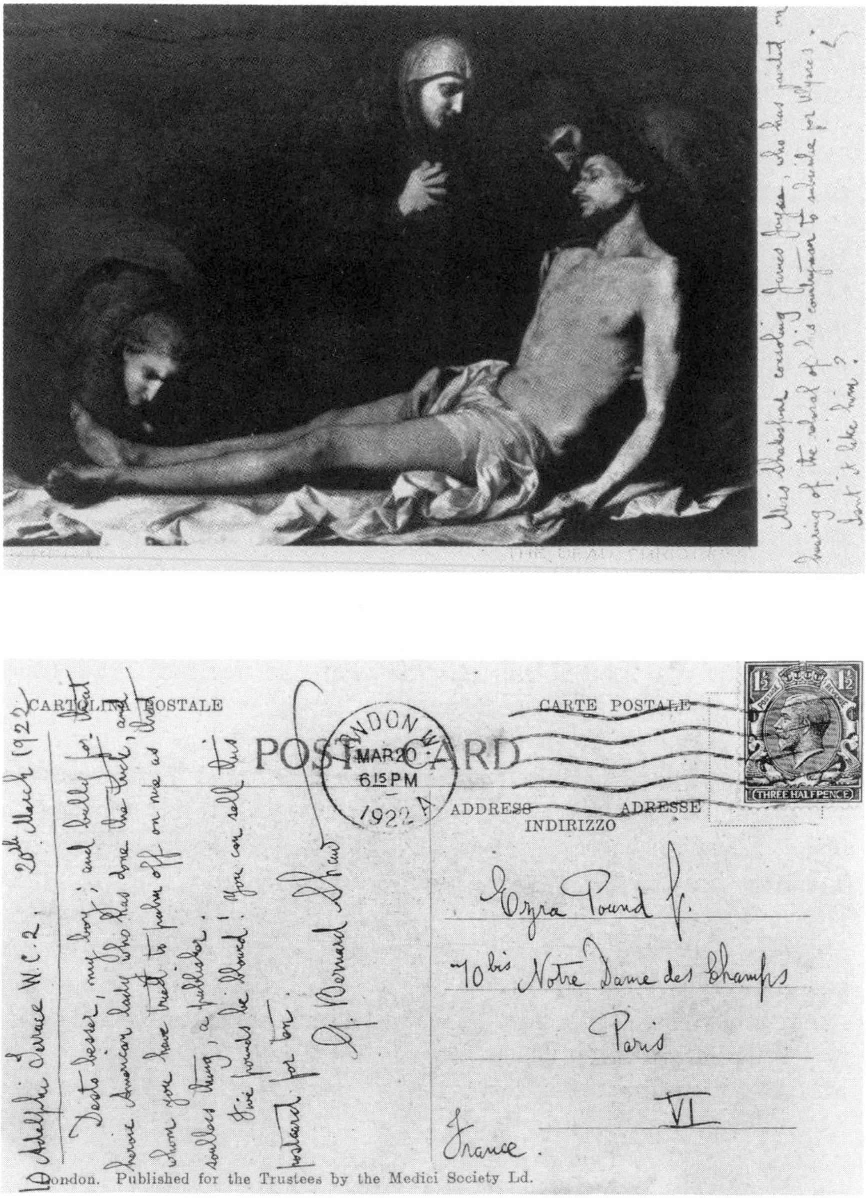

Fig. 10. Shaw's March 1922 postcard to Ezra Pound on subscribing for a copy of Joyce's *Ulysses*. Shaw's wicked humor in using the reproduction of Ribera's painting *The Dead Christ* was prompted by the plethora of art postcards available to him in Italy. Courtesy Manuscripts Department, Lilly Library, Indiana University.

A few lines later came a comment that appears to recall the first, "Telemachus," episode of the novel. "If a man holds up a mirror to your nature and shows you that it needs washing—not whitewashing—it is no use breaking the mirror. Go for soap and water." Early in *Ulysses*, in the Martello tower, Stephen Daedalus watches Buck Mulligan lather his face and shave while holding a cracked mirror that he confesses he had "pinched . . . out of the skivvy's room." Stephen observes, possibly parodying Oscar Wilde, "It is a symbol of Irish art. The cracked lookingglass of a servant." In *Intentions*, a dialogue that G.B.S. knew, Wilde had quipped, "I can quite understand your objection to art being treated as a mirror. You think it would reduce genius to the position of a cracked looking-glass." Shaw's comment, deliberate or inadvertent, may be an echoing of his own reading in the early pages of *Ulysses*. (Yet almost certainly not as far as the "Circe" episode, where Lynch, pointing to Bella and her whores, observes, "The mirror up to nature.")

Shaw would have had to read nearly two hundred pages into *Ulysses* to discover that Stephen Daedalus's teacher recommends as a commentator on Shakespeare a "George Bernard Shaw," who among other things "draws for us an unhappy relation with the dark lady of the sonnets," but for the lower-case, the last six words of a Shavian play that had followed *Blanco Posnet*. And he would have had to read further hundreds of pages into it to find that a phrase that he had first applied to Ireland in the preface to *John Bull's Other Island* had turned up in the "Eumaeus" chapter as "Ireland, her Achilles heel." Shaw had written, during a decade of invasion jitters that would spawn a dozen prophecy-novels, "The Irish coast is for the English invasion scaremonger the heel of Achilles."

Aside from general Dublin atmosphere and geography, at least two other aspects of Joyce's novel should have especially intrigued Shaw. When he was a boy living in the Dublin shoreline suburb of Dalkey he was sent to a private school in Lawson's Terrace, Sandycove, only a couple of hundred yards from the squat round Martello tower in which *Ulysses* opens. "Sonny" Shaw was only nine at the time, but Shaw in his sixties could not have missed recognizing the memorable round tower. If he read a little farther into the novel, he would have discovered that Molly Bloom, whose girlhood and nubile adolescence as the daughter of Major Brian Cooper Tweedy (and of a Spanish Jewess) was spent on the British rock of Gibraltar, could have been suggested by a character in one of his own plays. The languid Mrs. Sally Lunn, in the farce *Overruled*, is reminded by her aspiring lover, the energetic Sibthorpe Juno, of Sally's "southern blood."

"My what?" she asks.

And he, the type of Joyce's Hugh (Blazes) Boylan—also a singer—, recollects that when he had sung "Farewell and adieu to you dear Spanish ladies," she had reminded him that she was "by birth a lady of Spain." Further, Sibthorpe adds, "Your splendid Andalusian beauty speaks for itself."

"Stuff!" she objects. "I was born on Gibraltar. My father was Captain Jenkins. In the artillery."

Undeterred, Sibthorpe Juno goes on, ("*ardently*" in Shaw's stage directions), "It is climate and not race that determines the temperament. The fiery sun of Spain blazed on your cradle; and it rocked to the roar of British cannon."

Mrs. Lunn is used to having men make a fuss over her ("about three times a week ever since she was seventeen"), and the occasions range from having "rather a taste for it" to "a mild lark, hardly worth the trouble . . . [but] valuable once or twice as a spinal tonic. . . ." To the more passionate Molly Bloom, remembering at the close of *Ulysses* "the glorious sunsets and the figtrees in the Alameda gardens yes and all the queer little streets and pink and blue and yellow houses and the rosegardens and the jessamine and geraniums and cactuses and Gibraltar when I was a girl where I was a Flower of the mountain yes when I put the rose in my hair like the Andalusian girl used . . . and how he kissed me under the Moorish wall and I thought well as well him as another" only reinforces her ardor, although not for her husband. Of course there is a possible *Odyssey* relationship for both Molly and Gibraltar in that there is a Penelope side to her character; and Gibraltar—"Calpe's rocky mount" to Joyce—is sometimes considered as a stopping-place for Odysseus, although most opinion has Homer take him no farther west than Tunisia and Sicily. (The Greek name for Gibraltar was *Kalpe*, and there is a suggestion in it of Calypso, who lives on an isle that is a "navel of the sea.") But Mrs. Bloom, we learn in the "Calypso" episode of the novel, is, like Mrs. Lunn, born on Gibraltar, where, with a trace of "blood of the south," she grows up "to peerless beauty."

The parallels between Sally and Molly are striking—birth and girlhood on Spanish/British Gibraltar, army-officer father, the references to Andalusia and to southern blood, the lover who sings. Are these mere coincidences? We know that the book version of Shaw's play was published soon after Joyce began his novel, but also that the play was not among the 600 titles—a number of them Shaw plays—that Joyce *left behind him* in Trieste when, in 1920, he moved to Paris. However, that does not mean that he could not have taken a volume including *Overruled* with him, or have read the play (which had been produced in 1912) in an earlier form. Joyce claimed the composition dates of *Ulysses*—noted on the last page of the novel—as 1914–21. While he lived in then-Austrian Trieste, *Overruled* was published, on 23 March 1913, in the easily accessible *Neue Freie Presse*, the leading Viennese newspaper; and in May 1913 it was published in the *English Review*, which Joyce read, and to which he had vainly offered *Dubliners* the year before. Perhaps there is something of Sally ("Seraphita") Lunn* in Molly Bloom.

Reproducing some of Shaw's words in a 1933 book on Joyce, Louis Golding inexplicably invented the myth that Shaw "threw his copy of *Ulysses* into the fire." (He may have been thinking of Frank Harris's *My Life and Loves*, an inscribed copy of which Mrs. Shaw threw into the fire to prevent contamination of the maids.) In June 1939 the cranky critic Geoffrey Grigson, in an article in the London *Picture Post*, happily retold the tale that Shaw was disgusted by *Ulysses* and burned his copy "in the grate." Exasperated, Shaw protested to the editor that "Somebody has humbugged Mr. Grigson. The story is not true." Rather, he wrote, "Having passed between seven and eight thousand . . . days in Dublin I missed neither the realism of the book nor its poetry. . . . If Mr. Joyce should ever desire a testimonial as the author of a literary masterpiece from me, it shall be given with all possible emphasis and with sincere enthusiasm."[13] What Shaw did not add is that he could not have thrown into his fireplace a book he had never owned nor read.

The first furor over *Ulysses* had hardly faded when *Saint Joan* resulted in a Shavian apotheosis and with it the 1925 Nobel Prize for Literature. He was seventy, and impatient with what he called a lifebelt thrown to a swimmer who has already reached the shore. He even threw congratulatory letters into the wastebasket. All but one. "Allow me to offer my felicitations to you on the honour you have received," read one letter from Paris, "and to express my satisfaction that the award of the Nobel prize for literature has gone once more† to a distinguished fellow townsman." The only letter Shaw preserved was from Joyce.[14]

Still, there were differences that kept the two ex-Dubliners apart. When a

---

*The closest we get to her name in *Finnegans Wake* is "Sally Lums" (249), which may be no clue at all. A more persuasive link may be Joyce's use of *Overruled*'s subtitle (and original title, *Trespassers Will Be Prosecuted*). Its Joycean metamorphosis (503), "*Trickspissers vill be pairse-cluded*," describes what happens in the play.

†Yeats had been honored in 1923.

magazine in the U.S., *Two Worlds Monthly*, began pirating chapters of *Ulysses* late in 1926, mutilating the work and paying Joyce nothing, a protest petition was initiated to put moral pressure on the publisher while legal action ground on slowly. The 167 signers included great names Shaw admired—Albert Einstein, Benedetto Croce, Maurice Maeterlinck, H. G. Wells, D. H. Lawrence. But Shaw, with Joyce's felicitations he had appreciated only three weeks earlier still fresh in his mind, nevertheless would not sign, bluntly querying Sylvia Beach, "Is it in copyright in the United States or not? . . . If, however, the work is in the public domain by simple neglect to secure copyright, I am afraid there is nothing to be done. . . . The protest is all poppycock: nobody that the pirate cares about will blame him for taking advantage of the law. But Mr. Joyce can point out that the law [that declared the book immoral in the U.S.] has produced an absurd situation. Instead of suppressing the book, which is its object, it is inviting every bookseller to rush out an edition of it, and thereby increase the author's reputation enormously."[15] Was Shaw remembering Joyce's unauthorized productions in Zurich in 1918, and reacting accordingly? Almost certainly he had long forgotten the trivial matter and was only trying to inject some needed realism into a situation in which idealists had poured impractical enthusiasm. The fact was that Joyce was more famous than ever. Now, Shaw thought, Joyce should take advantage of that happy fact by publishing something new. Fragments of the new work in progress, *Finnegans Wake*, would indeed appear at intervals, but the book itself would be years more in gestation.

Although Shaw had refused to sign the piracy complaint, a few years later Joyce was again tempted to use Shaw's name, this time with that of H. G. Wells, in protesting the inadvertent use of the Joyce by-line by the *Frankfurter Zeitung* in 1931, over the German translation of a story by the younger and little-known writer Michael Joyce. Other than sowing brief and minor confusion, the mistake did Joyce no harm, but he was eager to seek damages until his lawyers warned him that he could win £25 at best. In any event, Joyce changed his mind before Shaw could refuse, and had determined to press the names of T. S. Eliot and Sean O'Casey into the fray instead, when the newspaper published a retraction that, although it did not satisfy Joyce, made the matter moot. Still, Joyce was not yet through enlisting his Dublin townsman in Joycean affairs. He had taken a flat in the Kensington section of London that year, hoping to spend more time where the English language was spoken and read; however in April 1932, when he went with his wife and daughter to the *Gare du Nord* in Paris to get the boat train to Calais, Lucia screamed that she hated England and would not go. She had long suffered from schizophrenia, but Joyce was convinced that her insanity was curable. After he had their luggage removed from the train and carted to a Paris hotel, he determined that a new approach was necessary. He would have Lucia assisted by Bernard Shaw.

Joyce's strategy—about as insane as anything that Lucia might have thought of—was to suggest inferentially to the one-time music critic and drama critic that Lucia, who had received some dance and voice training, might be worth having her career promoted by G.B.S. Whether Shaw was actually approached is not clear from Joyce's letter of 22 July 1932 to Harriet Weaver about Lucia: "I thought that if she sent three letters . . . to Shaw on the 26th (they have the same birthday) he might like her talent. But I am afraid Shaw has lived too long on the boreal side of La Manche* to appreciate silly things like that. Perhaps he is right too." When Joyce died early in 1941, Lucia was still insane. G.B.S. would have had his hands full.

The only prize within Shaw's gift would be offered to Joyce a few months later (in 1932), when W. B. Yeats worked with Shaw to found an Irish Academy of Letters. "Of course the first name that seemed essential both to Shaw and myself," wrote Yeats to Joyce, "was your own. . . . If you go out of our list it is an empty sack indeed." Nevertheless, Joyce refused. "Please convey my thanks also to Mr. Shaw whom I have never met," he wrote Yeats, explaining that he did not feel he belonged.[16] The most intriguing words in the letter are not the expected ones disavowing any Irish professional associations, but the regret at the continuing distance between himself and Shaw.

They would never meet. But it is possible that their meeting of minds, at least in the case of Joyce, was more productive than imagined. Joyce, according to Sylvia Beach, had been fascinated by Shaw's suggestions of Wilde's gigantism (acromegaly) in his afterword to Frank Harris's biography and had rushed over to look at the "Giant's Grave" in Cornwall. "As early as 1922, I think, Joyce seemed to be interested in giants; he said to me that what particularly struck him in Frank Harris's *Oscar Wilde* was the preface [sic] of Shaw's in which he speaks of the gigantism of Wilde." Is this a link to Joyce's extrapolation of the mythic Irish giant Finn McCool (MacCumhal) in his last fiction, begun in 1923?[17] Whatever the reasons, in the encyclopaedic dream-vision that became *Finnegans Wake*, Joyce would evoke Shaw over and over again in guises still emerging with each reading.

*The north side of the English Channel.

Some are obvious; however Shaw (so he said in his nineties) "never had
time to decipher" the work. His 1924 comment that Joyce, having got the
dirt of Dublin right, had shown that Dubliners needed washing, not
whitewashing, had been widely printed and reprinted. Very likely it did not
escape Joyce himself, for often in the *Wake* we find Shaw, who had once
facetiously published letters to the press under the anagram *Redbarn Wash*,
now anagrammed as *Wash*. (And elsewhere in the *Wake* as *wush*, *Haws*,
whas and other variations of *S-H-A-W*.) The large cast of Shavian characters
in the *Wake* suggests that the bleary-eyed Joyce had scrutinized G.B.S.'s
plays far more than suspected, although Richard Ellmann's extrapolation of
Joyce's library in 1920 includes thirteen early books by Shaw representing
seventeen works.

One page of *Finnegans Wake* alone (211)[18] puns on the Hertfordshire
village in which Shaw lived, Ayot St. Lawrence, and refers to three
characters in *Heartbreak House*: Billy Dunn, Ellie Dunn (no relation) the
ingenue, and Hesione Hushabye. Other characters suggested elsewhere in
the *Wake* include Major Barbara and her father Andrew Undershaft ("Sainte
Andree's Undershift"), John Tanner (and his alter ego, Don Juan), Ann
Whitefield (and such others from *Man and Superman* as Octavius and
Mendoza), the Man of Destiny (the young Napoleon), and Saint Joan.
There is a Magnus *(The Apple Cart)*, a Valentine *(You Never Can Tell)*,
and a Blanco *(Posnet)*. And after the injunction, "Plays be honest!" there is,
after a one-sentence break, another that begins with the suggestion of a
Shavian play, "Candidately . . ." (396). Later in the novel—we have already
heard of his "tanner voice" (182)—is a further hint of *Don Juan in Hell* (the
talkative Juan, one will recall, spends the play arranging for his transfer from
Hell to Heaven) in the line, "After poor Jaun the Boast's last fireless words
of postludium of his soapbox speech ending in'sheaven. . ." (469). Hardly a
play escapes, although, like some titles, the sermonizing Juan's name is
twisted perversely.[19] There is even a "St. Mumpledum," Joyce having
again remembered the ruffian soldier who sings hoarsely of "Old Saint
mumpledum" in the play about Joan of Arc. And not only are the
jabberwocked variations on Shaw's name (where he is identifiably in mind)
numerous, from Barney the Bark to Paddishaw and Wildeshaweshowe: even
Shaw's long-time (and well-known) secretary, Blanche Patch, turns up (83).

Old G.B.S. himself, "the doblinganger . . . with a sandy whiskers" (490),
emerges once more, in his wrinkles and vegetarianism and music-critic past,
in "the wrinkles of a snailcharmer and the slits and sniffers of a fellow that
fell foul of the county de Loona and the meattrap of the first vegetarian"

(465). Joyce had read Shaw's 1935 preface to *London Music*, collecting his 1888–89 columns from *The Star*. "As I had no name worth signing," Shaw wrote, "and G.B.S. meant nothing to the public, I had to invent a fantastic personality with something like a foreign title. I thought of Count di Luna (a character in Verdi's *Trovatore*), but finally changed it for Corno di Bassetto, as it sounded like a foreign title, and nobody knew what a corno di bassetto [a basset horn] was."[20]

It has also been suggested that the Burrus-Caseous episode (161–68) is a burlesque Shavian preface with *Caesar and Cleopatra* in mind as well as Shakespeare's *Julius Caesar*. Perhaps the Shavian dimension is even foreshadowed several dense pages earlier (159), as the Burrus-Caseous element is being introduced, for Joyce begins, "No applause, please! Bast!" This is exactly where Shaw's preface to *Caesar and Cleopatra* ends, with the god Ra's soliloquy closing, "Farewell; and do not presume to applaud me." Although Joyce's explanation that follows has the usual multiple meanings, again one might be Shavian, including a comparison of their rhetorical strategies. "Horosehoew!" exclaims Joyce's narrator, weaving into his expletive an Egyptian god and G.B.S.'s surname. "I could love that man like my own ambo"—an *ambo*, in early Christian churches, was a reading desk from which the sermon was given—"for being so bailcycliaver though he's a nawful curillass and I must slav to methodiousness." (The juxtaposition of *slav* and *Horosehoew* suggests still another, non-Shavian dimension, since the Russian *khorosho*—meaning *good* or *well*—also works, possibly the deliberate corruption echoed by the Joyce-minded Anthony Burgess in his *Clockwork Orange* expletive *horrorshow*. *Finnegans Wake*, after all, is constructed upon a strategy of opposing voices that we can only partially reconstitute. Words, in Hugh Kenner's description, "are pulling every way at once, in search of enabling contexts," subverting our familiar thought processes registered in "dictionary words [laid out] in perspicuously consecutive sentences."[21] A Shavian context does not eliminate other overlapping contexts, nor do these rule out, in Joyce's carefully orchestrated Babel, his seemingly obsessive Shavian reverberations.

Perhaps the Schoolroom scene (300–303) is Joyce's final ambivalent revenge on Shaw since the *Wake*'s anatomical equating of the *Force Centres of the Fire Serpentine* with seven major Irish writers includes, opposite Pshaw, the Italian word *fontanella*. In slang usage the term can refer to the small village fountains where water spurts from the penis of a naked figure. Whether G.B.S. knew any of this, including that scatological Joyccan joke, is doubtful: he had kept a respectful distance from *Ulysses*, and almost certainly never read more than a few lines of the *Wake*. "I tried Finnegans Wake," Shaw wrote an inquirer in 1949, "but had to give up after a page or two because I had not time to interpret it. I might have persevered when I was 20; but at 93 time is precious and the days pass like flights of arrows."[22] That he tried it at all would have pleased Joyce's shade.

Notes

1. 7 December 1906; Joyce's letters are quoted from *Letters of James Joyce*, ed. Richard Ellmann (New York: Viking, 1966), vols. 2 & 3, unless otherwise specified.

2. "Ibsen's New Drama," *Fortnightly Review* 67 (1 April 1900), 575–90.

3. "Shaw's Battle with the Censor," *Il Piccolo della Sera* (5 September 1909), translated by Ellsworth Mason in the *Shaw Bulletin* 1:7 (January 1955): 7–9.

4. Quoted by William White in "Irish Antitheses: Shaw and Joyce," *Shavian* 2:3 (February 1961): 26.

5. The translation by Lindley W. Hubbell was sent to Shaw by Herbert Cahoon. Shaw's only comment, dated 21 July 1949, ignored the review. It is in the Yale University Library.

6. Quoted by White, p. 28.

7. Shaw to the B.B.C., 22 January 1950. Ellmann's misinformation is on p. 429 of the 1959 edition of the biography *James Joyce* (New York: Oxford University Press, 1959); William White corrects this in "G.B.S. on Joyce's *Exiles*," *TLS* (4 December 1959), quoting the Stage Society ballot then in the Feinberg Collection and now in the Morris Library, Southern Illinois University, Carbondale.

8. Whether Shaw actually spoke is now unclear; John MacNicholas in "James Joyce's *Exiles* and the Incorporated Stage Society," *ICarbS* 4 (Spring–Summer 1978): 14–16, notes that corroboration is lacking. Unable to verify it, Ellmann dropped the suggestion from the 1982 edition of his biography.

9. Joyce, sending a copy to Robert McAlmon on 10 October 1921, refers to Shaw's letter as dated 11 June 1921. The letter was first reproduced in Patricia Hutchins, *James Joyce's Dublin* (London: Grey Walls Press, 1950). A partial text had been published by David Dempsey in the *New York Times Book Review* earlier in the year (23 July 1950).

10. *Selected Letters of James Joyce*, ed. Richard Ellmann (New York: Viking, 1975), p. 302.

11. Sylvia Beach in *Shakespeare and Company* (New York: Harcourt, Brace, 1954), pp. 53–54, conflates the correspondence into a single postcard, adds several tearful Marys to the picture, and improves Shaw's prose. For the full texts of the four cards, see *Bernard Shaw, Collected Letters 1911–1925*, ed. Dan H. Laurence (New York: Viking, 1985), pp. 763–67. The dates, respectively, are 8 March, 16 March, 20 March, and 24 March 1922.

12. Henderson, *Table-Talk of G.B.S.* (New York: Harper & Brothers, 1925), reproduced in *Bernard Shaw's Nondramatic Literary Criticism*, ed. Stanley Weintraub (Lincoln: University of Nebraska Press, 1972), pp. 214–15.

13. *Picture Post* (3 June 1939), quoted in *Letters of James Joyce*, 3:444–45n. William Hull, in "Shaw on the Joyce He Scarcely Read," *Shaw Bulletin* 1:6 (September 1954): 16–20 notes, too, that Golding invented such additional Shavian dialogue as "It only proves that Dublin men and boys are as incorrigibly filthy-minded now as they were in my youth." It is still quoted erroneously as Shaw's.

14. 26 November 1926, Ms. British Library; reproduced in *Letters*, vol. 2.

15. 18 December 1926; quoted in *Letters*, vol. 2.

16. 5 October 1932; quoted in Ellmann, *James Joyce*, p. 573.

17. The suggestion is quoted by White, p. 32. Shaw's "preface" is actually a letter to Harris printed as afterword to his *Oscar Wilde*.

18. Page references in parentheses are to the standard text (New York: Viking, 1939).

19. Most Shavian allusions escape Adeline Glasheen's three encyclopaedic *Census* volumes on *Finnegans Wake* and are my own inferences.

20. I owe this insight to B.S.M. Horne of the University of Nagoya from a paper read at the July 1990 IASAIL conference in Kyoto.

21. Hugh Kenner, *A Colder Eye: The Modern Irish Writers* (New York: Knopf, 1983), pp. 224, 227.

22. The letter, dated 13 November 1949 and to an unnamed correspondent, is in the Lockwood Memorial Library, State University of New York at Buffalo, and is quoted by White, p. 54.

The Playwright and the Pirate

Bernard Shaw and Frank Harris

In his dozens of bantering yet benevolent letters to Frank Harris over more than thirty years, Shaw regularly inserted references to Harris as "buccaneer" and "ruffian," and the old pirate objected. But, reduced to living off nostalgia for the good years past and begging letters that deflated the pride in the old buccaneering sails, Harris protested too much. The mostly well-earned reputation that had helped to do him in was, in his last decades, his only negotiable currency.

Harris often reminded Shaw that both had emerged on the London intellectual scene almost at the same time, in the early 1880s, as journalists and reformers, and had achieved fame on the same journal, Harris as editor-proprietor of the *Saturday Review* and "G.B.S." (as he signed his columns) as its highly visible—and quotable—theater critic. Yet Harris, for once, had been deliberately modest, perhaps a gesture aimed at drawing Shaw's support for one of the pirate's dubious propositions at a time when Shaw was world-famous and Harris was down and out.

In truth Shaw had sought for years after his emigration from Ireland (at twenty, in 1876) to find a measure of literary success but did not see his first play produced, and that unsuccessfully, until he was thirty-six. He was nearly forty when he joined Harris's paper. Harris, on the other hand, was a boy immigrant from Ireland who became an American citizen and then returned to the Old World to make his fortune. By 1885, when he and Shaw were both twenty-nine, Harris was the upstart young editor of the London *Evening News*. Shaw, who had been an unemployed writer of unsalable novels, in 1885 had finally acquired the opportunity to write anonymous reviews of third-rate books for the *Pall Mall Gazette* and equally poorly paid notices for the *Dramatic Review*. Two years later Shaw was still writing reviews of third-rate books and was also tramping the galleries for unsigned art columns in the *World*. Meanwhile Harris, already a pompous, commanding figure in London, had married a widow of forty-eight with wealth and social position, was editor of the *Fortnightly Review*, and contemplated standing for Parliament.

Later, when Shaw's play royalties were pouring in, and Harris, grasping in his old age for something to publish, sent his old friend a questionnaire. Shaw answered (18 September 1930), "You want to know what it feels like to be a rich man. Well, you should know; for if you are not a millionaire at this moment, you have been one for an afternoon, or for a week, or if rumor be true, for perhaps a year when you married a lady in Park Lane and spent all your money consorting with Randolph Churchill. . . ."[1] Shaw was applying salt to an old wound, for in almost every way it had been downhill for Harris after that, and a precipitous ascent for Shaw as critic, playwright, and social philosopher; yet at one point their careers had converged. In the mid-1890s Harris had taken over the moribund *Saturday Review*, hired clever but largely unknown writers such as H. G. Wells, Arnold Bennett, Robert Cunninghame Graham, John Runciman, and D. S. MacColl to write for him, and turned out a weekly that was the most lively in London. For his drama critic Harris wooed away from the *World* a music critic who had begun in yet another paper under the pseudonym of "Corno di Bassetto." Then writing as "G.B.S.," Shaw had achieved his aim of making even Philistine stockbrokers who cared nothing about the arts read his column.

Harris had gone after Shaw even earlier. When editor of the *Fortnightly*, he had wanted some of Shaw's energetic prose in his own paper and had proposed an article in a letter now lost. In a letter dated 7 November 1891 to his critic friend William Archer, Shaw began, "I have just had a letter from Frank Harris asking me to put my oar into the discussion on criticism. I have refused on the ground that I have said all that need be said in the appendix to the Quintessence [of Ibsenism]." Then he went on at gossipy length on the very subject about which Harris had asked him, addressed two envelopes, and put his "no" to Harris in Archer's envelope and mailed his Archer letter instead to Harris.[2]

The puzzled Harris returned it four days later with the comment, "I will confess to a sense of mystification upon reading the enclosed letter of yours, which none the less has afforded me much amusement. I tried to look on it

as the eccentricity of a clever writer, but failed to comprehend its drift. . . .
I felt as Alice may have felt in Wonderland."

"Horror on horror's head!" Shaw wrote to Archer when he discovered the
blunder; at the bottom of the letter that Harris had returned, he added the
postscript, "Has anything more unspeakably awful ever happened than my
sending this to Harris & his letter to you?"[3] Still, Harris wanted Shaw in the
Fortnightly and persisted in suggesting ideas until one appealed.

What won Shaw was an invitation to contribute to a series, "What Mr.
Gladstone Ought to Do." In the *Fortnightly* for February 1893 Shaw had
little advice for the Prime Minister: "What on earth can Mr. Gladstone do
with such opinions as his, except precipitate the inevitable smash?"

"The Religion of the Pianoforte," perhaps Shaw's finest musical essay,
was written for Harris for the February 1894 issue, and another political
piece followed later in the year. The first commission in 1893 even resulted
in his first meeting with Harris, at the offices of the *Fortnightly*. He would
not see Harris again until December 1894, by which time the editor had
moved to the proprietorship of the *Saturday Review*, where the wooing of
G.B.S. would begin in earnest.

The inventive Harris later reminisced that he had invited Shaw by letter
to write a weekly theater article. Shaw replied in "a letter somewhat after
this fashion," Harris later wrote, in pure Harrisian, "How the Dickens you
knew that my thoughts had been turning to the theatre of late and that I'd
willingly occupy myself with it exclusively for some time to come, I can't
imagine. But you've hit the clout, as the Elizabethans used to say, and, if
you can afford to pay me regularly, I'm your man so long as the job suits me
and I suit the job. What can you afford to give?" According to Harris, his
answer was equally prompt and to the point: "I can afford to give you so
much a week, more, I believe, than you are now getting.* If that appeals to
you, start in at once; bring me your first article by next Wednesday and we'll
have a final pow-wow."[4]

In reality the business seems to have been settled at the meeting on 4
December, after which Shaw gave appropriate notice to the *World* that his
musical column would cease. "I return to town tomorrow afternoon," Shaw
wrote Archer from Folkestone on 28 December, "to take up the duties,
fairly forced on me by Harris, of dramatic critic to the Saturday Review. . . .
It is questionable whether it is quite decent for a dramatic author to be also

---

*In actuality, £6 a week, nearly a pound more than he had been paid as music critic for the *World*,
and an opportunity, besides, to influence London theater in other ways than as a playwright.

a dramatic critic; but my extreme reluctance to make myself dependent for my bread and butter on the acceptance of my plays by managers tempts me to hold to the position that my real profession is that by which I can earn my bread in security. Anyhow, I am prepared to do anything which will enable me to keep my plays for twenty years with perfect tranquillity if it takes that time to educate the public into wanting them."[5]

Harris, then, was the right person at the right time, for after six years as music critic Shaw was eager for a change and happy to make more money in the process. The only part of the operation Shaw disliked was the Monday lunch that Harris held for the staff and contributors at the Café Royal. He struggled impatiently through several months of them with the sense that they wasted his time and degenerated quickly into "brag and bawdry." Then, early in May 1895, in the midst of the Wilde trials (Oscar had come only once to the lunches, with young Lord Alfred Douglas in tow), Shaw reviewed a mediocre play by R. C. Carton, *The Home Secretary*. In the review were passages scoffing at the attempts to make a bogey of anarchism. Harris—thinking of his market—cut the offending lines, leaving only Shaw's remark that the "stuff" about "abysses of revolution opening at the feet of society" was a "mischievous kind of absurdity." It kept Shaw's point intact but gave him the excuse that the meetings provided—at least in his case—no meeting of minds. He never went again.

Long interested in the stage—Harris would write for it, largely unsuccessfully—he would try out his ideas on impresarios who craved coverage in the *Saturday*, usually the conservative ones since Harris was curiously old-fashioned about everything but journalism. (Even in sex he was a Victorian—but of the Henry Ashbee persuasion.) At 91 Shaw recalled to drama critic J. C. Trewin (ca. 9 June 1947) a West End example from the 1890s, "X" apparently standing for Shaw:

X and F.H. meet at the stage door of Wyndham's Theatre.

X. What on earth are you doing here, of all places?

F.H. I am going to read a play to Wyndham.

X. Ah, well, he is half a century out of date; but he is a really great comedian; and you may pick up a hint or two from him.

F.H. The pump will give water if you PEE in it.[6]

Outrageousness appealed to Harris. Shaw (in the same reminiscence to Trewin) remembered Harris's description of Lady Colin Campbell, a statuesque beauty painted by Sargent and Whistler, and Shaw's designated successor as art critic on *The World* in 1889.

x. By the way, do you know Lady C.C.
F.H. DO I know that fat arsed bitch!!!

She did in fact lace her corsets so tightly, said Shaw, that she was "dorsally on the Hottentot side." But Harris's epithet, Shaw thought, resulted from her having "no doubt snubbed F.H."

"No typing or printing," he added, "can convey the effect of F.H.'s resonant voice, audible to everyone within a range of hundreds of yards indoors or out, and of his perfect elocution. No man could express scorn as he could in the language of a buccaneer but with the bearing of a prophet."

Although the Café Royal lunches themselves soon faded as a Harris institution, the weekly he had rejuvenated remained animated, and the years through 1898 were the apex of his reputation as editor. He had an eye for writing talent and an ear for lively controversy. A predilection for libel suits and for bad investments, however, would force Harris to look for ready cash, and his only asset was the *Saturday*.

At just the point Harris was preparing to sell, Shaw would leave, but not as a deserter. As drama critic for the *Saturday* he had become the most feared and most respected, as well as the most entertaining, columnist in London, but a foot infection and subsequent surgery would keep him from the theaters. It was his opportunity to resign and to turn more of his energies to playwriting, but he could hardly have done more as a critic. As he explained, not entirely facetiously, in a valedictory column (21 May 1898) when he turned over his assignment to Max Beerbohm,

> For ten years past, with an unprecedented pertinacity and obstination, I have been dinning into the public head that I am an extraordinarily witty, brilliant, and clever man. That is now part of the public opinion of England; and no power in heaven or on earth will ever change it. I may dodder and dote; I may potboil and platitudinize; I may become the butt and chopping-block of all the bright, original spirits of the rising generation; but my reputation shall not suffer: it is built up fast and solid like Shakespear's, on an impregnable basis of dogmatic reiteration.

Shaw had taken his leave of Harris just in time. By 1900 Harris was clutching at any opportunity to retrieve his fortunes. Once he had lost the

Saturday, he would edit a series of journalistic disasters, beginning with the *Candid Friend*, each a greater money loser than its predecessor. It was rumored that Harris recouped his losses and sustained his high living by quietly blackmailing other high-living Londoners with the threat of exposure in his seldom-successful magazines, which became increasingly ridden with scandal. One libel suit that resulted when, as proprietor of *Modern Society*, his last English venture, he published something he should only have threatened to publish, even put him in jail. He had lost his wife, who was jealous of his affairs with younger women even before they happened—and they did happen, again and again. He was publishing his own fiction, some of it, such as *Montes the Matador and Other Stories*, not bad for its time, but few critics noticed, and few readers bought any copies. A career as a playwright would end after one significant play—significant primarily because Harris had purchased the scenario from Oscar Wilde at a time when Wilde would have sold anything for a few pounds; and indeed Oscar sold *Mr and Mrs Daventry* to several would-be dramatists, each transaction conferring exclusivity to the purchaser.

Shaw, meanwhile (having married an Irish millionairess in 1898), was arriving as the leading playwright in the language and one of his era's major public personalities. Harris was hurtling headlong in the other direction. Never quite respectable, he had been tolerated—even courted—as an amiable vulgarian when he was a rising star. His booming voice and four-letter language, his inability to look like anything other than an Albanian highwayman even when dressed in tails, and his gluttinous gormandizing and insatiable womanizing quickly made him a pariah in the circles where his income had been found. As his opportunities as editor and writer dwindled during the Edwardian years, he took on a paranoid air.

The *Candid Friend* had appeared on 1 May 1901, with society photographs, gossip, political and theatrical articles—and advertising. Shaw contributed an article, "Who I Am, and What I Think," to an early issue. Even practical advice to ladies on coiffures and costume, competitions, and prizes failed to pick up circulation, and Harris then added exposé articles. After Countess Cowley sued for libel when Harris claimed in print that she had demonstrated "contemptible snobbery" by retaining her title after her divorce and remarriage, the *Candid Friend* went under, although the court awarded her only £100. The last issue was 9 August 1902.

Harris, as Shaw had suggested, turned to playwriting. *Shakespeare and His Wife* (later *Shakespeare and His Love*) produced an option from Beerbohm Tree for £500 but was not produced and was published only in 1910.

Black China would have the hero a thief, a role Tree refused to play. It was neither published nor produced. Eventually there would be *The Bucket Shop*, given a Stage Society production at the Aldwych in 1914, and *Joan La Romée*, privately printed in Nice in 1926, but Harris's career as playwright was, after *Mr and Mrs Daventry*, as futile as Shaw's was successful.

Turning again to magazines, Harris planned an *Automobile Review* that never published an issue. What resulted, however, was *Motorist and Traveller*, which he began editing in 1905 with backing from the Dunlop Tyre Company. The blend of gossip and travelogue, however, failed to hold together. When the venture ended in 1906, Harris's £500 annual salary ended with it. Quickly he turned to other friends and made £400 editing and peddling, to Macmillan, Winston Churchill's biography of his father.

With promises of borrowed money Harris then attempted to get back into magazine or newspaper publishing through the purchase of an existing organ. Among others, the proprietors of *The Times* declined the offers, but Harris did land the struggling *Vanity Fair*, producing his first issue early in 1907. To keep it from toppling into bankruptcy he even regally revisited the United States in search of funds and of copy. Only the latter materialized, and he published his accounts of the Far West in his own journal, later turning them into his purported memoirs of cowboy days, *On the Trail*. Chicago also produced the material for his novel about the 1886 Haymarket Riot, *The Bomb*. Meanwhile Harris cultivated lawsuits—on behalf of his shaky investments and alleged libels, piracies, and persecutions. A number of them added to his notoriety as blackmailer; some cost him money he did not have. *The Bomb*, which he wrote in two months of furious activity, was designed—but failed—to recoup his fortunes.

It was English hypocrisy and Philistinism that was bringing him down, he insisted, not the inability of Frank Harris to rein in his gift for self-destruction. And no help came from the pretty young Nellie O'Hara, who called herself Mrs. Harris all her life and had expensive tastes that kept Harris in debt. Only when the real (and long estranged) Mrs. Harris finally died at a great age in 1927 could Frank make an honest woman of Nellie, but Shaw through the years politely referred to her as if she and Harris were living together with full benefit of clergy; and termagant as she could be, she nevertheless tolerated Harris's indulgence of his sexual itch among servants, subeditors, and assorted females who wandered into his wide orbit. ("Sex," Harris assured his young assistant on *Modern Society*, the future novelist and playwright Enid Bagnold, "is the gateway to life," and she duly went through the gateway.)

Before Harris became a literary confidence man and let his journalistic hand falter, he possessed the confidence and aplomb of the successful late-Victorian man of letters. Yet there was a vulgarity about him that Shaw chose not to see. Harris had, Shaw wrote in his preface to *The Dark Lady of the Sonnets* in 1910, a "range of sympathy and understanding that extends from the ribaldry of a buccaneer to the shyest tenderness of the most sensitive poetry" and could be all things to all men. "To the Archbishop he is an atheist, to the atheist a Catholic mystic, to the Bismarckian Imperialist an Anacharsis Klootz,* to Anacharsis Klootz a [George] Washington, to Mrs Proudie a Don Juan, to Aspasia a John Knox: in short to everyone his complement rather than his counterpart, his antagonist rather than his fellow creature. Always provided, however, that the persons thus affronted are respectable persons."[7]

The lines explain much about the Shaw-Harris relationship. Shaw was cool, scrupulous, precise, generous, and humane. Beneath the post of self-advertising egoist he was a shy man; beneath the clown's motley he masked a philosophic mood; beneath the Bunyanesque preacher he was a sentimental Irish romantic. While Shaw's sexual temperature was low, the Irish-born Harris, who fancied himself a sentimental romantic, possessed a compulsion for lechery that, when he became impotent in later years, became transmuted into erotic "autobiography" that was more fantasy than fact.

Harris's finer feelings often did him credit, yet the real Harris he could never recognize in himself was more often unscrupulous and ungenerous. While Shaw was quick to own up to the "pantomime ostrich" he played, beneath the pose of Good Samaritan and altruist was a self-indulgent Frank Harris who saw himself only as a model human being. When he claimed that he had offered to help Oscar Wilde in his extremity, he really thought he had, although he had grossly exaggerated his assistance *ex post facto*. When in 1898 he had offered to assist Harold Frederic's mistress at her trial for manslaughter (she had treated Frederic's fatal stroke with Christian Science) and pay half the court costs, he actually did sit with her at the trial, and he even wrote a *Saturday Review* editorial defending her. That he stayed away at the end and failed to remember his offer to pay her legal bills never occurred to him as a flaw in his character. So it went through his life. "Frank Harris," Wilde concluded in his prison letter, "has no feelings. It is

*Jean Baptiste Klootz (or Clootz), who called himself Anacharsis, after the sixth-century B.C. Athenian friend of Solon, was a German revolutionary guillotined in Paris in 1794.

the secret of his success. Just as the fact that he thinks other people have none either is the secret of the failure that lies in wait for him somewhere on the way of Life."[8]

Major Barbara's father in Shaw's play was always embarrassing his wife by doing the right thing for the wrong reasons, as Shaw might have done, while Harris was doing the wrong thing for the wrong reasons. Yet both might have claimed that they were somehow right and that each was following his own conscience. Perhaps Harris was an attractive personality to Shaw exactly because he was Shaw's complement rather than his counterpart, because there were qualities in him, exaggerated to be sure, that Shaw saw the lack of in himself. To Shaw, Harris was not "vulgar, mean, purblind, spiteful," which he was to other men—and women. And to Shaw, Harris lacked humor "because scorn overcomes the humor in him." Later, he would see a pathetic humor in Harris, but he contented himself in the *Dark Lady* preface with the prophetic line about his old friend: "Nobody ever dreamt of reproaching Milton's Lucifer for not seeing the comic side of his fall . . ." (*CP* 4: 277).

In Harris's dealings with others in person and in print Shaw often thought he saw a "capacity for pity," but it would become an obsessive self-pity when each attempt to recoup his fortunes would end in misfortune. Harris had immense capacities for bouncing back after defeat, but each resurrection required some help from his friends, and soon there were few who could stand the strain of such a friendship. The longest-standing friendship remained Shaw's, but it required lending no money and seeing Harris in person as little as possible while keeping Harris at arm's length via correspondence. Their exchanges of letters kept the relationship going, and at the level Shaw was willing to tolerate—not only for old times' sake. Harris was a walking melodrama, and Shaw enjoyed the roles he had created for the two of them, although Harris would regularly try to break out of his because he did not know that he was playing Frank Harris. Had he known, his pride would not have permitted it. When Harris once objected to a jocularly accurate Shavian description of him, Shaw rose to the bait:

> You must not take my comments on your personal characteristics as sneers and disparagements. If you do you will find me an impossible man to have any relations with. I tell you you are a ruffian exactly as an oculist might tell you that you are astigmatic. I will tell you now more precisely what I mean—if I have done so already you have brought the reputation on yourself.

Somebody in London society who likes interesting people meets you and invites you to dinner. He asks you to take in a bishop's wife. You entertain her with deep-voiced outpourings of your scorn for the hypocrisy and snobbery of the Church, finishing up with a touch of poetry about Mary Magdalene and her relations with Jesus. When the poor lady escapes to the drawing-room and you find yourself between the bishop and Edmund Gosse, you turn the conversation on to the [pornographic] genius of [Felicien] Rops, and probably produce a specimen of his work, broadening your language at the same time into that of the forecastle of a pirate sloop.

And if you observe the least sign of restiveness or discomfort on the part of the twain, you redouble your energy of expression and barb it with open and angry scorn. When they escape upstairs in their turn, they condole with one another. Gosse says, "My God, what a man!" The Bishop says, "Oh, impossible; quite impossible!"

Now though this particular picture is a fancy one, it is not founded on any lies that people have told me. I have seen and heard you do such things; I have been condoled with, and have had to admit that you are a monster, and that clever as you are, it is impossible to ask anyone to meet you unless they are prepared to stand anything that the utter-most freemasonry of the very freest thought and expression in the boldest circles can venture on. . . .

"You can't write to me or about me without calling me names," Harris complained with unfeigned concern. "I have never felt this inclination towards anyone and so cannot understand it in you. . . . What you call my 'ruffianism' is revolt against convention which you incarnated almost as strongly in London as I did. You . . . seem even more unconscious of it in yourself than I am." The "sex business" that he confessed he had trouble getting printers to print was as essential to his art as he knew it was to Shaw's, but somehow Shaw managed to tuck it safely between the lines. Harris did not have that alternative, he told Shaw, for "you cannot know a man without knowing his faith and practice in this respect; and I wanted to state them about the men I knew. . . . You, on the other hand, seem to have no difficulty in this matter." Harris could never understand, Shaw explained to J. C. Trewin, "why publishers would not commission him to write a life of Christ, whom he regarded as the nearest thing to himself that humanity had ever produced."[9]

Not seeing any possible relationship between Harris's principles and her husband's practice, Charlotte Shaw insisted that the first volume of Harris's notorious *My Life and Loves* be burned, page by page, in the fireplace; and she would tolerate neither another volume nor Harris. G.B.S. patiently indulged his old companion-in-arms of *Saturday Review* days, sometimes paying a heavy price for permitting the often-desperate Harris to exploit him. In part Shaw sincerely wanted to assist Harris, who was helpless to help himself; and since Shaw had been forced by his excess of public visibility to restrict the character of his benevolence, he wanted to furnish assistance within the confines he permitted himself. He would not write prefaces that might enable authors to peddle bad books. He would not recommend bad business bargains to London publishers on the strength of his name. He would not provide outright charity, which he felt broke the spirit. But he indulged Harris within characteristically Shavian limits, permitting him to publish letters that had been composed as disguised articles or prefaces or afterwords, and when autograph Shaw letters began bringing substantial prices from collectors and Harris was even more down and out than usual, Shaw would carefully write a long, entertaining letter by hand rather than mail a typed letter that would bring less in the market place. Yet this would happen only years later. (Shaw would tell him, honestly, after one begging letter, "I always hate the people I have to give money to; and they always—very properly—loathe me.")

Gaps in correspondence, especially between 1908 and 1915, suggest that some letters are missing. Yet Harris obviously saved all or most of Shaw's letters, and Shaw regularly filed his correspondence. Some letters may have been pilfered by secretaries or maids; some may yet be in private collections. It is clear, however, that these were years when the two had fallen out of sympathy and out of contact. Harris had moved from magazine to magazine, and Shaw had ceased furnishing him with copy as the journals became more gossip-ridden and scandalous and Harris's financial speculations leaned more and more over the edge of the law.

After Shaw had published his Shakespeare play, *The Dark Lady of the Sonnets* (1910), and Harris had accused him of pilfering from a Harris play about the Bard, *Shakespeare and His Love*, Shaw reviewed the book in the *Nation* (24 December 1910), owning up to cribbing from everyone who had ever written on the subject, including Harris. But Harris's work was "impoverished by his determination not to crib from me. . . ." What was, to Shaw, most Harrisian was not the picture of Shakespeare as an Elizabethan Frank Harris but Harris's picture of himself as Shakespearean disciple:

> This remarkable portrait has every merit except that of resemblance to any Frank Harris known to me or to financial and journalistic

Fig. 11. Frank Harris as drawn by "Owl" for *Vanity Fair*, 12 November 1913. Despite his dapper appearance, Harris was beginning his slow slide into editorial failure and debt, both of which would be accelerated in 1914 when he supported Germany in the Great War.

London. I say not a word against finance and the founding of weekly journals; but if a man chooses to devote to them what was meant for literature, let him not blame me for his neglected opportunities. The book . . . with a preface accusing me of having trodden a struggling saint into darkness so that I may batten on his achievements, might just as well have been published fifteen years ago. If they have been suppressed, it has been by Mr. Harris's own preoccupation with pursuits which, however energetic and honorable, can hardly be described as wrestling with angels in the desert in the capacity of one of "God's spies."

Harris's nonliterary activities (including amorous ones) had been sufficiently questionable to have provoked regular comment in the press, and Shaw did not need to detail them to his readers. "I have never disparaged his activities, knowing very little about them except that they seemed to me to be ultra-mundane; but I feel ill-used when a gentleman who has been warming both hands at the fire of life, and enjoying himself so vigorously that he has not had time to publish his plays and essays, suddenly seizes the occasion of a little *jeu d'esprit* of my own on the same subject . . . to hurl them, not into the market, but at my head. If he had been neglected, he has himself to thank." But Shaw was not finished. Dropping personalities, he concluded that if Harris wished "to keep in the middle of the stream of insult which constitutes fame for fine artists today," he had to furnish the public with "plenty of masterpieces to abuse" rather than a few desultory works "of the kind that our Philistine critics and advertisement managers do not understand even the need of reviewing. . . ."

Such sharp words, however witty and well meant, could only drive Harris farther apart from Shaw, but Shaw was in no mood to condone the fruits of Harris's Edwardian years. It would only be when both Shaw and Harris, for widely different reasons, found themselves in the wartime wilderness in 1915 that there was a reason for a rapprochement.

It took the war to initiate the interchange that would continue unabated until Harris's death. The beginning was not a letter from one to the other but Shaw's spirited defense of his old friend's war stance—which Shaw used indirectly to defend his own embattled position resulting from his icono-clastic supplement to the *New Statesman* the previous November, "Common Sense about the War." Harris, who had returned to the United States shortly after the war began, had contributed a number of articles on the war to the *New York Sun* that were then revised and issued as a book, *England or Germany?* On 19 June 1915, although the book bore the imprint of a New York publisher, it was reviewed in the *New Statesman*, where both Harris and the book were condemned. Since Harris was considered an Englishman in America, the review declared, his "decidedly mischievous" anti-British writings were widely quoted. As a contribution to controversy the book was derided, but "as an event or symptom it has, by reason of the author's personality and career, a certain international significance." Harris's career was then recounted, including the seamy side. Between literary enterprises, the reviewer wrote, "Harris would appear in the courts in connection with cases of a curious shadiness; and about a year ago he closed his career in England with a short spell in a London prison. . . . It is extraordinary, we may agree, that a man like Frank Harris should be able in any circumstances to attain a position which invests with importance the things he does and says; but so it happens in this world of incalculable chance." Harris, it concluded, "a fugitive from England, is an advocate of German civilisation and German sins. There is, to be sure, nothing original in his articles or his book, except the impassioned denunciation of English law and the English prisons—product of a painful personal experience."

Shaw reacted in a letter to the editor of the *New Statesman*, published in the issue of 26 June 1915:

> To the Editor of The New Statesman.
>
> Sir,—Your article on Frank Harris gives me an excuse for a comment on his book and on himself which may perhaps supply a needed touch or two to the portrait of the man. I have just read the book, and am struck by its intense British feeling. It is a consistent and indignant attack on England, a plea for Germany, and an express repudiation of the author's connection with England (Frank declares himself a naturalized member of the United States Bar); and yet it all through expresses a sounded concern for England, and a high, if bitterly disappointed ideal of England, which, unreasonable as it may seem in its application to the war, makes it more bearable to seriously proud Englishmen than most of the professedly patriotic explosions with which so many of us are now relieving our feelings at the expense of making our country ridiculous, besides informing the enemy loudly of his mistakes, a service which, one would think, we might offer first to our own side.
>
> The book must be read with due discrimination. For instance, the chapters which deal with the author's personal misadventures in our courts must obviously be taken goodhumoredly as the petulances of a sensitive man who never could be got to understand that illiterate Philistines have rights as against men of genius. When Frank Harris really edited a paper, he edited it very well, as the files of the *Fortnightly* and the *Saturday* shew. But when, preoccupied by more fascinating activities, he left the office boy to edit it, the results were disastrous. . . .

Harris lacked any vestige of a sense of humor but appreciated any defense whatever, and Shaw was his only public champion in England. The result would be a growing Harrisian dependence on a now-benevolent but cautious Shaw and a burgeoning correspondence that would end only with Harris's death in 1931.

World War I left Harris a shipwreck. He had barely escaped England ahead of his creditors and critics, the latter having multiplied because Harris, half out of bitterness with John Bull and half out of affection for the Germany he had known for several years as a student, had taken to observing publicly and often that England might be as war-guilty as Kaiserdom. In New York he struggled with yet another magazine, *Pearson's*, which he turned to socialism, sensationalism, and pro-Germanism and which survived only because whenever *Pearson's* was forbidden entry into the American mails, it received a new wave of publicity and Harris pocketed a few more handouts from supporters. Although he could no longer find publishers for his books in the United States or abroad, he nevertheless wrote volume after volume of reminiscences of the great men he had known (or, in some cases, read about), his *Contemporary Portraits*. They were not, Shaw told him in 1915, "like anybody else's attempts at the same kind of thing. They are really much more like what used to be called Characters than the sort of stuff we do nowadays. I doubt if any of our Savile Club scribes would venture to defend them." But, Shaw said in praise, "When you tackle a great man, you really do know the sort of animal you are dealing with. . . ." Among the less savory aspects of the "portraits" were not only Harris's pioneering emphasis (for reasons less historical than commercial) on his subjects' sex lives, but his suggestions, few with any validity, that he had more than a little to do with the biographee's success. Contemplating his own inevitable biography, Shaw tried to torpedo that treatment in advance with a letter that included a hilarious spoof, "How I Discovered Frank Harris," in which a penniless and starving Harris is discovered huddled on a bench on the Embankment and is catapulted to fame by an insistent G.B.S.

Harris nevertheless produced a portrait in which he was shown as actively involved in furthering Shaw's career. It concluded,

> I have always thought of him as Greatheart in Bunyan's allegory, a man so high-minded and courageous he will take the kingdom of heaven by storm and yet so full of the milk of human kindness that he suffers with all the disadvantages of the weak and all the disabilities of the dumb. He is the only man since William Blake who has enlarged our conception of English character; thanks to the Irish strain in him he encourages us to hope that English genius may yet become as free of insular taint as the vagrant air and as beneficent as sunshine.

To Shaw he wrote, in sending him a copy, "All I can say is, if you don't like it, your taste for sugar must be excessive for I have written it con amore." Clearly amused at the Harris blend of fulsomeness and egomania, Shaw followed it up with a lengthy self-portrait, "How Frank Ought to Have Done It," in which, in the third person, he parodied Harris's style, opening broadly:

> Before attempting to add Bernard Shaw to my collection of Contemporary Portraits, I find it necessary to secure myself in advance by the fullest admission of his extraordinary virtues. Without any cavilling over trifles I declare at once that Shaw is the just man made perfect. I admit that in all his controversies, with me or anyone else, Shaw is, always has been, and always will be, right. I perceive that the common habit of abusing him is an ignorant and silly habit, and that the pretence of not taking him seriously is the ridiculous cover for an ignominious retreat from an encounter with him. If there is any other admission I can make, any other testimonial I can give, I am ready to give it and apologize for having omitted it. If it will help matters to say that Shaw is the greatest man that ever lived, I shall not hesitate for a moment. All the cases against him break down when they are probed to the bottom. All his prophecies come true. All his fantastic reactions come to life within a generation. I have an uneasy sense that even now I am not doing him justice: that I am ungrateful, disloyal, disparaging. I can only repeat that if there is anything I have left out, all that is necessary is to call my attention to the oversight and it shall be remedied. If I cannot say that Shaw touches nothing that he does not adorn, I can at least testify that he touches nothing that he does not dust and polish and put back in its place much more carefully than the last man who handled it.

The parody was meant as fun and indeed contained some probing self-analysis as well as some jabs at Harris's approaches and style that would have deflated a less desperate man. Harris merely seized it, rushed it into print, and accepted the dollars it brought without embarrassment.

While the next decade saw Shaw's apotheosis with *Saint Joan* and a Nobel Prize, the 1920s were agonizing years for Harris. He left his American magazine, *Pearson's*, having sold the debt-ridden enterprise for $2,000—enough to get him and Nellie to Paris and then to the Riviera. Each succeeding volume of the half-imaginative *My Life and Loves* brought him as much legal and postal trouble as income, and at the last, racked by asthma and heart trouble, Harris proposed a full-length biography of Shaw.

Fig. 12. Frank Harris on the Riviera in 1926. Courtesy Harry Ransom Humanities Research Center, University of Texas at Austin.

As negotiations proceeded, Shaw was alternately amused and concerned. Eventually he wrote to Harris,

> What a chap you are! You can of course compile a life of me as half a dozen other people have done—the sort of life that can be published whilst all the parties are still alive. . . . Also you can write an autobiography, as St Augustine did, as Rousseau did, as Casanova did, as you yourself have done. . . . A man cannot take a libel action against himself; and if he is prepared to face obloquy, and compromises no one except himself and the dead, he may even get a sort of Riviera circulation in highly priced top shelf volumes with George Moore and James Joyce. But you cannot write that way about other people. You have a right to make your own confessions, but not to make mine. If, disregarding this obvious limitation you pick up what you can from gossip and from guesses at the extent to which my plays are founded on fact (in your Shaksperean manner), what will happen? Your publisher, believing me to be fabulously rich and an ill man to cross, will send me the MS and ask me whether I have any objection to it. . . . I will say that I have every possible objection. . . .

Further, Shaw reminded him in 1926, Harris's selfstyled masterpiece, the play *Joan la Romée*, written because Shaw had "just reopened the medieval theatre market for saints," was "hopeless" as drama. Harris, he charged, had "reduced the subject to a story of a very young Virginian female, a few dullards, two crooks, and a very modern American executioner cheeking an English lord and snapping his fingers at the Holy Office. . . . Just like O. Henry, with the Harrisian style superimposed."

B. D. Kentner, Harris's secretary in Nice, confided to the publisher, Lincoln Torrey, that Harris was despondent over Shaw's reaction, especially the sarcasm that in creating his Joan of Arc, Harris had taken "the fool's cap" from Anatole France, whom Harris despised. "This from Shaw whom Mr. Harris regards as about the greatest of critics. . . . May I say in the *strictest confidence* (please BURN this letter) Mr. Harris is in a critical condition—the fear of poverty is either going to cause him to lose his mind, or resort to suicide. . . ."[10]

At the very last, Shaw had to rescue Harris, after some concern that he had confessed too much too explicitly to the old pirate, by permitting him to secure a large advance from an American publisher in order to concoct a

G.B.S. biography largely out of Shaw's many autobiographical letters, texts of which Shaw censored and bowdlerized for publication, sometimes to Harris's great disappointment. But Harris made use of whatever he could, sometimes changing the first person to the third person and sometimes making no change at all. Yet even that turned out in the end to be not enough help to the failing Harris (who was beyond help) and his ghostwriter Frank Scully. When, in 1931, Harris died in the south of France, in self-exile from both England and America, Shaw felt that he had not only to complete the book but to rewrite it—in the pompous Harrisian style—to pay for Harris's obsequies and provide for the aging Nellie's uncertain future. Then he wrote a characteristically paradoxical postscript in his own name to give the book a further push.

It was a curiously appropriate end to a relationship that had been less than a friendship but undescribable by any other name. For a moment in time they had been valuable to each other professionally. After that the two flamboyant self-publicists were linked only by the conscious need of one for the propping up of a faltering ego and a fading reputation, and the unconscious desire of the other for basking in his hard-won self-esteem and for preening himself via his own memoir writings while helping a down-and-out colleague who had been unable to cope with his too-quick success. Grasping at straws at the end, the ill and increasingly desperate Harris even suggested, since he had preserved most of his letters from Shaw (who had earlier urged Harris to sell them while the market was right), that all their correspondence be published, as was Shaw's with Ellen Terry. Shaw was cool to the idea. "We have never had a correspondence in that sense," he explained to Harris on a postcard, and "my occasional attempts to persuade you that the world is not yet populated exclusively by Frank Harrises would not make a book even if they were fit for publication."

Piteously, Harris appealed:

> Such a threat [to forbid quotation] is worse than unfair. I have already months ago entered into a contract and received the money from the publisher for giving him my life of you and some of your own letters. Now 6 months afterwards you forbid me to use a word. Three months ago you wrote: "I have written the information you want in my own hand; sell it and have a spree with Nellie." And now you forbid and threaten me. . . . What am I to do? I cannot rewrite the whole book. . . . Do be sensible. You talk of [Archibald] Henderson's 600 pages as the only authorized biography. There is

hardly a gleam of Shaw in the whole tome. . . . If you had put "private" at the head of any letter I would have regarded it as an order. . . . You say you have 5 to 10 thousand £s a year—I have nothing. . . .

Such a close to the affair, with Shaw teasing the hard-up and ailing Harris with the prospect of making his book from Shaw's letters and then alternately withdrawing and restoring permission to quote; censoring the mildly objectionable—and hardly Harrisian—parts after tantalizing the pathetic Harris with them at Harris's request; and finally (in an excess of guilt or self-protectiveness, or both) rewriting the book as well as seeing it through the press for Harris's widow, suggests an unsatisfactory side of Shaw. Perhaps it is an unappetizing aspect of all of us reflected in much of the Shavian side of the exchange. That for years he had been toying with his old friend while making efforts to help him suggests an element of unrecognized cruelty in the underside of benevolence. Yet it was Shaw who saw the relationship as that of the playwright and the pirate. In Harris's view it had been that of two old cronies (which they never were), who had shared a heyday before one fell upon bad luck. But they saw each other as each viewed his world—Harris as melodrama, Shaw as tragicomedy.

Notes

1. The annotated texts of both sides of the correspondence between Shaw and Harris, 1895–1931, appear in Stanley Weintraub, ed., *The Playwright and the Pirate. Bernard Shaw and Frank Harris: A Correspondence* (University Park: Pennsylvania State University Press, 1982). It also includes substantial extracts from Harris's "Contemporary Portraits" biography of Shaw and Shaw's spoof-rejoinder.

2. *Collected Letters 1874–1897*, ed. Dan H. Laurence (New York: Dodd, Mead, 1965), p. 32.

3. Ibid., pp. 321, 322.

4. Harris, "George Bernard Shaw" in *Contemporary Portraits, Second Series* (1919) as reprinted in *The Playwright and the Pirate*, p. 122.

5. *Collected Letters 1874–1897*, pp. 472–73.

6. Shaw to theater critic J. C. Trewin, assigned by Dan H. Laurence to 9 June 1947 in *Collected Letters 1926–1950* (New York: Viking, 1988), p. 796. Trewin had asked Shaw for examples of Harris's "earthy" manner of speech, and Shaw complied.

7. *The Bodley Head Bernard Shaw: Collected Plays with Their Prefaces* (London: Max Reinhardt, 1972), 4: 275–76. Hereafter *CP* in the text.

8. Oscar Wilde to Lord Alfred Douglas, January–March 1897 (often referred to as "De Profundis"), in Rupert Hart-Davis, ed., *The Letters of Oscar Wilde* (London, Hart-Davis, 1962), p. 538.

9. *Collected Letters 1926–1950*, p. 796.

10. Quoted as item 325 in the Sotheby sale catalogue of English Literature and History, 18 July 1991, London. Shaw's letter of 20 May 1926 was the document in question.

"LAWRENCE OF ARABIA"
Bernard Shaw's Other Saint Joan

G.B.S.'s friendship with T. E. Lawrence was still rather new on 1 December 1922 when he wrote to him that "perhaps I shall put you into a play, if my playwriting days are not over."[1] Since completing *Back to Methuselah*, his longest and most complex play, Shaw at sixty-six had felt written-out, barren of new inspiration. Still, the throwaway line, the sign-off sentence in the letter, had implications that Shaw was not about to reveal. He *was* going to put his strange new friend in a play he had yet to begin, and in the most curious of disguises.

The Epilogue to the play had been gestating for a decade, at least—since a series of five picture postcards to Mrs. Patrick Campbell, for whom he had written the Eliza Doolittle role in *Pygmalion*. The Shaws had been traveling in what G.B.S. called the "Joan of Arc country," and on the back of one card dated 8 September 1913, he wrote,

> I shall do a Joan play some day, beginning with the sweeping up of the cinders and orange peel *after* her martyrdom, and going on with Joan's arrival in heaven. I should have God about to damn the English for their share in her betrayal and Joan producing an end of burnt stick in arrest of Judgment. "What's that? Is it one of the faggots?" asks God. "No," says Joan, "it's what is left of the two sticks a common English soldier tied together and gave me as I went to the stake; for they wouldn't even give me a crucifix; and you cannot damn the common people of England, represented by that soldier

because a poor cowardly riff raff of barons and bishops were too futile to resist the devil."

That soldier is the only redeeming figure in the whole business. English literature must be saved (by an Irishman, as usual) from the disgrace of having nothing to show concerning Joan except the piffling libel in Henry VI, which reminds me that one of my scenes will be Voltaire and Shakespear running down bye streets in heaven to avoid meeting Joan. . . .

On 23 April 1923 he would actually begin the play, stirred, very likely, by Joan's canonization in 1920. But the personality of Joan first escaped Shaw, who kept his interest in the subject quiet after the postcards of 1913, until he questioned Father Joseph Leonard about her in a letter of 11 December 1922, ten days after his cryptic comment to T.E.L. He had met the Vincentian priest, an Irishman who taught at a Catholic college in Hammersmith, while on holiday in Derry in 1919, and they had become friends. "I always forget to ask you about an historical question in which I am interested," Shaw began. "It is about Joan of Arc."

Suddenly Shaw had been boning up on Joan's history, however offhand he made the query seem. His letter made it obvious that he already knew a good deal about her, possibly from the *Catholic Encyclopaedia* since evidence from his play script suggests he had employed it. But he had a specific query: "Where can I find a record of the proceedings?" Three days later Father Leonard replied, suggesting that Shaw read T. Douglas Murray's Englishing of J. E. J. Quicherat's nineteenth-century French version of the Latin *procés* of 1430–31.

Shaw may have already had it at home, without realizing it, since Sydney Cockerell, director of the Fitzwilliam Museum at Cambridge, who had first introduced Lawrence to Shaw in March 1922, claimed later that the proceedings of Joan's trial and rehabilitation had so filled him with "excitement" that he shared it by giving copies to some of his friends. Charlotte Shaw apparently located it and left it out for G.B.S. to read. If Cockerell were as involved as he later claimed, it was his second service to the future of *Saint Joan*, for not long after he had brought Lawrence to Shaw's door at Adelphi Terrace, T.E.L. followed up the encounter by offering Shaw—only to read—one of the eight privately printed copies, run off on the presses of the *Oxford Times*, of *Seven Pillars of Wisdom*.

Most of the reading during the first few months the Shaws had the enormous narrative—330,000 words—was done by Charlotte, who read out portions to G.B.S. Involved in politicking for Labour in the General Election, Shaw did not get to it himself until late in the year, but both from what he had read and from what Charlotte had read to him, the connections between the medieval saint and the modern soldier were becoming compellingly clear. Shaw kept that to himself.

The day Lawrence responded to Shaw—27 December—was T.E.'s end of innocence. Exposed by the *Daily Express*, he was revealed as the "UNCROWNED KING" of Arabia, serving pseudonymously in the Air Force ranks as J. H. Ross. The next day he was headlined as "PRINCE OF MECCA ON RIFLE PARADE." The embarrassed R.A.F. released Lawrence forthwith, and in March 1923 he took Shaw's name on joining the army as a private, again trying to lose himself in the ranks.[2] Shaw, meanwhile—the real Shaw—had offered to help edit the sprawling manuscript, which he overestimated at 460,000 words, into shape for actual publication. Thus as he began drafting his stage chronicle of a military commander even more unorthodox than Lawrence, he had at his elbow Lawrence's *Seven Pillars of Wisdom*, in many striking ways the chronicle of a modern Joan. The coincidence may have been of vital importance to the play.

Visitors to Ayot St. Lawrence during 1923—the year in which G.B.S. began and completed *Joan*—usually were treated to an admiring display of, and lecture on, Lawrence's epic, and the more customary reading of a fragment from the current Shavian work-in-progress. Sidney and Beatrice Webb, for example, were accorded the dual honor, and Beatrice duly recorded the episode in her diary. Meanwhile, Shaw, busy with preliminary reading and planning of *Saint Joan*, had little chance to finish *Seven Pillars* himself. That his enthusiasm for the book survived both sporadic reading and Charlotte's missionary zeal for it is a key to the playwright's real feelings about the literary merits of Lawrence's book. He took it in brief nightly stints when he was at Ayot that winter and spring, for the Oxford edition of the book was too massive to be regularly carried about for reading in railway carriages (a favorite practice of Shaw's). By mid-April, just as he began the actual writing of *Saint Joan*, he still had forty pages of *Seven Pillars* to go, but was convinced, even apart from his wife's panegyrics, that Lawrence had written one of the era's great books. Sydney Cockerell, patiently waiting to read the Shaw copy, had to be put off by a G.B.S. note that the book had to be finished to the last morsel before it could be released.

In May, Lady Gregory, Yeats's great friend and patron, arrived for a stay with the Shaws and carefully noted all the details in her diary. They provide a crucial contemporary link between the personality of Lawrence and Shaw's conception of Joan:

> *May 19, 1923.* Came down to Ayot by train. . . . G.B.S. drove me home and talked of his Joan of Arc play. He has not read Mark Twain, is afraid of being influenced by him. He has read a little of Anatole France and is reading the evidence at the trial, it was published some years ago. He does not idealise her as Mark does, and defends the Church, "it didn't torture her." I think there will be something good about the English soldiers. He tells me that Lawrence, who fought in Mesopotamia,[3] had been to see him, is an extraordinary man, very small, living as a private in the army, having resigned his command, and has written a wonderful book, has had five [*sic*] copies linotyped, and lent him one. "It will be one of the great books of the world. He describes every blade of grass and flower and noxious insect, and all the fighting and the terrible crimes of the Turks and the terrible vengeance he and his men took on them. He has not a religious mission like Gordon but must have a touch of his nature. His brother is a missionary in China, or wants to be one, and his mother has the same desire." He thinks (G.B.S. hears) that all his family will die out because they are all mad.
>
> *May 20, 1923.* He showed me in the evening this book, and I read a few sentences and said, "It seems as good as Doughty," and G.B.S. said, "Lawrence is a great admirer of Doughty." This probably gives him his style.
>
> G.B.S. has been working at Joan without talking [further] about it. . . .
>
> G.B.S. says he chose Joan of Arc because of Bernhardt and others having played so many parts turning on sexual attraction, he wanted to give Joan as a heroine absolutely without that side. . . .
>
> I am reading the Lawrence book, it is enthralling, each sentence rich and complete.
>
> Charlotte says Lawrence was a Don at Cambridge [*sic*]. . . .
>
> He had come to lunch with the Shaws while (as he still is) a private, but dressed extremely well, and although he said that a couple of weeks ago he had been washing plates for the sergeants' mess, she could hardly believe it because his hands were so well cared for. He was charming, but one hears of his thrusting away approaches of friendship with some rudeness. . . .

May 21, 1923. We have been to Cambridge. . . . Cockerell met us at the Fitzwilliam Museum. . . .

Then we had lunch at "The Bull," ordered by G.B.S. . . . There was good deal of talk of Lawrence and his book. Cockerell says it (the book) is to be kept secret, but G.B.S. says, "When Lawrence gets into a secret place it is in the limelight. If he hides in a quarry, he puts red flags all around."[4]

While attempting to pull strings in Whitehall to get Lawrence—Private Shaw—out of the army and back into the air force, from which he had been discharged because of the publicity his presence created, G.B.S. was completing *Joan*, finally writing on 27 August to aspiring actress Molly Tompkins, "Saint Joan is finished (except for polishing): a magnificent play,—and I thought I should never write another after Methuselah! I am certainly a wonderful man; but then historical plays hardly count: the material is readymade." By September 1923, only the arrangement of the stage business remained to be done, and by early October he was staying with Barry Jackson at Birmingham, planning for rehearsals of the new play early in the following year.

As Shaw researched, plotted, and wrote *Saint Joan*, he seems to have sensed the uncanny resemblance that the work in progress bore to the book at his elbow—*Seven Pillars*—and its enigmatic author. Whether the coincidences helped shape the play and its preface can only be surmised, but striking parallels *are* there and perhaps represent Shavian perspectives upon both the legendary Maid and the living legend of the ascetic former knight of the desert. As Shaw lived with the records and chronicles of one, and with the chronicle and person of the other, their figures seem in many ways to have merged into a single image, reinforcing the timelessness of Joan's experience: the experience of having the spirit within—adventurous, imaginative, ascetic, contemplative—made use of and then discarded by a world unready for idealism except as an instrument to serve political realities.

The great Dutch medieval historian Johan Huizinga has described Joan from contemporary details—the scanty data preserved by her cohorts, who were little interested in personal descriptions.[5] These were also documents Shaw read in researching *Joan*. Much of the picture of the Maid formed by her contemporaries strikingly fits Lawrence—Joan's shortness of stature, her eating and drinking sparingly, her avoidance of physical contact and generally asexual behavior, her combination of the laconic with the lighthearted, her "superior, irresistible, and infectious bravery."[6] Even her delight in beautiful horses and armor and the rich raiment she wore, which offended Church authorities, can be visualized in the contemporary terms of Lawrence's fascination with the flowing dress and ornaments of an Arab sheik—which scandalized other English officers—and (in the days G.B.S. knew him) his infatuation with his mechanical steed, a Brough motorcycle, which T.E. named as a medieval knight would christen his charger.

In many cases, except for the gender of the personal pronoun, it would be difficult to separate the personalities of these two figures, medieval and modern, with their immense appetites for glory, their abilities to put people in their pockets, their knack for unconventional strategy unconventionally set forth. "She lectured, talked down and overruled the plans of generals, leading troops to victory on plans of her own," Shaw wrote in his preface to the play, using contemporary terms better applied to Lawrence. "She had an unbounded and quite unconcealed contempt for official opinion, judgment, and authority, and for War Office tactics and strategy. . . . There were only two opinions about her. One was that she was miraculous: the other that she was unbearable."

In both cases we find the campaign's central figure inseparable from the nationalistic momentum to create a unified state from a feudal order and to set a monarch representative of that unity upon the throne of the nation-state. Joan's France under the Dauphin (later Charles VII) may have had as its contemporary parallel Lawrence's more naive dream, dashed at Versailles, of a Pan-Arabian kingdom under Sheikh Feisal.

By the time Shaw had begun *Saint Joan*, T.E. had once more retired to his hoped-for obscurity in the ranks, once saying of himself in a letter to Lionel Curtis in May 1923, when he was still attempting to adjust to Tank Corps life, that his was a strange form of lay monasticism:

> I want to stay here till it no longer hurts me: till the burnt child no longer feels the fire. . . . One used to think that such frames of mind would have perished with the age of religion: and yet here they rise up, purely secular. It's a lurid flash into the Nitrian desert: almost seems to strip the sainthood from Anthony. How about Teresa?[7]

What might Joan have done, had she lived? In his preface, dated May 1924, Shaw pondered, "Had she escaped she would probably have fought on until the English were gone, and then had to shake the dust of the court off her feet, and retire to Domremy. . . ." We may ponder further that Joan, "a young girl, pious and chaste; [whose] . . . excesses have been excesses of

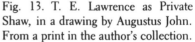

Fig. 13. T. E. Lawrence as Private
Shaw, in a drawing by Augustus John.
From a print in the author's collection.

religion and charity and not of worldliness and wantonness"—as the Inquisitor points out in the play's trial scene—might have found her postwar world
depressing and unsatisfying and sought fulfillment instead within the walls
of a convent, a medieval equivalent, perhaps, to Private Shaw's monasticism
of the barracks. In 1927, quoting an anecdote about Marshal Foch, G.B.S.
wrote that Lawrence's self-imposed retirement after the First World War
saved England a delicate problem—the question of the young colonel's
future. The Marshal, the story went, was asked how Napoleon would have
fought the war. "Superbly," he said; "but what the devil should we have
done with him afterwards?" Flatteringly equating Lawrence's achievement
with Napoleon's, Shaw added, "The Prince of Damascus solved the problem
for Britannia. He simply walked away and became a nobody again under
another name."[8]

Several years after connecting the Foch anecdote to Lawrence's situation,
Shaw applied it to St. Joan. The occasion was a B.B.C. radio talk delivered

on the five-hundredth anniversary of the burning of Joan at the stake, 30 May 1931. The question of what is to be done with them after their period of accomplishment, Shaw pointed out, arises with many people of extraordinary ability. He went on to pick a case from the newspaper—that of Leon Trotsky. Stalin's former rival—a thick-spectacled civilian whose military exploits from his railway car headquarters, Shaw thought, rivaled those of history's great commanders—was then in precarious exile in Turkey. There were many reasons why, in 1931—if the omission from the anecdote were a conscious one on Shaw's part—it was best for him to leave Lawrence (for the moment) publicly unmentioned. Still, we sense a labyrinth of relationships in Shaw's mind in the Saint Joan anniversary talk, for G.B.S. had just completed the section of his play *Too True to be Good*, in which T.E. is openly and affectionately caricatured as the infuriatingly undisciplined military genius, Private Napoleon Alexander *Trotsky* Meek.

"The Conflict between Genius and Discipline" is the heading of one section of Shaw's preface to *Saint Joan*. In it Shaw described the charismatic quality of the Maid's personality:

> Outside the farm she had no authority, no prestige, no claim to the smallest deference. Yet she ordered everybody about her from her uncle to the king, the archbishop, and the military General Staff. Her uncle obeyed her like a sheep, and took her to the castle of the local commander, who, on being ordered about, tried to assert himself, but soon collapsed and obeyed. And so on up to the king.

Lawrence, too, Shaw knew, had his equivalents to Bertrand de Poulengey and Jean de Metz, as well as to Joan's General Staff. A fellow officer in the Middle East, John Buchan (Lord Tweedsmuir), called Lawrence the only authentic genius he ever knew and confided, "I am not a very tractable person or much of a hero-worshipper, but I could have followed Lawrence over the edge of the world." There was no question about the compelling power of T.E.'s wartime leadership, however unmilitary and informal his Arabian operations were. G.B.S. embellished the facts slightly: "As to the British Army, its feelings when, after having to make Lawrence a colonel rather than be ordered about by a nobody, it found him leading his hosts to battle on camel-back in a picturesque Arab costume, can be more easily imagined in messrooms than described by me. Even the camel did not get its regulation meals."[9]

Not only was Lawrence "unbearably irritating" to his military superiors, but like Joan was regarded "as a liar and impostor." Shaw went on about Joan in language strikingly applicable as well to Lawrence:

> It is hard to conceive anything more infuriating to a statesman or military commander, or to a court favorite, than to be overruled at every turn, or to be robbed of the ear of the reigning sovereign, by an impudent young upstart. . . . Not only were the envy, snobbery, and competitive ambition of the baser natures exacerbated by Joan's success, but among the friendly ones that were clever enough to be critical, a quite reasonable scepticism and mistrust of her ability, founded on a fair observation of her obvious [military] ignorance and temerity, were at work against her. . . . [S]he must have seemed, to all who were not infatuated by her, so insufferable that nothing but an unbroken chain of overwhelming successes in the military and political field could have saved her. . . .

Lawrence's charisma even emerged regularly during his final incarnation as "Shaw," when he was in a rank remote from command level. An incident of 1929, recorded by Mrs. Clare Sydney Smith, wife of Lawrence's commanding officer, demonstrates as much. Flight-Lieutenant Brecky, who was in charge of R.A.F. marine craft at the Calshot station, and Mr. Robertson, of the Air Ministry's Press Section, had gone down to the slipway, discovering there a corporal transmitting some orders about a boat. "Who gave you those orders?" the officer inquired.

> "Mr. Shaw, sir."
> "Who is Mr. Shaw?"
> "Well, sir, Aircraftman Shaw."
> "And why should you, a corporal, take orders from an aircraftman?"
> "Well, sir, it seemed perfectly natural to take orders from Mr. Shaw."[10]

Mrs. Smith drew from the incident what she considered a key to T.E.'s "unconscious power of leadership," referring to Chapter XXV of *Seven Pillars*. There Lawrence had written,

> the work suffered by the creation of . . . a bar between the leaders and men. Among the Arabs there were no distinctions, traditional or

natural, except the unconscious power given a famous sheikh by virtue of his accomplishment; and they taught me that no man could be their leader except he ate the ranks' food, lived level with them, and yet appeared better in himself.

It is unlikely that these lines escaped G.B.S. in 1923. Shaw's Joan, perhaps out of the same instinctive power of leadership, insists (as play and preface point out) on having a soldier's dress and arms, horse, and equipment and on treating her escort of soldiers as comrades, sleeping side by side with them on the floor at night as if there were no difference of sex (or rank) between them. Yet both youthful warriors, medieval saint and medieval scholar, were essentially unmilitary individuals—novices at war yet in love with its trappings and its heady thrills. To the village girl whose sole military experience has been to see the soldiers pass by, Dunois comments, "You have the makings of a soldier in you. You are in love with war." So too, in 1916, was the former archeology student from Oxford.

How both Joan of Arc and Lawrence of Arabia were able to triumph as military tacticians has puzzled historians and encouraged skeptics. And as Shaw realized about Joan, as early as her rehabilitation trial and for centuries thereafter, there were evasive answers to questions about the quality of her military genius and its actual tactical effect: whether her role was more moral and emotional than strategic, arising from the example of her undoubted courage. G.B.S. assumed that both warriors had real military skill. The facts of accomplishment and the testimony of comrades-in-arms were both plentiful. The Duke of Alençon had praised Joan, Shaw read, as being "in war . . . very expert, whether to carry a lance, to assemble an army, to order a battle, or to dispose artillery." But Shaw knew that neither Joan nor Lawrence needed, in the relatively uncomplicated military situations of Joan's day or the primitive conditions that were Lawrence's stage, more than a pick-up knowledge of the simple weaponry, penetrating common sense, spectacular courage, and a charismatic personality. Lawrence's war, E. M. Forster suggested in a review of *Seven Pillars*, was "probably the last of the picturesque wars . . . waged under archaistic conditions, . . . the last effort of the war-god before he laid down his godhead and turned chemist."[11]

The reports about Lawrence's disinterest in such conventionalities of living as love and marriage were borne out by his choice of friends and his ascetic barracks life as much as by his letters. The "conflict of sex," as Shaw put it in his description of Joan, was given little encouragement to manifest itself:

The evident truth [Shaw wrote of Joan] is that like most women of her hardy managing type she seemed neutral in the conflict of sex because men were much too afraid of her to fall in love with her. She herself was not sexless: in spite of the virginity she had vowed up to a point, and preserved to her death, she never excluded the possibility of marriage for herself. But marriage, with its preliminary of the attraction, pursuit, and capture of a husband, was not her business: she had something else to do.

Shaw comprehended Lawrence's personality only partially—the part represented by what Shaw called moral passion in an individual, such as he saw in Joan. This kind of hero does not control his passions by any rational process. His physical passions are overwhelmed by a greater passion, the passion of virtue, which is a passion of the mind. For Shaw, thought is a passion, as he demonstrated to his own satisfaction in many of his later plays, from *Back to Methuselah* (completed shortly before Shaw met Lawrence) to the play of Shaw's ninety-third year, *Farfetched Fables*. It is at the close of the *Fables* that Raphael insists that there are passions far more exciting than the physical ones: "On the contrary: intellectual passion, mathematical passion, passion for discovery and exploration: the mightiest of all passions." To Shaw's discomfort, however, he sensed in another part of Lawrence's design—his choice of ranks—a quest for a living martyrdom rather than a quest for an ascetic way of living. To Shaw, martyrdom was

> a waste of vitality and a triumph of illusion over reality, since it produces a sort of hypnosis upon its witness. Men develop fixations upon the cross, the act of martyrdom itself, while doing their best to ignore the implications of the martyr's ethical conquest. As Joan remarks, "It is the memory and the salvation that sanctify the cross, not the cross that sanctifies the memory and the salvation. . . . I shall outlast the cross."[12]

A Shavian reflection of this attitude is the evidence that as he worked on *Saint Joan* he pressed his efforts—against Lawrence's own wishes—to pension T.E. out of the service altogether and into creative literary work. The outcome was another of T.E.'s tactical successes: Shaw failed.

There is even some internal evidence in *Saint Joan* that Lawrence or his chronicle influenced some of the play's dialogue, particularly in the fourth scene, in the exchange between Warwick and Cauchon. Cauchon paints

Joan as a Mohammed, with her own collection of Arabs, who follow her through force of her personality. "What did the camel driver do at the beginning more than this shepherd girl is doing?" he warns. Warwick, the Englishman, is unimpressed: "I am a soldier, not a churchman. As a pilgrim I saw something of the Mahometans. They were not so ill-bred as I had been led to believe. In some respects their conduct compared favorably with ours." Cauchon, displeased, answers sharply: "I have noticed this before. Men go to the East to convert the infidels. And the infidels pervert them. The Crusader comes back more than half a Saracen. Not to mention that all Englishmen are born heretics."

It is easy to imagine that the dominant metaphors of the dialogue were unlikely to have occurred to G.B.S. before his friendship with the young man who wrote an Oxford thesis on "Crusader Castles" and a personal memoir of his leadership of a motley Arab camel corps, during which he described having discovered that Arab ethics compared favorably with those of his native England.

Although both Lawrence and Shaw enjoyed the discipline of sitting for portraits and busts, and the reflected glory of looking at them, neither playwright nor subject ever confessed to seeing Lawrence of Arabia in the Joan of Arc that G.B.S. shaped. T.E. received several copies of the play over the years, the last inscribed "To Shaw from Shaw to replace many stolen copies until this, too, is stolen." An earlier one, which disappeared from T.E.'s barracks, had been signed, "To Pte. Shaw from Public Shaw." Had G.B.S. owned up to it, he might have written instead, "To Bernard Shaw's other Saint Joan."

There can be no doubt at all that the Private Meek of *Too True to Be Good* is Lawrence as he was in 1931, when the play was written. Enjoying the caricature of himself as Meek (never was a man less so), T.E. even helped with the dialogue and the military terminology so that G.B.S. would get it exactly right. Yet he was more than Meek in the comedy, as he understood when he let his guard down, just before the premiere, in a letter to Mrs. Shaw. Often writing indirectly to Shaw through Charlotte, he asked her to tell G.B.S. that Meek was "probably the finest acting thing" the playwright had ever done. The slip came in a worried afterthought—that Cedric Hardwicke, a fine actor who had already created the difficult role of King Magnus in Shaw's political play *The Apple Cart* (1929), would let T.E.'s own conception of Aubrey in the play "frantically down. He will never understand what he represents. I shall dread seeing the play acted, for fear it does not come up to what it is. . . ." The implication is that Lawrence himself did. And Lawrence, it seems, understood what may have been an unspoken secret he shared with the Shaws—that *Too True to Be Good* was too true to be comfortable, an analysis of his motives and nature far beyond the obvious implications of Private Meek and Private Shaw. There were subtleties and complexities in the character of Aubrey, the confidence man, that T.E. could not own up to. These make Meek, the happy warrior of the play, almost a reverse image of the troubled Aubrey.

Whether G.B.S. recalled Lawrence's *Seven Pillars of Wisdom* for any of the raw material from which he molded his warm caricature of Private Meek is no longer a matter for conjecture. Shaw hardly needed to go back to the book since his familiarity with its contents included having edited it. Although there are some parallels to *Seven Pillars*, we find rather an evocation of some of the many sides of the younger Lawrence who loved to make a game of war and military customs and proprieties, who could dominate as well as enrage helpless superiors—and who could get his job done. Obvious details of Colonel Lawrence—Aircraftman Shaw—appear in the script of the play: his appearance, authentic in physical particulars and in insignificant stature; his pseudo-meek quick-wittedness, combined with modest omniscience; his voluntary descent down the ladder of rank from colonel to private; his knowledge of dialects and tribal psychology (as in his suggestion that his commanding officer keep an offered bribe because the chieftain "won't believe you have any authority unless you take presents"); his charismatic leadership qualities; his technical facility with mines in blowing up bridges and trains (the mines replaced farcically by colored flares in the play); his freedom from need for woman or wife; his unseen but ear-shattering postwar motorcycle.

This is Lawrence at his happiest, the incarnation as Private Meek displaying all the facets of Arabian, Army, and Air Force life in which T.E. found satisfaction in the employment of his peculiar talents. He found additional pleasure in surveying this side of himself from the perspective of the finished play and in suggesting ways by which the affectionate caricature could be improved and married even more closely to military reality. He made nearly two dozen specific recommendations for alterations in the text, and G.B.S. adopted all of them—a turnabout from the days when T.E. meekly accepted G.B.S.'s wholesale alterations and excisions in *Seven Pillars of Wisdom*.

Although Lawrence feared that mere actors might not be able to comprehend and convey—as he phrased it—"my conception of Aubrey," he made no attempt to alter, clarify, or simplify Shaw's characterization of Aubrey as he had done with Meek. Possibly he realized that he had already said too much.

It was always obvious that Private Meek, complete to the long head adorned with Wellingtonian nose, was a portrait of Private Shaw, but it has not been as easy to see that Aubrey Bagot, ex-R.A.F. combat officer and now a professional thief, represents the "Colonel Lawrence of Arabia" side. Here is the young officer plucked from civilian innocence and thrust into the horrors of military necessity so graphically described in *Seven Pillars*, from the murder of helpless prisoners and the execution of offenders at point-blank range to the mercy-killing on the field of battle of mortally wounded friends and the massacre of civilians in mined railroad cars. Lawrence had left Oxford and a promising career as a scholar-archeologist, but he could not return to it after demobilization. "Digging up old civilizations"—as G.B.S. later put it—was deprived of meaning by a war that demonstrated how precarious our own civilization and its values really are. The seeming irrationality of Lawrence's postwar behavior seems, from this perspective, almost inevitable.

Shaw's Aubrey Bagot, who had left behind his university education, and his ordination in the Church of England, to join a combat service, is so warped by his wartime experience that he cannot resume his life at the point war interrupted it, and he lapses, like Lawrence (but in his own way), into irrational behavior. "I was hardly more than a boy," Aubrey recalls, "when I first dropped a bomb on a sleeping village. I cried all night after doing that. Later on I swooped into a street and sent machine gun bullets into a crowd of civilians: women, children and all. I was past crying by that time. And now you preach to me about stealing a pearl necklace!" He had been awarded (in his description) "a very poorly designed silver medal" for the wartime deeds for which his conscience tormented him. "What am I?" he asks: "A soldier who has lost his nerve, a thief who at his first great theft has found honesty the best policy. . . . Nature never intended me for soldiering or thieving: I am by nature and destiny a preacher. . . . But I have no Bible, no creed: the war has shot both out of my hands. . . ."

Bagot bears additional resemblances to Lawrence that are only partially disguised by differences in detail. Aubrey, for example, loses a brother in the war and recalls bitterly the waste of his death, while Lawrence was shocked when his brothers Will and Frank were both killed in action. Aubrey is contemptuous of his silver medal, while Lawrence, summoned at the end of the war to an audience with King George V to receive a decoration, allegedly refused to accept it, leaving the startled monarch with the box in his hands. Further, Aubrey, who has lost his faith—Lawrence had none—confesses to his father that the war only completed the religious deterioration begun at home when he was a boy. His father (The Elder)—an unbeliever—insists that this could not be true, for he had shielded Aubrey from a religious education. "You thought you did, . . ." Aubrey replies, "but you reckoned without my mother. . . . You forbade me to read the Bible; but my mother made me learn three verses of it every day, and whacked me if I could not repeat them without misplacing a word. She threatened to whack me still worse if I told you."

The "incorrigibly superstitious mother" (the Elder's term) seems almost certainly to have had her origin in Lawrence's own mother, who overcompensated for her marriage and family being without benefit of clergy. (Lawrence's father Sir Thomas Chapman had left his wife and four daughters to live with her.) "Mrs. Lawrence" had had a strict Calvinist upbringing and became so overwhelmed by her sense of sin and guilt that she strove for atonement in the only way her background allowed—by extremities of religious devotion, including attempts to make her children intensely religious. T.E. was profoundly—but negatively—affected, something we may see, in Shavian exaggeration, in the evangelical passion of the lengthy oration with which Aubrey ends the play. Seeking affirmations to preach, in his deep disillusion he is unable to find them. It is possibly an ironic pun that Aubrey's postwar existence has been that of confidence man. "I shall spend another six years on the make," he tells his father, "and then I shall retire and be a saint." The mood and the terminology, incidentally, seem like parodies of Lawrence's repeated references to his diminishing term of enlistment, his retirement, and his proposed withdrawal from active life.

Too True to Be Good becomes, then, more than a discreet probing into the motives for Lawrence's behavior disguised slyly as a caricature of his "Private Shaw" side. It is a play, G.B.S. warns, about living precariously in a world in which the comfortable old values have been rendered obsolete by wars past and—prophetically—future. And there is more than a little of G.B.S. himself in Aubrey, who has a compulsion to "preach and preach and preach." Yet because we appreciate the play as comedy or as polemic, we lose sight of the fact that one of the most enigmatic personalities of our century is partly hidden in it—hidden, oddly enough, because he is also so obvious in another role. Lawrence may have been Shaw's other Saint Joan, but he was also the split personality divided into Aubrey and Meek.

Notes

1. All G.B.S. letters are from *Collected Letters 1900–1925*, ed. Dan H. Laurence (New York: Viking, 1985) unless noted otherwise.

2. For details of the Shaw-"Shaw" relationship from 1922 until T.E.'s death in 1935, see my *Private Shaw and Public Shaw* (New York: George Braziller; London: Jonathan Cape, 1963). The fullest account of Lawrence in his "Private Shaw" years is H. Montgomery Hyde's *Solitary in the Ranks: Lawrence of Arabia as Airman and Private Soldier* (London: Constable, 1977). It adds nothing relevant to the record and has only two pages on *Too True to Be Good*, largely about T.E.'s reaction to a performance. Jeremy Wilson's "Authorized Biography"—authorized by A. W. Lawrence, T.E.'s last surviving brother, representing the T. E. Lawrence trustees, is *Lawrence of Arabia* (London: Heinemann, 1989; New York: Atheneum, 1990). It has a paragraph on *Too True*, in which T.E. "amused himself suggesting the kind of things that Meek might have said to his superiors."

3. Lady Gregory's geography was erratic.

4. Lennox Robinson, ed., *Lady Gregory's Journals 1916–1930* (New York: Macmillan, 1947), pp. 192, 193–94.

5. Johan Huizinga, *Men & Ideas* (New York: Doubleday, 1959), esp. pp. 218–19.

6. Shaw, Preface to *Saint Joan*.

7. Lawrence to Lionel Curtis, 14 May 1923, in David Garnett, ed., *The Letters of T. E. Lawrence* (London: Jonathan Cape, 1938), p. 416.

8. Shaw, Preface to *Catalogue of an Exhibition of Paintings, Pastels, Drawings and Woodcuts Illustrating Col. T. E. Lawrence's book "Seven Pillars of Wisdom"* (London: Ernest Brown & Phillips, The Leicester Galleries, 1927), pp. 7–13.

9. Shaw, *Exhibition Catalogue*.

10. Clare Sydney Smith, *The Golden Reign* (London: Cassell, 1940), p. 109.

11. E. M. Forster, *Abinger Harvest* (New York: Harcourt, Brace, 1936), p. 146.

12. R. F. Dietrich, "Shaw and the Passionate Mind," *Shaw Review* 4 (May 1961): 9.

SHAW'S OTHER KEEGAN

Sean O'Casey and G.B.S.

In November 1919 Shaw received yet another request to write a preface to someone else's manuscript. His policy on such appeals from aspiring authors was clear, and he would eventually prepare a printed postcard that would inform disappointed applicants that they could not count upon an introduction by G.B.S. to boom their work. The newest entreaty came from an unknown writer in Dublin who was aware of Shaw's wartime writings on Irish questions and had put together a book of his own—*Three Shouts on a Hill*, on Irish labor, nationalism, and the Gaelic language—from articles he had produced for the *Irish Worker* and *Irish Opinion*.

Shaw had no idea that the "Shaun O'Casey" who signed the letter was an impecunious, self-taught union organizer and journalist already nearly forty. His kind response, nevertheless declining to write still another preface, suggested that he thought he was dealing with an earnest young man.

"I like the foreword and afterword much better," Shaw began, "than the shouts, which are prodigiously overwritten." Like other writers who wanted a Shavian preface to help get a book published, O'Casey received instead more questions than answers. Shaw wondered why O'Casey appeared ambiguous on labor issues and was impractical enough a nationalist to come out against the English language. "You ought to work out your position positively & definitely," he advised. "This objecting to everyone else is Irish, but useless." Besides, it was "out of the question" for O'Casey to assume that a preface by an established author would advance him as a writer. "You must go through the mill like the rest and get published for your own sake, not for mine."[1] Although O'Casey would carry the letter in his wallet for years, until it was frayed and cracked at the creases, the relationship appeared unlikely to prosper.

Shaw went on to produce *Heartbreak House*, which he had completed during the war, and to write his play cycle *Back to Methuselah* as well as *Saint Joan* before hearing of O'Casey again. Meanwhile O'Casey had been reading Shaw's plays as they were published and was now writing some of his own, offering them to a cautious Abbey Theatre management. The first three scripts, politely turned down, included *The Crimson in the Tri-Colour*, which Lady Gregory in November 1921 found "extremely interesting" but "disagreeable." Yeats proved "down on it," leaving no chance for O'Casey to bargain the play into production via revision.[2] It was, he recalled to Jack Carney twenty years later, "really 'a play of ideas' moulded on Shaw's style. It had a character posed on A[rthur] Griffith, a Labour Leader, mean & despicable, posed on whomsoever you can guess, & the 'noble proletarian' in it was later 'The Covey' in the 'Plough and the Stars,' as was a carpenter who developed into 'Fluther' " (28 March 1942).

Eventually O'Casey's stylistic exuberance and colorful characterization would win over Lady Gregory's colleagues Lennox Robinson and W. B. Yeats, and by 1924 the Abbey had produced three, increasingly longer, O'Casey plays: *Kathleen Listens In*, *Shadow of a Gunman*, and *Juno and the Paycock*. He hoped, O'Casey wrote Lady Gregory, with whom he discussed Shaw's and Mark Twain's versions of *Saint Joan* (Mark Twain's was a "supplement"), that Eamon de Valera would read *Back to Methuselah* and acquire broader vision. It was already clear from the published text of *Shadow of a Gunman* that year that O'Casey had also been reading the earlier Shaw. The self-styled "poet and poltroon" Donal Davoren, the first page of stage directions declares, has been "handicapped by an inherited self-developed devotion to 'the might of design, the mystery of colour, and the redemption of all things by beauty everlasting.' " O'Casey was quoting from the deathbed credo of Shaw's rogue artist Louis Dubedat in *The Doctor's Dilemma*, and Davoren's romantic idealism provides an ironic contrast to the amoral, courageous Dubedat. G.B.S., O'Casey confided to Mrs. Shaw years later, had been his "anamchara—soul-friend—as we say in Ireland" for many years before he "met him in the flesh."

That March, when *Juno and the Paycock* opened at the Abbey, gripping its audiences and turning O'Casey into a local hero, veteran playgoer Joseph Holloway had a chat with the new playwright in the theater vestibule. "He told me," Holloway noted in his diary, "that when he started to write plays he thought he was a second Shaw sent to express his views through his characters, and was conceited enough to think that his opinions were the only ones that mattered. It was Lady Gregory who advised him to cut out all expressions of self, and develop his peculiar aptness for character drawing."³ O'Casey was rarely able to eliminate himself from the dialogue of his characters. The indebtedness to Shaw would be emerging in more ways than this misunderstanding of Shavian dialogue (based so much on debating technique), where even the Devil in *Don Juan in Hell*—or the Inquisitor in *Joan*—has to be given persuasive lines.

O'Casey's intentions may have been otherwise, but Juno herself is, in a number of her appeals, reading an O'Casey editorial, however eloquent. Yet echoes from Shaw were more apparent in *Juno and the Paycock* in the "paycock" figure of Captain Boyle, who may be O'Casey's genial parody of *Heartbreak House*'s Captain Shotover, the aged and philosophic retired seaman who warns mankind of impending apocalypse. In *Juno* the dark vision is reduced to absurdity in Boyle's repeated declarations that "the whole worl's in a state o' chassis!" And Shotover's nostalgic recollections of living to the fullest demands of body and spirit, as opposed to the softness he sees in the younger generation, are again turned to absurdity by the lazy and unemployable Jacky Boyle and Joxer Daly, his parasite. "I was ten times happier on the bridge in the typhoon, or frozen into Arctic ice for months in darkness," Shaw's seafaring patriarch tells young Ellie Dunn. "At your age I looked for hardship, danger, horror, and death, that I might feel the life in me more intensely. I did not let the fear of death govern my life; and my reward was, I had my life."⁴ Boyle, his wife Juno observes, had earned his "Captain" designation the easier way. He was only in the water "in an oul' collier from here to Liverpool, when anybody, to listen or look at you, ud take you for a second Christo For Columbus!" The sarcasm is quickly forgotten by Joxer and Boyle. Joxer recalls the "young days when you were steppin' the deck of a manly ship, with the win' blowin' a hurricane through the masts, an' the only sound you'd hear was 'Port your helm!' an' the only answer, 'Port it is, sir!' "

"Them was days, Joxer," says the Captain. "Nothin' was too hot or heavy for me then. Sailin' from the Gulf of Mexico to the Antanartic Ocean. . . . Ofen, an' ofen, when I was fixed to the wheel with a marlin-spike, an' the win's blowin' fierce an' the waves lashin' an' lashin', til you'd think every minute was goin' to be your last, an' it blowed, an' blowed—blew is the right word, Joxer, but blowed is what the sailors use. . . ."

For an audience familiar with *Heartbreak House*, the shiftless braggart Captain Boyle may have been meant to have special irony, reinforced when we recall that Shotover's "seventh degree of concentration" can be reached at his age only with the aid of rum. Jacky Boyle prefers to induce forgetfulness (rather than perception) with whiskey, and in the last scene, drunk, he mumbles something about "Irelan' sober . . . is Irelan' free" and recalls only that the world remains "in a terr . . . ible state o' . . . chassis!" The desolated flat that Juno and Boyle have occupied is O'Casey's first Irish version of Heartbreak House.*

In Boyle's romanticizing of tawdry reality—his philosophy as well as his religion come to him in a bottle—can be seen the symptoms identified in Larry Doyle's lament in *John Bull's Other Island*, that gentle satire of Irish ways apparently interpreted more harshly by O'Casey in play after play. "Oh, the dreaming! the dreaming!" Doyle observes,

> the torturing, heart-scalding, never satisfying dreaming, dreaming, dreaming, dreaming! No debauchery that ever coarsened and brutalized an Englishman can take the worth and usefulness out of him like that dreaming. An Irishman's imagination never lets him alone, never convinces him, never satisfies him; but it makes him [so] that he cant face reality nor deal with it nor handle it nor conquer it; he can only sneer at them that do, and be 'agreeable to strangers,' like a good-for-nothing woman of the streets. It's all dreaming, all imagination. He cant be religious. The inspired Churchman that teaches him the sanctity of life and the importance of conduct is sent away empty; while the poor village priest that gives him a miracle of a sentimental story of a saint, has cathedrals built for him out of the pennies of the poor. He cant be intelligently political; he dreams of what the Shan Van Vocht said in ninetyeight. If you want to interest him in Ireland you've got to call the unfortunate island Kathleen ni Houlihan and pretend she's a little old woman. It saves thinking. It saves working. It saves everything except imagination, imagination, imagination; and imagination's such a torture that you cant bear it without whisky.

In O'Casey's *The Plough and the Stars*, produced at the Abbey in 1926, we are reminded of the sardonic thrusts of *Major Barbara*. "I am rather interested in the Salvation Army," says Barbara's father, the armaments

---

*Later O'Casey would insist that *Heartbreak House* was Shaw's finest play, once arguing the point with Charlotte Shaw, who stood by *Saint Joan* (*Autobiographies*, 6: 248).

manufacturer Andrew Undershaft. "Its motto might be my own: Blood and Fire." Shocked, one of his prospective sons-in-law insists that it could not be "your sort of blood and fire, you know." "My sort of blood cleanses," insists Undershaft, and "my sort of fire purifies."

O'Casey's play invokes the Irish Citizen Army, not the Salvation Army, when the shadowy figure of one of its ruthless officers is silhouetted and heard through the pub window. "It is a glorious thing to see arms in the hands of Irishmen," he exhorts the unseen crowd. "Bloodshed is a cleansing and sanctifying thing, and the nation that regards it as the final horror has lost its manhood. . . ."

Fluther's sentiments in the play, says critic Saros Cowasjee, have the ring of Shaw. "Fight fair!" Fluther asks about the Easter rising. "A few hundhreds scrawls o' chaps with a couple of guns an' Rosary beads, again' a hundhred thousand thrained men with horse, fut, an' artillery . . . an' he wants us to fight fair! [To Sergeant] D'ye want us to come out in our skins an' throw stones?" Shaw, Cowasjee reminds us, had published a protest against the British executions in May 1916, observing that the rebellion "was a fair fight in everything except the enormous odds my countrymen had to face."[5]

Although it would have been poor strategy for O'Casey to point to these apparent echoes of Shaw—even if he recognized them himself—he would, nevertheless, mention G.B.S. when precedents or examples were useful. When Lennox Robinson, then running the Abbey, objected, on behalf of actress Eileen Crowe, to allegedly indelicate language in *The Plough and the Stars*, O'Casey pointed out that Shaw had used "bastard" in *The Devil's Disciple*, which the Abbey had produced six years earlier. It was not Miss Crowe's only objection, and when she refused to speak her lines as written, she was replaced. O'Casey would have increasing difficulty with Irish prudes as well as with Irish patriots. The patriots, of course, objected to everything in *The Plough*, and in a letter to the *Irish Independent* the playwright again invoked the name of Shaw, who, he said, hated patriotic sham, pointing to the description of the supposedly heroic cavalry charge in *Arms and the Man* as "slinging a handful of peas against a window-pane."[6]

The author of *Gunman*, *Juno*, and *Plough* had read and seen all the Shaw he could find in Dublin but almost certainly thought that the only indebtedness to Shaw in his plays was his deliberate quotation from *The Doctor's Dilemma*. Irish productions of Shaw in the mid-1920s included *Saint Joan* and *Man and Superman*, both of which O'Casey attended. The *Man and Superman* presentation, he thought, was bad indeed, "a helter-skelter performance" in which "all the actors were subdued by the relentless enthusiasm" of F. J. McCormick, who played John Tanner. Thinking innocently that with the successes of his plays at the Abbey he was "among old friends," he spoke his mind. The reaction was a choked hush. Then McCormick, who had overheard, pushed close to O'Casey and warned, "I hear you've been criticising our rendering of Shaw's play. You've got a bit of a name now, and you must not say these things about an Abbey production. If you do, we'll have to report it to the directors; so try to keep your mouth shut."

O'Casey was bewildered by the crude blast but went home and naively wrote a long letter to the play's director, Michael J. Dolan, pointing out the flaws he thought he saw in the production, adding that the letter might be utilized in any way that could be helpful. "It's just like Sean," said Lennox Robinson. When the letter was posted on the Abbey's notice board, it ended O'Casey's access backstage. The next time he came by, Sean Barlow, a property man, asked what he was doing there. He was on his way to the Green Room, O'Casey explained. "There's none but the actors and officials allowed on the stage," said Barlow, "and we'd be glad if you came this way no more."

By the time O'Casey's next dispute with the Abbey and its public erupted, he was living in London, deliberately keeping his distance; and he had met Shaw, whose aid he soon needed in person. Shaw, in fact, seeing that O'Casey needed funds, quickly introduced him to Ivor Montagu, who was eager, G.B.S. said, to "experiment" on *Juno and the Paycock* as a film, and had his father's money to bankroll him. In the end it was Alfred Hitchcock who did the film—a reel of which was publicly burnt in the streets of Limerick in 1930. It did not solve O'Casey's chronic financial problems, which would be compounded by each new play. In the dispute over *The Silver Tassie*, Shaw would put in more writing time than any preface for another author would ever cost him.

O'Casey's struggle with the Abbey management over *The Silver Tassie* in 1928 permanently embittered the playwright's relations with the theater that most needed him, confirmed his estrangement from the soil that had inspired him, and left him without a regular audience or theater for his work thereafter. Shaw would not only come to his defense but help him find a producer in London.

O'Casey had sent a copy of the play to Shaw, who answered through Charlotte that both had read *The Silver Tassie* with *"deep interest"* and enthusiasm and wanted to have both Sean and Eileen to lunch to talk about it. As Shaw himself put it to O'Casey in a separate letter before the luncheon at Whitehall Court, "What a hell of a play! I wonder how it will hit the public." By then he knew how it had hit the directors of the Abbey. W. B. Yeats, Shaw explained, was "not a man of this world; and when you hurl an enormous smashing chunk of it at him he dodges it. . . ." Yeats had hectored O'Casey on writing about the Great War (in which neither had participated) rather than the Irish struggle, "You never stood on its battlefields or walked its hospitals and so write [entirely] out of your opinions." "Was Shakespeare at Actium or Philippi?" O'Casey had countered. "Was G. B. Shaw in the boats with the French, or in the forts with the British when St. Joan and Dunois made the attack that relieved Orleans?"

To Lady Gregory, with whom Shaw interceded, the author of *Saint Joan* wrote that Yeats "should have submitted" to *The Silver Tassie* "as a calamity imposed on him by the Act of God, if he could not welcome it as another *Juno*." But the elderly Lady Gregory, who, Shaw told O'Casey, was really on his side, was in no position to countermand Yeats, Walter Starkie, and Lennox Robinson. "Playwriting," Shaw explained in a note on the back of another of O'Casey's letters, "is a desperate trade."

Despite the uproar, which had resulted in newspaper editorials and letters to the editor, Macmillan was willing to take its chances on publishing the play, and O'Casey secured Shaw's permission to use portions of his "hell of a play" letter on the jacket of the book—an unusual gesture for G.B.S. O'Casey then attempted to use the quotation further, for a critic in the *Irish News* of Belfast had attacked the play he had not seen by observing, confidently, "Bernard Shaw would never have put his name to *The Silver Tassie*." But in effect Shaw had, came the O'Casey rejoinder, and he quoted the "hell of a play" paragraph from Shaw's letter. On 7 July the paper, staunchly Roman Catholic and nationalist, reported receipt of the letter and its inability to print it "unamended." There was a censorable word in the quotation from G.B.S., which the *News* took as another example of O'Casey's bad taste.

Hearing softened words from Yeats and Robinson, who needed a palatable O'Casey, Shaw urged conciliation, which O'Casey saw as impossible. The Abbey management, he insisted, had "turned a Playhouse into a silly little temple, darkened with figures past vitality. . . ." By this time Eileen was in contact with Charlotte Shaw, who agreed with her that it was a period when Sean "wants a lot of looking after" and offered G.B.S. as intermediary wherever useful. But Shaw's advice was not always heeded. After C. B. Cochran had lost money on a splendidly mounted production of *The Silver Tassie* and had warned O'Casey in Shavian fashion that he needed to write things that were not only fine but had some expectation of "material reward," O'Casey turned to political plays with no chance of commercial success and to a story that the English printer considered too immoral to set in type.

To Cochran, Shaw suggested that he had earned a place in a producer's Valhalla. The play would pass "into the classical repertory," he wrote, "and it was a magnificent gesture of yours to produce it. The Highbrows *should* have produced it: you, the Unpretentious Showman, *did*, as you have done so many other noble and rash things. . . . If only someone would build you a huge Woolworth theatre (all seats sixpence) to start with O'Casey and O'Neill, and no plays by men who have ever seen a five-pound note before they were thirty or been inside a school after they were thirteen, you would be buried in Westminster Abbey." The criteria did not quite fit G.B.S. himself, yet it came close.

In 1932 Yeats decided that Ireland needed its own academy of letters and induced Shaw to become its first president (with Yeats himself as vice president). The first thirty-five writers invited to become founding members included O'Casey. But they also included, obviously, Yeats as well as the Abbey's impresario, Lennox Robinson. Bitter at the Abbey's treatment of him, for which he blamed Yeats, O'Casey found reasons to refuse admission, pointing to the dangers of implicit censorship through the approval or disapproval of the academy. Besides, he added in a letter to the *Irish Times*, the whole idea was a "literary cocktail" rather than anything truly useful for Ireland. That he saw Yeats as the evil genius behind the academy, he made no attempt to hide. That the invitation to join came over Shaw's signature made it, O'Casey later wrote in his memoirs, "the hardest refusal he had ever had to face," the "one favour" Shaw had ever asked him. A letter of refusal was sent to Shaw, O'Casey recalled, "but no answer came back." No such letter has turned up. Perhaps O'Casey had let his public statements stand for him and only imagined the letter later. In any case, Shaw knew what it would have cost O'Casey's pride to join something that had been Yeats's brainchild.

That year O'Casey was slipping deeper into debt. His income from minor journalism was not supplementing his meager royalties enough to arrest the slide. While preparing the prompt copies of his plays for Samuel French he received an offer from the publisher to purchase half the amateur rights to *Gunman, Juno*, and *Plough* for £300. He consulted Shaw, who warned him against the "absurdly bad bargain" and enclosed a loan of £100. "My advice," Shaw added, "is to let wife and child perish, and lay bricks for your

Fig. 14. Shaw and the self-exiled Sean O'Casey in the early 1930s. Courtesy the late Eileen O'Casey.

last crust, sooner than part with an iota of your rights." O'Casey needed more than that but was reluctant to ask Shaw, who at about the same time was extricating his old friends Sidney and Beatrice Webb from assorted difficulties with a check for £1,000. O'Casey signed away his rights to French, only to discover later that the publisher was holding £350 in royalties for him, claiming that they had been unable at the time to locate his address. At least once Shaw would complain that O'Casey had repaid a loan, calling the gesture "Swank" in hopes the label would keep further repayments from occurring. "This is," Shaw insisted, "an improvident, extravagant . . . and entirely unnecessary proceeding, most inconsiderate to your wife and children."[7]

A rare opportunity for reciprocity came to O'Casey in the early 1930s. To

Charlotte he had described Shaw's *Too True to Be Good* as a "rare title" and a "terrible [meaning terrifying] philosophy," and in the *Listener* he wrote a long review of *Too True* and *On the Rocks*, Shaw's next political-prophetic play. *Saint Joan*, he wrote, was easier to take, "like an illuminated Book of Hours that one can finger and fondle, and be amused by the quaint pictures, thanking God all the time that we are not as other men were." On the other hand, Shaw's apocalyptic plays set in the near present were "flames of courageous thought which some day, sooner or later, will burn to ashes the hay, straw, and stubble of god mercy and truth and righteousness and peace that find their vent in the singing of hymns, piling of law upon law, and the pampering of the useless and the unfit."[8] But O'Casey was not merely championing Shaw, he was pointing implicitly to his own increasingly uncommercial playwriting perspectives—visions of apocalypse in the present.

Within the Gates, an example of O'Casey's current method, had opened a month before his essay had appeared, and the playwright had brought Shaw to sit with him at the Royalty Theatre on opening night. The play, however, needed more than that. An essentially plotless, poetic, sentimental denunciation of hypocrisy and misery, it was Strindberg's *Dream Play* set in Hyde Park and peopled with contemporary types. What the public wanted was another *Juno* or *Plough*—Hibernian poetic realism rather than Strindbergian dream visions. He was not about to turn back, instead telling Shaw that he should write a play about the rebellion of Jack Cade. Shaw "could make a Communist St. Joan of him." O'Casey, rather, would begin a new symbolic play, *The Star Turns Red*, which would have no chance of either critical or commercial success. Having read it, Shaw found that a good reason to stay away from the opening, writing O'Casey afterward that the bad press "shewed up the illiteracy of the critics."

With little hope of burgeoning play royalties and with work on his "semi-autobiography" going slowly, O'Casey lived frugally and in debt. With his children growing into school age, he and Eileen warmed to Shaw's suggestion that living away from the London area could be both inexpensive and valuable for schooling, especially if the O'Caseys could find a place near the modern Dartington Hall School in Devon.[9] A spacious Victorian house in Totnes was available at £85 a year, very little by London standards, but the landlord (a dentist), seeing O'Casey and his brood, asked for a co-signer of the lease to guarantee his rent.

Not wanting to bother G.B.S. directly, O'Casey asked Charlotte, who invited him to the Whitehall Court flat to talk about it over lunch.

Businesslike, she asked about the house, the rates, and whether O'Casey was working on anything remunerative. O'Casey flushed at the means test, and G.B.S. barked, "Oh, give it to him!" The questioning halted, and everything seemed settled, but the landlord refused to accept a woman—even a millionairess—as guarantor. G.B.S. quickly obliged, writing O'Casey on 17 October 1938, "Your landlord, being a dentist, has developed an extractor complex. He proposed a lease in which I was not only to guarantee all your covenants, but indemnify him for all consequences." Since Shaw loved haggling over contracts and vetting other people's legal documents, nothing could have made him happier. "I said," Shaw told O'Casey, "[that] I did not know his character, but knew enough of yours to know that the consequences might include anything from murder to a European war: so I re-drafted the agreement. The lawyers, knowing that their man was only too lucky to get a gilt-edged (so they thought) security, and that his demands were absurd, made no resistance."

To Charlotte Shaw (G.B.S. was difficult to thank so directly) O'Casey wrote that he indeed needed the financial guarantee but—he took Shaw's joking remark literally—"I'm not going to ask anyone to guarantee my morals." Then he added, documenting what must have been the beginning of the Shavian impact upon him, "I have always had to fight like the devil for life; but you must blame your husband, G.B.S., for whatever sharpness and wit that have come into my fighting qualities; and [as well] my young Dublin comrade, member of the Fourth Order of Saint Francis, who first put the green-covered copy of *John Bull's Other Island* in my then reluctant hand."

"Read *John Bull's Other Island*," Kevin O'Loughlin had promised, "and the Ireland you think you know and love will vanish before your eyes."

"Well, that's a damn fine recommendation!" O'Casey had said skeptically, but when payday came, he had gone to Jason's bookshop and purchased the six-penny paper edition. By the time of his letter to Charlotte, *John Bull* had taken on an almost metaphorical quality to him.

By then, too, O'Casey was again a father (Shaw sent the infant Shivaun fifty pounds) and working on a play that he hoped would combine what he wanted to do with what he hoped the public would accept. The result was the comic fantasy *Purple Dust*, a try at social criticism through a symbolic decaying country house and characters who might have come out of *Heartbreak House*. Saros Cowasjee, rather, sees a bond between *Purple Dust* and the play that had first turned O'Casey to Shaw a generation earlier. Still, as Cowasjee observes, Shaw had probed deeply into both Irish and

English psyches, while O'Casey, who lived largely self-insulated from his surroundings, was unable to see profoundly into the English milieu. Shaw's characters can be absurd without being puppets or fools. In *Purple Dust*, O'Casey did not get beyond being cantankerous and colorful, but whether or not his inspiration had been *John Bull* or *Heartbreak House*, the result was one of his rare later plays that had some box-office success in his lifetime.

There are close resemblances in structure as well as theme to *John Bull's Other Island*, as Ronald Rollins notes. Both comedies utilize the device of English expeditions to a backward Ireland, a portion of which they propose to rehabilitate, and both expose fraudulent sentiment, spiritual torpidity, paralyzing class antagonisms, and consequent economic stagnation. "Excessive, neurotic fascination with imaginative splendors and/or glories of the past makes people, so Shaw and O'Casey suggest, inept participants in the present, rendering them victims and enemies of change, innovation, and progress."[10]

John Bull's Other Island reverberates through O'Casey's plays, although perhaps nowhere so much as in *Purple Dust*. Larry Doyle's penetrating analysis in *John Bull* of the Irishman's dreaming imagination, which "never lets him alone," permeates O'Casey's characters from Donal Davoren to the Irish dreamers of *Purple Dust*; and Cowasjee sees in both *John Bull* and *Purple Dust* the same portrayal of the "irresponsibility of the Irish, their sense of humor, their pride, their flattery of the English, the poetic brilliance of their speech and their queer love-making. . . ." The apocalyptic ending, however—a flood rather than a bombing—echoes *Heartbreak House*, and the warnings of imminent catastrophe are reminiscent of the prophecies of Shotover and Hector (and even echo the spoof of English respectability in *Caesar and Cleopatra*, about the dying of their bodies blue by Britannus and his confreres, so that even when stripped of their clothes they could not be robbed of their respectability). Says Philib O'Dempsey (the 2nd Workman) of the English interlopers for whom he must work at reclaiming a dilapidated mansion on the edge of a river that regularly overflows its banks, "Hammerin' out handsome golden ornaments for flowin' cloak and tidy tunic we were, while you were busy gatherin' dhried grass, and dyin' it blue, to hide the consternation of your middle parts; decoratin' eminent books with glowin' colour an' audacious beauty were we . . . when you were still a hundred score o' years away from even hearin' of the alphabet. Fool? It's yourself's the fool, I'm sayin', settlin' down in a place that's only fit for the housin' o' dead men! . . . Wait till God sends the heavy rain, and the floods come!"

Later O'Casey would describe *Purple Dust* in *Heartbreak House* terms as without partisan politics—not an attack on England, "not even on any particular class in the country. . . . It is to some extent, a symbolic play, and unconsciously, a prophetic one too. The auld hoose, beloved by so many for so long, is in a bad way; old things are passing away, and new things are appearing in the sky, on the horizon, and right here in the middle of us. The house is falling, and we hardly know where to pick up the bits."

The move to Devon, prompted by Shaw, would prove to have the drawback for O'Casey that he was no longer in easy visiting distance.

"Sean missed him exceedingly," Eileen O'Casey remembered, for the war years, then beginning, were years of decreased mobility because of wartime restrictions and O'Casey's increasingly failing eyesight. It would have been such a help, Eileen thought, if her husband "could have talked to somebody who really loved the theatre and who was in harmony with him." It was time, Shaw wrote O'Casey in 1943, that he produced a "money-spinner"; but written exhortations were the best that Shaw could do at eighty-seven, worn down himself with age and with care for Charlotte, who had died that year of a crippling bone ailment. O'Casey had received letters from Shaw just before Charlotte's death, he told Gabriel Fallon (3 April 1945), "saying 'we are terribly lonely, & feel damnably old.' " As for money-spinners, O'Casey would write three volumes of what he would describe to Shaw, early in 1945, as "semi-biography." They would make up financially for the poor box office of such new plays as *Oak Leaves and Lavender*.

Loyally, in his fashion, O'Casey would refuse requests to write puffery for ninetieth-birthday volumes planned for Shaw, which smacked of publishers' profit scheming to him. "If an article would lift 50 years off the 90," he assured G.B.S., "I'd do it quick." Beset by depression after Charlotte's passing and by an avalanche of mail in anticipation of the birthday, Shaw failed to respond to half a dozen O'Casey letters, and Sean wondered to George Jean Nathan whether he had said anything in the autobiographical books to offend. Finally, in 1948, there was a postcard. O'Casey had found the sure way to provoke one, asking Shaw to write a preface to an IRA memoir by Tom Barry, *Guerilla Days in Ireland*. He knew Shaw's attitude on prefaces. "So the postcard came," O'Casey wrote to Nathan, "saying he had written to the IRA author setting down reasons for refusal."

Shaw was writing fewer and fewer letters, which O'Casey blamed, in his own case, on Fritz Loewenstein, who had insinuated himself into Shaw's confidence and become his anointed bibliographer. He was really Shaw's "Iron Curtain," O'Casey told Nathan. Loewenstein "calls himself Shaw's

Bibliographer and Remembrancer," O'Casey noted, seeing the role as evidence of Shaw's weakness for self-publicity—something to which he also attributed Shaw's interest in photography, especially in pictures of himself. Yet soon O'Casey was writing to his publisher, Daniel Macmillan, about his friend Francis McCarthy, who had been a sergeant on a troopship torpedoed in the Pacific by the Japanese. "He floated about for 26 hours before they picked him up, & sent him to Japan, where he was a prisoner until the war ended. He saved nothing but a photograph of Bernard Shaw that he had in an oilskin cover lying on his chest, & tied around his neck. A curious scapular!"

A variety of ailments, from heart trouble to near blindness, kept O'Casey at home in Devon, but at G.B.S.'s invitation, Eileen went to Ayot St. Lawrence early in 1950 to have tea with him. As the link between the two frail old Irishmen, Eileen did her job well, but pride would prevent her from doing what was clearly in the back of Shaw's mind. He would get no hint from her of the state of the O'Casey finances. "The old warrior," Sean reported to Nathan, "is as alive as ever; still gets indignant at stupidity; still has his cascading laugh: and takes an hour's walk every day in the garden, whatever the weather. And him goin' on for 94!" Shaw had greeted Mrs. O'Casey with, "Well, Eileen, you've still got your good looks." Irish diplomat John Dulanty, the friend who had driven Eileen to Ayot, recalled in a note on the meeting, "I wandered out of the room to give them the opportunity of a mild flirtation."

The revival of the relationship continued. Eileen had brought to Ayot a picture of the O'Casey family, and Shaw wrote that he had hung it on his wall. O'Casey was pleased and proud. In May 1950 Shaw told him that Irish Catholics were still sending him "medals of the Blessed Virgin, guaranteeing, if I say a novena, that she will give me anything I ask from her, to which I reply that the B V needs helpers and not beggars." While over the years Shaw had been generous in many ways to the O'Casey family, Sean himself had never begged anything after the abortive request for a preface but the lease guarantee, which had cost G.B.S. nothing more than his signature. The genteel poverty in which the O'Caseys were surviving in Devon was something Shaw never realized, and in the immediate postwar years, when the self-styled Green Crow seemed to be turning out plays and polemics with regularity, Shaw had assumed the best, although O'Casey's cranky new comedies made little money. He would never find out otherwise.

After Shaw's fall at Ayot in September 1950, in which he broke a hip and became bedridden in his final months, Dulanty and Eileen returned at their first opportunity to see Shaw. It was October, and Shaw was frail and clearly failing, "caged now," as O'Casey would write, "in his own home." Privately, to Dulanty, Shaw asked how the O'Caseys were doing, and Dulanty confided that he did not think they were "all that good." When Shaw told him that he had heard, rather, that they were "in clover," Dulanty urged Eileen to tell him the truth. Afterward, as Shaw and Eileen talked of the children and the daily lives of the family, Shaw suddenly asked, "And how is Sean financially?" Unwilling to be a supplicant, she replied, as she recalls in her memoir, *Sean*, "Of course, we are perfectly all right." (Shaw "said he had heard we were in clover, and was relieved about it.") He went on to talk of his loneliness after the passing of so many friends and contemporaries, and Eileen felt that it was time to return to London, where she had been staying. It was the O'Caseys' last chance to be remembered in his will, and it had passed by. *

A few days later Shaw asked to see her. He opened his eyes when she walked in and said faintly, "I really think I am going to die." His musical voice, weakened to a whisper, was still clear. He was ready to go, he announced, for he was tired of dependence and especially disliked having to be minded by people he did not know. He had willed his death, he said. "I want to go now; it is better to go now. It'll be interesting, anyway," he suggested, smiling, "to meet the Almighty."

"I'm sure," said Eileen, "that the two of you will get on splendidly together."

"I'll have a helluva lot of questions to ask Him," said Shaw.

"Take it calmly till Sean gets there, and then you can start a row."

"I'll find it hard to take it calmly, for I've always been a fighter."

He asked her to stroke his forehead, and—according to Sean—"he murmured that it was fine to feel the touch of a soft Irish hand & hear the soft sound of an Irish voice." When he fell asleep, Eileen strode out, but within ten minutes the sickroom bell rang. Shaw wanted to see Eileen again, to say good-bye. "I'm finished," he said, "and now it's up to Sean."

"No," she said, frankly, realizing that O'Casey was seventy and nearly sightless, "Sean is too old." At his request she kissed him good-bye, and he sank back into sleep. He died two days later, on 2 November 1950. O'Casey's

---

*Later, O'Casey, on his own deathbed in 1964, wept to Eileen that he was leaving her nearly penniless. "You could have married a millionaire," he said, remembering what a beauty she had been when he, at forty-seven, had married her thirty-seven years earlier. "If you hurry up," said Eileen gently, "I still can."

tribute "to a Fighting Idealist" appeared in the first *New York Times Book Review* issue to be printed after Shaw's death.

In *Sunset and Evening Star* (1954), the sixth and last volume of his autobiographies, O'Casey would publish a long chapter he titled "Shaw's Corner," lovingly detailing his relationship with G.B.S. (Yet O'Casey had never been to "Shaw's Corner"—in Ayot St. Lawrence—having visited the Shaws only in London.) No one has been more eloquent or more persuasive about the poetic element in Shaw's plays (so often labeled as nonexistent). O'Casey saw poetry not only in Shaw's prose but in the Shavian theatrical imagination:

> Some critics say there is no poetry in Shaw's plays (how often have the Dublin bravos signed this in the air with a sawing hand!); and no emotion. There is poetry in the very description of the Syrian sky at the opening of *Caesar and Cleopatra*, in the way the Bucina calls, in the two great figures dwarfed between the paws of the Sphinx, in the rush of the Roman Legion into the Palace, halting to cry Hail, Caesar, when they see him sitting alone with the Queen of Egypt; poetry, and emotion, too. There is poetry and fine emotion in the scene on the banks of the Loire in the play of *Saint Joan*, and in the Saint's sorrow when she sees that while the world venerates her at a safe distance, the same world wants her no nearer; here is ironical emotion, shot with sadness stretching out to the day that is with us, for, with Christians now, it is not, Get thee behind me, Satan, but Get thee behind me, God. . . . There is poetry and emotion in *Candida*; poetry of a minor key in the way the doctors regard the thoughtlessness of the artist, Dubedat, rising into a major key at the death of the artist when the play is ending; it flashes through every scene of *Heartbreak House*; and stands dignified and alone in the character of Keegan in *John Bull's Other Island*; the poetry and emotion gleams out in the revelation that God is close to Feemy Evans, the fallen woman of the camp, though the respectable humbugs wouldn't let her finger-tip touch the bible. The English critics are afraid to feel: Eton and Harrow seem to have groomed them against the destitute dignity of tears. . . .

O'Casey had been writing his memoirs since the early 1930s, and the third, *Drums under the Windows* (for which he had designed his own jacket, with the figure on the left, looking over a toy-town Dublin, meant to be

Shaw),[11] had included nearly a dozen pages on the epiphany that was his encounter with *John Bull's Other Island*. "Near naked, Ireland stood, with the one jewel of [Father] Keegan's Dream occasionally seen sparkling in her tousled hair, attaching poverty to pride; a shameful figure, but noble still, though her story was hidden and her song unsung." The spurned O'Casey could identify readily with the reputedly mad, unfrocked Keegan, in O'Casey's words "banished from the altar, hinging himself more closely to his breviary than ever, torturing himself delightfully with the vision of a country where the state is the church and the church the people; three in one and one in three; where work is play and play is life; where the priest is the worshipper, and the worshipper the worshipped; three in one and one in three; carrying the vision around with him to pour it into the loneliness of a round tower: the dream of a madman, but the dream of an Irishman, too." In the mirror in O'Casey's house he could always confront the face of Father Keegan.

Notes

1. Shaw's letters are quoted from the notes to David Krause, ed., *The Letters of Sean O'Casey*, I: *1910–41* (London and New York: Macmillan, 1975); II: *1942–1954* (London and New York: Macmillan, 1980); and from Eileen O'Casey, *Sean* (New York: Macmillan, 1972). Mrs. O'Casey's *Cheerio Titan: The Friendship Between George Bernard Shaw and Eileen and Sean O'Casey* (New York: Scribner's, 1989) largely recycles previously published memories and letters.

2. David Krause, ed., *The Letters of Sean O'Casey*, I: 96, quoting Lady Gregory's analysis.

3. Robert Hogan and Michael J. O'Neill, *Joseph Holloway's Abbey Theatre* (Carbondale: Southern Illinois University Press, 1967), entry for 18 March 1924, p. 227.

4. Shaw's plays are quoted from *The Bodley Head Bernard Shaw: Collected Plays with Their Prefaces*, 7 vols. (London: Max Reinhardt, 1970–74). O'Casey's plays are quoted from *Selected Plays of Sean O'Casey* (New York: Braziller, 1954).

5. Saros Cowasjee, *Sean O'Casey: The Man Behind the Plays* (London: Oliver & Boyd, 1963), pp. 77–78.

6. O'Casey's letters are quoted from Krause.

7. Shaw to O'Casey, 4 July 1935, quoted in Sotheby catalogue of the 29–30 June 1982 sale, item 593, p. 252.

8. "G.B.S. Speaks Out of the Whirlwind," *Listener* (7 March 1934), Supplement III–IV.

9. Eileen's memories hereafter supplement the *Letters* and O'Casey's own autobiographies; *Mirror in My House* (New York: Macmillan, 1956).

10. Ronald G. Rollins, "Shaw and O'Casey: John Bull and His Other Island," *Shaw Review* 10: 2 (May 1967): 60–69.

11. Ronald Ayling and Michael J. Durkan, *Sean O'Casey: A Bibliography* (London: Macmillan, 1978), pp. 71–72.

Indulging the Insufferable

Shaw and Siegfried Trebitsch

In bad times, which became more and more frequent, and which he brought upon himself, Frank Harris turned to Shaw in whining, pleading, begging, cadging insufferability. Yet Shaw indulged him. One puzzles over Shaw's encouraging such unsavory specimens of humanity to exploit him, from the impossible poetess and harridan Erica Cotterill to the German propagandist and probable spy George Sylvester Viereck. And while they used him, Shaw both indulged and abused them, often enjoying the game, but sometimes paying a steep price for the dubious pleasure.

In no case was the cost heavier than in his cultivation of the Viennese writer Siegfried Trebitsch as his authorized German translator. From the beginning in 1902, Shaw realized that Trebitsch knew insufficient English, possessed—as an Austrian—the wrong German, and lacked the imagination and the verbal dexterity to metamorphose a work from one culture and language into another. Whatever Trebitsch's successes over nearly half a century, often due to Shaw's patient oversight and the theatrical invulnerability of his creations, Shaw's reputation in German-speaking Europe would have been far higher, and his European income far greater, had he jettisoned his translator. Instead, he patched up Trebitsch's blunders where possible and kept him on, much as he did Augustin Hamon in France. Hamon's only virtue to Shaw, since the translations were execrable and kept the plays from finding French audiences, was that he was a doctrinaire Socialist.

With Trebitsch was the bond any more than the indulgence of a curious old friend to whom Shaw felt bound by lingering loyalties? Was he ever really a friend? Siegfried Trebitsch was an unlovable, unemployable Viennese hack writer fortunate to have some small family income that he proceeded to dissipate by living above it. At the beginning he beguiled Shaw with his broken-English enthusiasm. Unfortunately, most of Trebitsch's letters are lost, but the impression we get from Shaw's responses is unmistakable. Trebitsch became another of Shaw's soured investments in people.

Trebitsch's early literary accomplishments were few, but he did go to London to seek out Shaw and win him over more by persistence than by a record of performance. In Shaw's Edwardian heyday, Trebitsch was already his translator. Forty years later he was just as bad a translator as he had been in the days of *John Bull's Other Island*. But one owes him at least the innocent honesty of having bearded Shaw about his Communist blindnesses at a time when idealists worldwide were seeing the new Russian leaders as saintly utopians. "I am your pupil," Trebitsch wrote to Shaw (11 October 1921) politely after the playwright had been explaining the greatness of Lenin and Trotsky. Trebitsch acknowledged that the Bolshevik leaders had "brains and sense and ability," but he confessed ungrammatically that he was still by no means convinced by Shaw's praise. "[P]lease answer one question," he said; "why do you not reply with one single word to my just accuse that they are the greatest murderers of the universe." Naively he concluded with the disarming concession, "We must have a serious conversation about this question as soon as we meet again; one of the great moments I am still expecting in my life."[1]

Such comments by Trebitsch give some idea of his persistently inept English, and some idea of the relationship between the two men. His problems with English were insoluble. Even after he had been at it for almost half a century, in a failed attempt at literalness he first translated Shaw's title *Farfetched Fables* as *Weltweite Fabeln* (Worldwide Fables). The nonagenarian G.B.S. duly corrected his elderly pupil's error, and that seems to be the principal theme of five decades of Shaw's letters to Trebitsch: correction of his translator's errors—and not only in translation, but in responding to criticism, in dealing with copyright and other literary business, and in keeping impertinent German and Austrian directors or managers in line when they wanted to alter Shaw's texts. The relationship between Shaw and Trebitsch is nicely suggested in a photograph showing Shaw confidently leaning against one side of the pedestal on which was Rodin's bust of him at Ayot St. Lawrence in 1925, and gazing down at the visiting Trebitsch, who is standing stiffly and awkwardly on the other side of the bust, looking up worshipfully at both incarnations of the master.

On a visit to London early in 1901, Trebitsch had met William Archer,

Fig. 15. Shaw and Siegfried Trebitsch at Ayot St. Lawrence in 1925, with Rodin's bust of G.B.S. between them. Adolf Scharf's photograph courtesy of Samuel A. Weiss.

then best known as translator of Ibsen. When Trebitsch confided his interest in translating Shaw, Archer arranged a meeting for Trebitsch's next stay in London. Returning in the autumn, he called at Adelphi Terrace and enthusiastically offered his exposition of Shaw's dozen plays. "Upon my word," he quoted Shaw as saying, "you have made a pretty thorough study of my works! And what is it you are really after? What do you mean to do with me?"

He was determined, Trebitsch said, to translate Shaw's plays into German. He had set himself "the aim of conquering the German stage" for Shaw.

Shaw jumped up and climbed the stairs to fetch Charlotte. Trebitsch heard him shout as he went, "Charlotte, here's a young lunatic Archer's sent me whom I won't be able to make see reason! You come and try to calm him down."

She listened to Trebitsch expound more Shaw, then turned to G.B.S. "He is quite right," she said. "Why should the German theatre, which has made Shakespeare into a German poet, not give you the satisfaction that is still denied you in your own country?"

"So you want to be my Schlegel and Tieck?" Shaw said. And the bargain was made, but Trebitsch would prove to have little in common with the classic translators of Shakespeare. Even his German was not much. After Shaw read the first few pages of a story in Trebitsch's *Weltuntergang* he wrote to Trebitsch (22 October 1902), "Why don't you write your stories in English—a much easier language?" But to master German prose, Shaw bought "a devil of a big dictionary, also a grammar." His German would soon be up to Trebitsch's English. In the interim, to get a feel for Trebitsch's language he read from it three times a week (18 November 1902) "with a Fräulein who acts as my dictionary." But Trebitsch's work "must be most scandalous," he suggested, as his Fräulein "refuses to translate most of it. . . . She blushes and says it is nur dumme Zeug;* and my wife tells me to go onto the next paragraph."

By early December Shaw was correcting Trebitsch's German version of *The Devil's Disciple*, in which he found (10 December 1902) "48 appalling errors and ruinous oversights." He suggested reading the translations ten times to circles of friends before going to the printer with the text. But Trebitsch had no such circles of friends.

As early as March 1903, the troublesome signals from Germany were clear. An article in the influential *Frankfurter Zeitung* by Leon Kellner, "Bernard Shaw: Eine Charakteristik," blamed the failure of the German production of *The Devil's Disciple, Teufelskerl*, on Trebitsch's incompetence. Trebitsch was angered and appalled. Shaw wrote back (31 March 1903), "A failure is half a success when it leaves a controversy behind. . . . Kellner writes and speaks English quite as well as you do, and probably a great deal better. . . . Now you are the sort of man that never masters a foreign language, and for the life of me I cannot understand how you have forced yourself to learn as much as you know."

If Shaw did not realize then that he needed to jettison Trebitsch, he should have concluded that after his translator published a rejoinder. Kellner's piece was "ausgezeichnetissimus"—superexcellent—Shaw insisted. Creating his own German, he chastised Trebitsch, "Your article is totally utterly, completely, ausserorderlicherly, insanely out of the question. To begin with, it is a defence of yourself; and you must NEVER defend

*only nonsense

yourself. Worse than that, you reply to a thrust clean through the body with a pin prick. . . . You mustnt pick up *little* stones to throw at your adversaries: they dont hurt & they always get thrown back.

"In fact you are all wrong, because you are not accustomed to be shot at in the newspapers. As for me, I am all over bullet marks; and I have come to enjoy the noise of the fusillade: it advertises me."

Shaw felt indebted to Trebitsch as his translator, and also some affection for him as he blundered energetically along. But the tone of their exchanges is mostly one of exasperated yet half-humorous rebuke for Trebitsch's easygoing reach for triteness, for commonplace language. "The fact is," said Shaw forgivingly, "you are young and still sentimental." But one serious mistake in *Candida* was also "stupid" (7 January 1903). Trebitsch, he pointed out patiently, was disabled as an adapter of drama because he was a *Spiegelmann*. "A Mirrorman, a Looking Glass man," Shaw explained. "What is a Looking Glass? A thing that reflects what is before it with exquisite fidelity, but that has neither memory nor hope, neither reason nor conscience. And that is what you are as a translator. You translate a sentence beautifully," Shaw praised, laying on the excessive compliment for diplomatic reasons, "but you do not remember the last sentence, do not foresee the next sentence, and when you finish the play it goes out of your head just as your head vanishes from the mirror when you have finished shaving."

Trebitsch was no better with stage directions, as would be proven with each new play. Directors, to be safe, had to check Shaw's original or hazard absurd uses of players and the stage. Writing about the staging of *Caesar and Cleopatra* (10 August 1903) as the translator had misunderstood it, Shaw pronounced Trebitsch "mad as a hatter." He was warned not to omit "the smallest detail[s]. . . . If they work from your stage directions, which are DISASTROUSLY inaccurate—the whole play will be thrown into confusion." Yet Shaw sent him more plays—and more advice.

The long correspondence—616 surviving letters and postcards and cables on Shaw's side—reveals a sort of partnership between the two men, but with Shaw overwhelmingly the senior partner. Not only was Shaw twelve years older, and the author of the plays that were making Trebitsch (who lied about his age by a year) famous, but he regarded himself—correctly—as infinitely wiser than his partner-pupil. In 1905 (27 July), although he found Trebitsch's *Frau Warrens Gewerbe* "as far as I can judge, so expert a piece of work that I have taken a good many of the words I dont understand on trust" he proceeded to give the translator a little lecture on the difference between the words "sensible" and "sensitive." "*I* am sensible," he offered as one of his illustrations; "*You* are sensitive."

The sensible Shaw had plenty of unwelcome advice for his sensitive pupil. Almost every letter included instruction of one kind or another, and such characteristic tutorial phrases are "Listen to me . . . ," "Do not forget . . . ," and "You must make it a rule in life. . . ." Shaw advised Trebitsch about everything from the arts of controversy and negotiation to avoiding, as a tourist, rebuilt medieval ruins. ("If you make a tour in Provence, do not be misled by the guide books into wasting time on Carcassonne. Pass it by and see Toulouse.") Some of the most valuable parts of the correspondence are Shaw's advice about how to translate particular words and passages. Trebitsch had, for example, originally translated the final line of *Saint Joan* in a way that had Joan asking God when the earth will be "*wert* [worthy]" to receive His saints. Shaw advised that he preferred "*bereit* [ready]" in that "I might have written worthy instead of ready; but I didnt, because it introduces an idea quite foreign to my meaning: The world will be ready to receive the saints when it is strong enough and big enough, not when its moral character is reformed."

Fortunately, Shaw knew just enough German to keep Trebitsch up to the mark, for his authorized German translator was so weak in English that in 1910, after Trebitsch had Germanized G.B.S. plays for eight years, Shaw had to hire a teacher of English, Wilhelm Lehmann, to help correct Trebitsch's errors. Still, the same year as this desperate move was taken, Shaw wrote a fulsome preface for the first German collected edition of his plays, "What I Owe to German Culture," in which he praised his stumbling translator: "There is no man in Europe to whom I am more deeply indebted or with whom I feel happier in all our relations, whether of business, or art, or of personal honor and friendship."[2]

Since Shaw preferred literalness to Viennese turns of phrase, he found style less crucial, but translating idiom required more than literalness, and letter after letter would find Shaw exasperated by Trebitsch's innocence of idiom and English usages in general. Shaw reacted almost merrily when Trebitsch's error-ridden lines turned less wooden. "The more you forget your English," Shaw assured him, "the better you translate." It was almost a suicidal approach to turning dialogue into another language, and indeed was exactly that in French, where Augustin Hamon was a good socialist but an execrable Frenchifier of Shaw's plays, and Shaw unhelpfully could barely order a breakfast in French.

Trebitsch, nevertheless, could extract laughs from Shaw's dialogue, but often in the wrong places and for the wrong reasons. His interpretation of a remark by William the Waiter in *You Never Can Tell* remains the classic case. Knowing his place in England's class-ridden society he firmly spurns an offer to join the Clandon family and friends at table, a group that includes his own barrister son. "I really must draw the line at sitting down," says William accurately in Trebitsch's German, after which in the German stage directions helpfully supplied by Trebitsch, William goes to the window and, before sitting down, draws the curtains.

"Laughter is my sword and shield and spear," Shaw had advised him in 1902, early in the collaboration, but Trebitsch's sense of humor was heavy and labored, requiring immense reserves of patience on Shaw's part. Inevitably, Shaw's equanimity exploded, although his wit was usually wasted on Trebitsch. The "hideous and devastating errors" were often, Shaw charged, "unashamed, intentional crimes." But instead of withdrawing his patronage, Shaw suggested to Trebitsch, "You must learn to laugh, or, by Heavens, you will commit suicide when you realize all the infamy of the world as it is. You must avoid literary people. . . . What is the use of people whose heads are full of the very same people you have read yourself? Keep with people who never read anything." When Trebitsch complained early on of the bad press his translations were getting, Shaw sympathized (31 March 1903), "The more we are written about the better. In such matters there is always the consolation that your enemy must either let you alone or advertise you."

Trebitsch also failed to understand Shaw's imperviousness to praise. The premiere of *Pygmalion* in Berlin, anticipating the London opening by half a year, was the complete success Shaw expected, and his ecstatic translator urged Shaw to send a message to the company. "I shall send my congratulations to the Burgtheater," Shaw growled (20 October 1913), "on the 500th night of Pygmalion. I take no interest in first nights. Every play has a first night. The success of the play, if it really proves a success, calls for no comment. I meant it to be a success."

In the early years there were more successes than failures, and even the controversies stimulated the box office. Shaw demonstrated his appreciation by literally giving Trebitsch something of himself—one of the copies he had Rodin make of his bust of G.B.S.—which, given Rodin's fees and reputation, was an enormous gift. But war came in 1914, and Trebitsch cautiously packed the enemy object back in its crate and hid it in the cellar. Shaw would have found the situation funny, but his humor always shocked

Trebitsch or was misunderstood by him, as with a proposed remedy that Shaw airily recommended (29 November 1920) to prevent future wars. Realizing that the Versailles Treaty was the ill-advised imposition of a conqueror, he jovially suggested instead that the victorious countries should be sunk below the surface of the Atlantic "for ten minutes. This would not spoil the machinery if it were quickly dried and oiled, and it would effectually remove all the obstructions to a resumption of those cordial relations without which civilization is impossible." No response from Trebitsch survives, but he must have taken Shaw appallingly seriously. He always did.

Rebukes from the German press seemed to reinforce Shaw's loyalty to Trebitsch. Hans Rothe, a colleague of the influential translator of Oscar Wilde, Max Meyerfeld, excoriated Shaw in the *Berliner Tageblatt* (30 November 1924): "Not all your exertions on your Siegfried's behalf will erase the incredible blunders which he has utilized for many years to make your works incomprehensible to us." Shaw was already doing the same for Trebitsch, offering to help Trebitsch out financially by adapting one of his plays into English, a feeble Viennese melodrama that Shaw turned into an English farce. Making *Jitta's Atonement* (1925) out of *Frau Gittas Sühne* was more like another of Shaw's lengthy corrections of Trebitsch's German than a proper translation. "You will find that in this final acting edition of the play I have committed some fresh outrages," Shaw confessed (17 June 1922). In places where the play returns to a previous scene, he explained, he cut the passages out. "Nothing has been lost by this except the characteristic Trebitschian brooding that is so deliciously sad and noble in your novels but that I could never reproduce. It would require a very special audience, in a theatre suitably draped and colored, with a mystically lighted stage and wonderful dark rich dresses. My method of getting a play across the footlights is like revolver shooting: every line has a bullet in it and comes with an explosion."

"How could you translate it when you don't know German?" Lawrence Langner of the Theatre Guild in New York asked on a visit to Shaw.

"I have a smattering," said Shaw. "Besides, translating isn't just a matter of knowing the language. The original play was a tragedy—which was all right for Austria where they like tragic endings—but it would never go that way in England or America. So I turned it into a comedy!"[3]

So Trebitsch's play was re-written in the Shavian manner (in a way that reveals a good deal, incidentally, about Shaw's dramaturgy). As Shaw had advised Trebitsch (29 March 1906) after reading an earlier attempt by his translator, "The whole play is really morbid & depressing because none of the people have any will: they are all flies on the wheel of Fate & Circumstance, like the people in George Eliot's novels. . . . [L]et the people in your next play have a little will and a little victory, and then you will begin to enjoy yourself and write your plays in the Shavian Key—D flat major, vivacissimo." With little to work with, the attempt was a commercial flop. Trebitsch, however, badgered Shaw about finding producers for *Jitta's Atonement* for thirty years thereafter, taking it to be Shaw's pension for him. (Shaw had actually purchased annuities for his hard-up French translator.) In addition, Shaw furnished Trebitsch with thousands of pounds aside from fees and royalties, using such pride-preserving technicalities as the purchase of German rights from Trebitsch of films and editions that would not be made and existed only theoretically. Nothing was ever enough. Always chasing quick income, in good times and bad Trebitsch constantly violated contracts, confidences and copyrights, selling articles and extracts and interviews, often to Shaw's embarrassment, sometimes to legal complications.

The two world wars added physical barriers to the relationship. Each time, to Shaw's relief, Trebitsch found himself unable to visit England. An outspokenly fervent German patriot, he imprudently hailed Shaw publicly on his sixtieth birthday in 1916 as a spiritual son and bold defender of Germany, not what Shaw, who was being vilified anyway for his anti-war statements, needed. Shaw had to joke about the German connection that he was having a large sign inscribed upon the roof of his country house at Ayot St. Lawrence to warn away Zeppelins that a kindred spirit lived there:

HIER WOHNT DER DICHTER SHAW
BITTE
FAHREN SIE WEITER

After the war, when Trebitsch and his wife Antoinette, widow of a Russian Grand Duke who had been killed in 1904 fighting the Japanese, were briefly in Switzerland, Shaw renewed epistolary relations, explaining that the Trebitsches were now in a country where writing to them would not get an Englishman "shot at dawn." His letters to Germany and Austria were still being opened by the branch of the Treasury overseeing the Trading with the Enemy Act. He was working, Shaw reported (20 July 1919), "at a huge tetralogy (like Wagner's Ring) called Back to Methuselah."

Anything Wagnerian was bound to appeal to the Germanophile Trebitsch and his haughty, aristocratic wife, who pretended with a nearly impenetrable obtuseness that her husband's Wagnerian name implied Nordic purity. Scion of a Moravian Jewish family that doggedly assimilated itself away from any taint of Jewishness, even to naming a son *Siegfried*, Trebitsch knew, or pretended to know, nothing of his heritage. Shaw assumed he was Catholic, like his wife, whom Trebitsch at thirty-nine had married in 1907. Less than a year later Shaw discovered that Trebitsch was the son of unbelieving Jewish parents who taught him nothing of Judaism or Christianity. Trebitsch even required lectures on biblical texts in order to translate Shaw's allusions properly. As late as 1938 G.B.S. was writing to Trebitsch, "Are you serious in asking me what I mean by uncircumcised? You really are the most complete heathen I ever met. Ask the nearest Rabbi or consult a dictionary if you can find one."

What had happened was that in the aftermath of the *Anschluss*, with the Nazis in full control of Austria, Shaw was trying to protect Trebitsch from himself, especially after the *Observer* in London had reported that despite G.B.S.'s translator's being Jewish, his plays were still being performed in Hitler's Germany. In the next Sunday's issue was a response from Shaw that Trebitsch was "an uncircumcised Lutheran German who has never . . . set foot in a synagogue." Technically Shaw was right: when Trebitsch had entered required army service and had to declare a religion, he claimed he was a Lutheran.

Neither his status as Tina's husband nor his parents' efforts at assimilation were of any avail, and Shaw's intervention staved off nothing. The couple had to flee, first to France and then to Switzerland, where they lived lavishly on earnings and borrowings from Shaw while lying to their benefactor that they had retreated modestly to a flat.

In the interwar years Trebitsch had prospered on Shaw's success and prestige, which reached a peak with the Nobel Prize (for 1925) in 1926. Nothing, however, seemed to help *Jitta's Atonement*, whether comedy or tragedy, in English or German. The few performances in England, admittedly hilarious according to critics, baffled them as well as audiences. Ahead of his time, Shaw had turned it into an absurdist play. But when Shaw explained his Nobel Prize for 1925 as Stockholm's relief that he had written nothing that year, Trebitsch pointed out that *Jitta's Atonement* had been produced.

The later 1920s and the 1930s were also the peak of Shaw's ambivalent love affair with European dictators, emerging in the plays in disdain for the incompetence of parliamentary democracies, admiration for Platonic philosopher-kings, and dramatizations of "born bosses." Even his political satire *Geneva* (1938), which Shaw had to keep revising in production to keep up with the bad news, was less than scathing about Hitler ("Battler"), Mussolini ("Bombardone"), and Franco ("Flanco"), and Shaw could be counted on all his life for unstinted praise of Stalin. For a while this made Shaw *persona grata* in Germany, even after Trebitsch had fled, but Shaw's refusal to issue a clear denunciation of Hitler was obviously painful to Trebitsch, who had been forced to come to terms with his origins. Many of Shaw's breezy, self-assured comments on the Nazis, which Trebitsch often had to translate, do not make pleasant reading, and there is a disagreeable, almost jeering, irony in Shaw's naive advice to Trebitsch (3 November 1939) in Zurich, with the war having already begun, "Leave these political questions to me: I have studied them for fifty years." One of the most chilling moments in the whole correspondence comes in a letter written on 9 March 1938, three days before the *Anschluss*. "What does Arisierung mean?" Shaw asked Trebitsch. "I can't find it in the dictionary." It meant Aryanization, the thieving Nazi policy pressuring Jews to transfer their properties at confiscatory prices to "Aryans." Shaw's claims to political sophistication were often baseless since he had read for fifty years with red-tinted spectacles.

From exile in Switzerland, Trebitsch was just as difficult as ever. He wrote pleading letters to Shaw to guarantee his debts but Shaw's replies were often misdirected because Trebitsch could not bring himself to confess that he and Tina were living at the luxurious Dolder Hotel in Zurich. Shaw was writing to Lausanne and assumed the war was responsible for the failure of his efforts to reach Trebitsch, who busied himself meditating on long walks in the forested grounds of the Dolder.

Needing funds to maintain his lifestyle, Trebitsch claimed an interest in the decades-old *opera bouffe* version—which Shaw had spurned—of *Arms and the Man*, the unauthorized but long-running *The Chocolate Soldier*. M-G-M wanted to film it, but Shaw had disowned it. "I cannot understand," Shaw wrote to a New York lawyer in July 1941, "on what ground Trebitsch can claim an interest in the English version of the Chocolate Soldier. He can claim an exclusive right to translate Arms and the Man into German; but the English version [of the musical] was translated from the libretto of [Leopold] Jacobsohn without any apparent reference to Trebitsch's Helden. That version infringes my copyright; and . . . I exercise my right to forbid absolutely any filming of the C.S."

M-G-M put the Oscar Straus music to the Ferenc Molnar play *The*

Guardsman instead since logic in an operetta was unimportant. Trebitsch had to look elsewhere for his income, German productions of Shaw everywhere having dried up in wartime. "Where do you get all the money you are spending?" Shaw had written to him suspiciously early in the war. Before long Shaw was explaining that wartime regulations prevented him from sending money abroad, and even if he could do so, there were others in even more dire straits. "I have just received a letter from Frank Harris's widow in Nice, in debt, and desperate." Soon he wrote, in response to Trebitsch's pleas, "You persist on treating me as a stingy millionaire. . . . The war has driven everyone mad."

The last thing he wanted was to have Trebitsch and his impossible Tina on his hands in England. "THE WAR WILL NOT LAST FOREVER COURAGE COURAGE" he telegraphed to Trebitsch early in 1942, after American entry into the conflict offered some new hope. A few weeks later he consoled Trebitsch with the observation that had he come to England he would have been interned, in the callous fashion that the British treated many refugees with "enemy" passports, "in a concentration camp in the Isle of Man." And he sent £100 indirectly through the American film production company United Artists.

"I omit my address," Shaw postscripted to one letter (8 August 1942), "as it may be objected to by the censors. But a letter addressed George Bernard Shaw, Wellknown author, England, will reach me. It is often used by Americans." The aside, like everything else about Shaw, whom he had known by then for forty years, baffled Trebitsch. It was not brag; Shaw was used to the kind of fame no previous author had ever known. Trebitsch's own visibility was a reflected glint off one facet of Shaw's reputation. Better translations would someday bury his; few translators, however happily they re-created a work, were remembered, and Trebitsch had long since ceased to concern himself about anything other than comfortable survival.

After the war, Shaw tried once more to keep the increasingly difficult Trebitsch away from England. Having never seriously considered an alternative German translator, it was far too late, but the relationship, always unsatisfactory on a personal level, remained at least tolerable at a distance. Trebitsch would come on his pilgrimage only to cajole and wheedle. Nearly ninety, Shaw had enough of that at home and rejected Trebitsch's postwar offers of renewal of old friendship before mortality intervened. "Do not be restrained by any of those delicacies and sentimentalities which are quite thrown away on me," he wrote back (13 March 1946), putting Trebitsch off. "What do you suppose I care about last meetings at my age? I never see anyone now without being conscious that it is probably our last meeting; and it does not trouble me in the least. When the cat leaves the room it may never see me alive again; but I don't cry about it."

Shaw had to keep the persistent Trebitsch away in letter after letter. He was "too old to be recognizable." He did not want anyone to contemplate his decay. Further, life in Switzerland had none of the privations England still lived under. He did not want to be interviewed only to provide Trebitsch with something to sell newspapers. Still Trebitsch came, and Shaw wrote diplomatically to Tina (28 April 1946), whom Trebitsch had left behind, that he was glad to see Siegfried, that their two hours together were "useful," and that, although he regretted the financial extravagance of the journey, it was "a very enjoyable incident for both of us." After Trebitsch returned, the bickering resumed.

Although Trebitsch's house in Vienna seized by the Nazis was returned to him late in 1946, he had no interest in returning to Austria and sold it to the Czech embassy. The windfall dissipated quickly as he remained in Zurich, and he continued making a mess of Shaw's German-language business arrangements, as usual, and a mess of his own life as well, selling rights that he had no authority to grant to anyone in Germany, Austria, and Switzerland who offered him money. "My licenses," Shaw wrote to him in renewed indignation (20 January 1947), "are not heritable, negotiable, nor transferable in any way."

The tragicomedy continued into 1948. Shaw was nearly 92, and cabled Trebitsch about a proposed new visit (26 April 1948), "DO NOT COME. I CAN DO ABSOLUTELY NOTHING FOR YOU. . . ." On the same day, not having seen Shaw's wire, Trebitsch announced that he was leaving for London that Friday. Shaw was baffled until he received a misspelled cable from Tina, "DID NOT SHOW YOUR HARTLESS TELEGRAM TO YOUR SUFFERING OLDEST FRIEND. . . ." Shaw frustratedly cabled again, "NEVER MIND THE HEARTLESSNESS DO NOT LET HIM COME."

A month later Shaw had simmered down enough to explain by letter (23 May 1948) to Trebitsch that the English rejected *"Empfindlichkeit"*—sensibility of the *mittel-europäische* variety. Friendship did not require physical contact. "I have had to forbid [Gabriel] Pascal to kiss me, as he did at first to the scandal of the village." His oldest friend, Sidney Webb, had recently died, he added. "You think I saw him every day. As a matter of fact, though he lived within a three hours motor drive from me I did not see him for years before his death, and we exchanged few letters. But our feelings were quite unchanged, as mine are towards you. I never shook hands with Webb in all my life; and I don't want to shake hands with you nor to contemplate your wrinkles. . . . You must understand that in England this is sentimental nonsense."

But Trebitsch, nearly eighty, could not understand, nor had he ever been able to understand, the perversely unsentimental Irishman who hid his feelings all his professional life beneath a gruff exterior that was his G.B.S. persona. Failing that perception, Trebitsch appealed for a gift of one of Shaw's play manuscripts, to sell in behalf of his lifestyle, and Shaw (22 June 1948) bluntly refused on the grounds that Trebitsch was too old for it to be a useful investment. "If I did such a crazy thing I should give it to a young man," Shaw wrote, but he preferred to offer his papers to "living and ageless public institutions."

Although by his doddering years Trebitsch had learned a little from Shaw's correspondence course of nearly half a century, it would never be enough. Shaw's only full-length postwar play, *Buoyant Billions*, went through several rounds of obtuse title suggestions for the German version until the playwright himself imposed *Zu viel Geld*. It was pithy and it was witty, he explained (17 July 1948), and it was "easy to say," unlike Trebitsch's *Weltverbesserers*, which was "the worst title in the world." But when it opened for its German premiere in Zurich, the audience was unprepared, for the English-language premiere at the Malvern Festival had been delayed by production problems, and the play had no performance history. *Buoyant Billions* concerned the idealistic, self-confessed "world-betterer," Junius Smith, and his relations with the too-rich Bill Buoyant and his love-smitten daughter Clementina, through whom Junius eventually learns that the way to make people better is to make better people.

Although such a plot summary drastically oversimplifies a play that was miraculously effervescent for a writer in his nineties, Trebitsch either missed the comedic elements as usual or decided, anyway, to make the message more Germanically serious, and he gave the dialogue what he thought was a "classical" tone. Shaw was legitimately unhappy with much of it and revised the translation "drastically," he told Trebitsch (8 July 1948) because he was assured by Fritz Erwin Loewenstein, an "echt Berliner" and refugee who did paperwork for Shaw, that "you do not know a word of German" and that the text was written in "a barbarous Austrian dialect."

Shaw had known that for nearly fifty years before Loewenstein's revelation, and it had made no difference. But he bridled (30 July 1948) at the play's metamorphosis into "a heavy highbrow profound dramatic poem."

What he did not realize was that the director, Berthold Viertel, was deferring, as was Trebitsch, to the conservative tastes of the Zurich audience, for whom the evening would even be extended, violating all Shavian practice, by having part of the preface read onstage. Shaw would call that "a silly outrage" and "an imbecility."

More successfully than in most of his efforts, however, Trebitsch managed to find reasonable German idioms for Shaw's English ones, or omitted the sticky problem altogether by dropping punch lines—which worked toward his more serious intent anyway.[4] An "Irish Deirdre" disappeared because the Swiss might have been baffled, while "a dog's chance" was dropped because Trebitsch could find no equivalent. Yet he effectively turned "The tiger has sprung" into the noun form *"Tigersprüngen"* and the plebeian "fish and chips" into the more culturally familiar *"heisse Würstchen."* Still, Trebitsch could not undo himself, and the errors often distort Shaw's meaning. It was, for example, Shaw's first post-atomic play, and he had a character discuss the need to "dilute and control and cheapen atomic power," a quite reasonable idea. Trebitsch converted that concept into improving the *"Atombombe."* In a stage direction in which Junius *"attacks the meal,"* Trebitsch diluted that to *"Er fängt an zu essen"*—which weakened the characterization.

The play survived, but it was about as much Shaw's as *Jitta's Atonement* had been Trebitsch's. Wearily, Shaw at ninety-two gave up, but not without a final injunction (5 August 1948), useless as far as Trebitsch's practice would go, yet still useful for any aspiring playwright or adapter. "You think," Shaw explained, "a play is a string of splendid sentences and epigrams, with every speech a poem that Goethe might have been proud of. You could not make a greater mistake. You might string a thousand splendid sentences and exquisite poems together without making a play. On the stage every speech must provoke its answer and make the audience curious to hear it. Every word that digresses and breaks the chain of thought, however splendid, must be ruthlessly cut."

The lesson, as usual, was lost on Trebitsch, who stubbornly saw German minds as responding differently to drama than British ones and who could not comprehend that mistranslations that warped the original meaning made any difference if the play worked for its new audience. There was no way for the nonagenarian Shaw to turn elsewhere: there were five decades of contracts in force. But he could refuse Trebitsch's continued entreaties to revisit the man who had given him whatever reputation and livelihood he had. Eleven months before his death (1 December 1949) Shaw repeated to

Trebitsch, "I do not want to see you" four times on four separate lines and insisted that they conduct further business through an intermediary. A week before, Shaw had pleaded, "For heaven's sake let us stop this correspondence." Yet it could not stop, having acquired a momentum of its own. "You will not understand," Shaw would write, or words to that effect, and his recipient would not understand. Insisting that Shaw owed his reputation in Europe to him, Trebitsch wanted to prosper on that reputation to his last hour, still trying to sell Shaw's copyrights, still trying to talk Shaw into purchasing an annuity for him, still trying to turn Shaw's buoyant English into a sluggish Viennese German, but never attempting anything on his own.

"You just do nothing, nothing, nothing, nothing, NOTHING, NOTH-ING!" Shaw had screamed (23 November 1949) in one of his last letters to Trebitsch. For he had long since become the translator as parasite, and for decades Shaw had indeed been giving him indirectly things to sell—the extraordinary run of Shavian letters that dealers could turn into money—and, more directly, every new Shavian work. As Shaw wrote on to the end, each new work was another opportunity to sell something. Once more Shaw assailed Trebitsch as *gehirnlos* (brainless), and when Trebitsch used his declining health as another excuse to beg, Shaw suggested that Trebitsch become a vegetarian. "Do you still eat meat? If I were to eat it," he explained in all seriousness, "my evacuations would stink, and I should give myself up for dead. They are entirely odorless. Are yours? . . . Why not try my diet?"

The last exchange, written 7 September 1950, three days before Shaw's fall in his garden, suggested, "We must stop squabbling and appoint an agent to transact our literary business. . . . I will say no more about your health. An invalid who thinks it 'coarse' to mention his bowels is impossible. . . . If you can afford your annual visit to London, you can please yourself, but . . . keep away from Ayot Saint Lawrence. . . ." Shaw was ninety-four.

When Shaw died two months later, Trebitsch eulogized him in an address in the Zurich *Schauspielhaus*. Early in the new year he completed his memoirs, *Chronik eines Lebens*, in which, after himself, Shaw was the leading character. Once that was done he no longer needed his chief treasure, his hoard of Shaw letters, but arranging to sell them took until 1956. As the editor of Shaw's letters to Trebitsch (only a few from Trebitsch survive), Samuel A. Weiss, describes the event, "Trebitsch went to his bank [in Zurich], retrieved the heavy bundle of correspondence, and suffered a heart attack. He was in his eighty-eighth year. On June 3, Siegfried Trebitsch—felled by the hand of his friend—died. . . ."

Why did Shaw suffer a donkey of a translator for nearly fifty years? At any time he could have pensioned him off and employed a better one. Did he enjoy bantering with him, even in Shavian German? Did he feel a debt—his breakthrough on the continent—that he could repay only in strained loyalty? One wonders from the beginnings of the relationship in 1901, when a young Austrian writer of stupefying mediocrity offered to become Shaw's translator, until late in 1950, when Shaw finally refused to have anything further to do with him while permitting him to hang on, why the playwright, who took pride in his prose, continued to condone translations that at best rose to adequacy. Was the hectoring role worth it? Could he have used someone else as a sounding board? Was he paying his heavy price to have someone to insult at his pleasure? Shaw had a long and checkered history of encouraging inadequate translators on the grounds that they were eager, or impecunious, or Socialist, or all three. Unlike the others, however, Trebitsch possessed a personality of unmitigated whimpering selfishness and demonstrated more than a little dishonesty in conducting Shaw's business. Shaw's keeping him on may tell us something about Shaw.

Notes

1. All quotations from the Shaw-Trebitsch correspondence are from Samuel A. Weiss, ed., *Bernard Shaw's Letters to Siegfried Trebitsch* (Stanford: Stanford University Press, 1986). Trebitsch's own recollections are from his *Chronicle of a Life* (London: Heinemann, 1953), trans. Eithne Wilkins and Ernst Kaiser.

2. "*Was ich der deutscher Kultur verdanke*" first appeared in *Neue Runschau* (March 1911), then as the preface to volume 1 of *Dramatische Werke* (Berlin: S. Fischer Verlag, 1911). Its first appearance in Shaw's original English was in *Adam International Review* (Spring 1970), pp. 5–16.

3. Lawrence Langner, *G.B.S. and the Lunatic* (New York: Atheneum, 1963; London: Hutchinson, 1964), p. 94.

4. Steven Joyce analyzes Trebitsch's version, *Zu viel Geld*, in several publications. His fullest account is *Transformations and Texts: G. B. Shaw's "Buoyant Billions"* (Columbia, S.C.: Camden House, 1992).

JESTING AND GOVERNING

Shaw and Churchill

"Mr. Bernard Shaw," Winston Churchill remembered, "was one of my earliest antipathies. Indeed, almost my first literary effusion, written when I was serving as a subaltern in India in 1897 (it never saw the light of day) was a ferocious onslaught upon him, and upon an article which he had written disparaging and deriding the British Army in some minor war."

London publications came to India late and stayed long—links with home too precious for mere time value. Almost certainly the article young Winston had seen in Bangalore or Hyderabad was "A Dramatic Realist to His Critics," from the *New Review* of July 1894. There Shaw had answered complaints about his Avenue Theatre production of *Arms and the Man*, which, he observed, "brought the misunderstanding between my real world and the stage world of the critics to a climax, because the misunderstanding was itself, in a sense, the subject of the play."

The war that Shaw mocked was ostensibly between two pathetically underdeveloped Balkan states, Serbia and Bulgaria, set in 1885–86, when for six months the defending Bulgarians, unskilled at war or anything else, became "a nation of heroes. . . . Their attempts at western civilization were much the same as their attempts at war—instructive, romantic, ignorant. . . . A nation of plucky beginners in every department."

In Shaw's theater audience were the Prince of Wales and his brother, Prince Alfred, the Duke of Edinburgh, who was also the Duke of Coburg, having inherited the year before a new wardrobe of uniforms as reigning duke that had required him to resign his admiral's commission in the Royal Navy. Between the lines of *Arms and the Man*, Victoria's sons sensed that the playwright was jeering at the British military and its ventures into embarrassingly difficult colonial wars against underarmed warriors from Afghans to Zulus. From their box they asked for the manager, and when Charles T. H. Helmsley inquired what he could do for his royal guests, the Prince of Wales asked who Mr. Shaw was, and "what he meant by it," while the Duke interrupted with "The man is mad, the man is mad."

If Shaw seemed mad to military types, it resulted from his undermining expectations about patriotism and heroism. In his satire, Major Sergius Saranoff, the play's unsophisticated military hero, has earned his honors in a cavalry charge, into enemy fire, only because his horse has run away with him. Captain Bluntschli, his adversary, is businesslike in logistics, hides in a young woman's bedroom when pursued, keeps chocolates instead of bullets in his cartridge case—and wins the Major's betrothed.

What was alleged as cowardice in the romantic view was only prudence, Shaw contended. And in the *New Review* he quoted Lord Wolseley, a general Churchill admired, as acknowledging, "One of the most trying things for the captain or subaltern is to make their men who have found some temporary haven of refuge from the enemy's fire, leave it and spring forward in a body to advance over the open upon a position to be attacked." And Wolseley's observation, Shaw noted, was not in a private memorandum but in the very public *Fortnightly Review* of August 1888. So much, the playwright concluded, for "your British soldier, who is quite as brave as any soldier in the world."

Wolseley had gone on, Shaw continued, to recall "a whole division literally crazy with terror when suddenly aroused . . . by some senseless alarm. I have even known officers to . . . wound their own comrades upon such occasions." And he described such a scare, which became too much for Churchill, even though Shaw went on to quote an American Civil War general, Horace Porter, to the effect that "Courage, like everything else, wears out."

Deploring the Irishman's lack of patriotism, Churchill seized his pen but found no takers at home for the polemic, his first attempt at writing for publication. Soon, however, he was in action on the Indian frontier with Afghanistan and was writing £5-a-column messages from the front for the *Daily Telegraph*, which he transformed into his first book, *The Malakand Field Force*. Moving to the Sudan, young Winston sent home more journalism, which became *The River War*.

After his escape from a Boer prison camp in South Africa and his letters to the *Morning Post* about still another war, Churchill was famous and on his way out of the Army and into a Parliamentary seat. His view of war, based on the feeling that all soldiers could be Young Winstons, was what both he and Shaw would describe as "an Adelphi melodrama." Such action-laden heroics, spoofed in *Arms and the Man* and in the 1897 *The Devil's Disciple*, had already forced Shaw into yet another riposte, "Trials of a Military Dramatist" (*Review of the Week*, 4 November 1899).

A few years later, now a war hero, a popular author, and a comer in politics, Churchill was taken to luncheon with Shaw by Jennie Churchill (Winston's mother), who had secured the playwright as a writer for her *Anglo-Saxon Review*, an expensive catch-all for notables kept going by her personality. By then Shaw had surprisingly revealed himself as a patriot in the South African business, opposing his own Socialist cronies who supported all nationalist movements. In the dour Afrikaners, Shaw saw only medieval throwbacks out of tune with the future.

Impressed by Shaw's lunch of fruit and vegetables and by his eschewing

Fig. 16. Winston Leonard Spencer Churchill as drawn by "Spy" for *Vanity Fair*, 27 September 1900. Churchill at twenty-seven was a new Tory M.P.

the wine for water, Churchill "rallied" him, "Do you really never drink any wine at all?"

"I am hard enough to keep in order as it is," said G.B.S.

"Perhaps," Churchill thought, "he had heard of my youthful prejudice against him," but Winston felt "instantly attracted by the sparkle and gaiety of his conversation." As he moved up in Edwardian politics they often exchanged banter while seldom agreeing on domestic issues or about Ireland. Through reading and in talks with the Webbs, Shaw, and Wells, Churchill learned that Britain's domestic problems were more complicated than his upper-class upbringing had revealed. Shaw wrote later, on reading Churchill's reminiscences, that when the "duke's grandson . . . was a child of seven he was sent to an expensive school where the discipline was more ferocious than would be permitted in a Reformatory for young criminals of twice that age." But Winston assumed that this was the way it had to be and that each class endured its own forms of discipline. Living under destitution, with a criminal code weighted against them, was merely the expected plight of the lower orders. Yet these people were gradually becoming voters, and they would not be Liberals (as Churchill then was) if a burgeoning Labour Party alone promised them a way out of oppression. It was in Churchill's self interest, aside from his genuine alarm at what he discovered about the condition of England, to offer the downtrodden a better future than mere assurances of an idyllic hereafter.

Liberals would soon furnish the beginnings of unemployment insurance and old age pensions, but first they would excoriate the Left as extremists. At a bazaar at the Free Trade Hall in Manchester in October 1906, Churchill, already a rising M.P., told an audience of social workers that he noticed that Shaw had already favored them "with his views upon the methods of human and social regeneration. Mr. Shaw was rather like a volcano. There was a great deal of smoke; and there were large clouds of highly inflammable gases, and there were here and there brilliant electrical flashes. There were also large volumes of scalding water and mud and ashes cast up in all directions, and here and there among the mud and ashes of extravagance and nonsense there was from time to time a piece of pure gold smelted from the central fires of truth." He did not himself dislike the volcano, Churchill said, but Shaw's solution for social ills was often "to cut off the Lord Mayor's head," which was only "undisciplined anger." Fortunately for the nation, Churchill joked, "it was not a very large volcano, though it was in a continual state of eruption."

Taking the young politician's jibe as good-natured, however inaccurate, Shaw may have recalled his success at getting politicians in 1904 interested in the matter of Ireland through his play *John Bull's Other Island*, to which the Prime Minister, Arthur Balfour, invited the leaders of both opposition parties. Even King Edward VII had demanded to see it, having forgotten his experience of *Arms and the Man*, and early in 1905 the Court Theatre had to lay on a Command Performance. Now Shaw apparently offered Churchill complimentary tickets to a new premiere: "I enclose two tickets for the first night of my new play, one for yourself and one for your friend, if you have one."

Whether fact or folklore, Shaw denied for years having taunted Churchill, but when he was 93 he allegedly recalled Winston's retort, "I am sorry I cannot attend for the first night, but I should be glad to come on the second night, if there is one."*

Could young Winston have seen himself in *John Bull's Other Island*? In the character of the English politician Thomas Broadbent, youngish, ambitious, and given to oratorical flourishes, and a candidate for a Parliamentary seat from an impoverished Irish constituency, Shaw took aim at the type if not the man. Elected M. P. from Oldham in 1900 at twenty-five, Churchill was guest of honor in January 1904—five months before Shaw began to write the play—at a widely reported dinner given by the Corinthian Club in Dublin. Replying to a toast, he offered an address in what seems to be Broadbentese. "I feel," said Churchill, "as St. Patrick must have felt when he landed to convert the Irish nation. I can only hope that I may have, if not the good fortune St. Patrick had, at any rate some proportion of that good fortune in driving out of Ireland the fiscal frogs and tariff toads." Reports of the address follow the labored witticism with *"Laughter"* and *"Hear! Hear!"* The impromptu political meeting that opens the fourth act, as its rhetoric—and perhaps the entire device of an enterprising young politician on alien turf in Ireland—may owe its conception to Churchill in Dublin.

Shaw and Churchill saw each other rather often in Edwardian days, sometimes in a theater-related way. Only a few months before Churchill's

---

*Two years earlier, in 1948, journalist Derek Tatham had asked Shaw to corroborate the exchange, now attributed to the Malvern Festival seasons beginning in 1929, but also linked elsewhere to the London premiere of *Pygmalion* in 1914 and later even to the London opening of *Buoyant Billions* in 1949. Shaw labeled the story "not only a flat lie but a political libel. . . . Publish it at your peril. . . ." The "friend, if you have one" jeer suggests a date before Churchill's marriage to Clementine Hozier in 1908.

Free Trade Hall fun at Shaw's expense, he had presided (11 June 1906) at a matinee benefit and public dinner in honor of Ellen Terry's fifty years on the stage, at which G.B.S. (as he signed his contribution) read a verse tribute to Miss Terry, asking whether it was

> . . . kind of Fate
> To make your youth so thrifty
> That you are young at fiftyeight
> Whilst we are old at fifty?

Home Secretary in 1910, Churchill had to contend with noisy and persistent suffragists and found Shaw on their side. Churchill had united with David Lloyd George to push through an unemployment insurance act to protect the working masses, and he did not appreciate Shaw's feminist interpretation of the income-tax rules. Lloyd George as Chancellor of the Exchequer had to raise more money, and Shaw had received an official request from the Office of the Special Commissioners of Income Tax to report "your total income from all sources" in order to determine the new supertax assessment, which had just become effective. Shaw replied (5 May 1910) that he had no knowledge of his wife's income and that "all that I can do for you is to tell you who my wife is and leave it to you to ascertain her income and make me pay the tax on it."

It was the irresistible force and the immovable object. There was a personal interview, during which Shaw insisted—he told *The Times*—"that we were both up against two obstacles—first, an oversight in the Income Tax Acts; and second, the suffragist movement."

"No one made a louder squawk than the already wealthy Fabian," Churchill later alleged, but Shaw's refusal on the grounds of law and principle eventually led to amendment of the regulations, permitting husband and wife to make separate returns—"The Bernard Shaw Relief Act," Churchill jibed. "An ex-Chancellor of the Exchequer," Shaw said later, "ought to know better. . . . When it became public vaguely that I had complained of something, it was concluded that it was the old grievance about being taxed at all."

In the Coronation year of 1911 the Liberal Prime Minister, H. H. Asquith, gave a party for George V and Queen Mary. For it, 10 Downing Street was turned into a theater, with the Cabinet and eminent guests as audience. *The Twelve Pound Look* by James Barrie and Act III of Shaw's *John Bull's Other Island* were performed, as directed by Harley Granville

Fig. 17. Winston Churchill as a young M.P. It is easy to visualize Shaw's Broadbent of *John Bull's Other Island* in the pose. Front wrapper, in red and black, of an anti-Socialist tract that utilizes as preface a speech delivered by Churchill in Dundee on 14 May 1908. Courtesy Pattee Library, Penn State.

Barker. With Home Rule for Ireland a hot topic in that hot summer, Violet Asquith, the Prime Minister's daughter, recalled "a moment of panic" when she overheard the King ask her father whether "this very appropriate play" had been "written for the occasion." Not only was the appalled Home Secretary within earshot, but also the playwright. Shaw reacted, so Violet Asquith remembered, "with exemplary loyalty."

Churchill—if not the King—remained on Shaw's mind when the "Home Rule" edition of *John Bull's Other Island* was published early in 1912. In fact, Shaw entertained the Churchills (including Lady Randolph) at lunch in London that January, and a week later he asked his secretary (and cousin) Georgina "Judy" Gillmore to have the publisher, Constable, send Winston an advance copy "if they can lay hands on one and find out where he is." It had a timely new preface, and Shaw was trying to influence politicians before the Irish matter became insoluble.

When Churchill, no longer Home Secretary in 1912 but now First Lord of the Admiralty, volunteered to "vindicate the right of speech" on Home Rule for Ireland by speaking out at a rally at the Celtic Park football ground in Belfast, Shaw weighed in once more. Four days before the public meeting, at which many feared violence, the London *Weekly Budget* (4 February 1912) published comments from "leading men" as to the wisdom of Churchill's intrusion, and Shaw observed, "I don't think anybody should go to Belfast. There are pleasanter places within reach. . . . Belfast has to choose between Free Speech and no politics." His "countrymen," Shaw felt, could be "depended upon" to see that if free speech were "applied at all," it would be "applied all around," and that it would be "quite as inconvenient for Sir Edward Carson as for Mr. Winston Churchill."

Home Rule became a war casualty in 1914, but Shaw managed to influence Churchill on another matter before the year was out. Soldiers, Shaw wrote to Mrs. Patrick Campbell, got fifteen shillings a week until they were shot dead, "when they get five." It gave the German bullet a doubled impact, killing the husband and starving the wife. In *The New York Times*, G.B.S. was quoted by a determined Irish-American lady journalist who had interviewed him, Mary Boyle O'Reilly, on the degrading pensions for service widows. London papers picked up the most controversial statements, and King George V wrote to Prime Minister Asquith to recommend greater generosity, bolstering his argument by quoting Shaw. When Asquith called for a vote in favor of a weekly widows' benefit of seven shillings and sixpence—then about two dollars—only Churchill raised his hand. Asquith and nine others voted for six shillings and sixpence while the laborers' ostensible champion, David Lloyd George, and eight others held out for the paltry five shillings.

Shaw's satiric invective against Asquith and Lloyd George in a later play was bitter, but he recognized that Churchill seemed always to act without hypocrisy. In *Common Sense about the War*, Shaw's notorious polemic in the *New Statesman* in November 1914, he observed that the "British Public" had "all along been behind Mr. Winston Churchill," whom he described as "an odd and not disagreeable compound of Junker and Yankee" whose "frank anti-German pugnacity is enormously more popular than the moral babble (Milton's phrase) of his sanctimonious colleagues."

As Churchill, after Gallipoli, was pushed farther out into the political wilderness, he even began sounding like Shaw. When the *Nation*, for which Shaw had been writing, fell under War Office interdict in 1917 on the grounds that a previous issue had been exploited by German propaganda (it had suggested a negotiated peace settlement), Shaw railed at the "mischief" of suppression, and Churchill delivered a brilliant condemnation from the benches of the House of Commons. "The administration of this country in regard to newspapers," he declared, "cannot be based on the caprice of a Munchausen department which collects tit-bits from the German wireless telegraphy."

"The worst of it," Shaw observed himself, was that "all the raving Jingo papers . . . are left free to provide Berlin with 'Sidelights on England.' " The ban was quietly removed in October 1917, by which time Churchill had been desperately plucked back into the Cabinet as Minister of Munitions. Afterward he was quoted as saying, almost as if he were a character in a Shavian political satire, "In the recent war we politicians had only two duties. The one was to persuade our admirals to put to sea, the other to persuade our generals to stop killing their own men. In both we were quite unsuccessful."

The prolonged tragedy of the war would lead Shaw to devote almost every play he would write thereafter to the subject of how humankind could be effectively governed. As he had a character put it in his futuristic satire, *As Far as Thought Can Reach* (1921), "There was a time when children were given the world to play with because they promised to improve it. They did not improve it, and would have wrecked it. . . ." In his Foundation Oration, delivered in March 1920 as he was finishing the play, Shaw observed that government was a skill not within the capabilities of the man in the street. "Let me expatiate on this," he added. "I was going to say Lord Randolph Churchill—that shews how very old I am—I mean Mr Winston Churchill, but the difference is not so great as you suppose. Mr Winston Churchill said the other day [that] the Labor Party could not govern. He was quite right. No party at present existing can govern."

The reason, he explained to his audience of London University students, was, "You are not taught to govern. Now, what it is that Mr Winston Churchill has had evidently in mind—God knows why—is that his people and his class can govern." In a way, Shaw explained, Churchill was right, in that a governing tradition "had grown up historically, largely by deliberate contrivance," which was the "ready-made machine" of Churchill's class.

Bringing G.B.S. into the debate, the now-Conservative Churchill, in an address in Woodford in October 1924, after the brief Labour government had fallen, declared that a "Socialist Government" ought never have existed since it had been a minority creation "directly contrary to the will of the people." Britain, he insisted, was not riven by "class division" as claimed.

> It is not classes against the masses. The Socialists proclaim a class war, but every class is represented in the Socialist ranks. They are delighted when they receive the adhesion of a gilded butterfly like Mr. [Oswald] Mosley, and they enjoy the support of a brilliant intellectual clown like Mr. Bernard Shaw. (Loud laughter and cheers.) . . . And when it comes to masses, after all, the Conservative Party has the largest mass of British democracy which exists in an organized political form in this country. (Cheers.) It is not a fight between the few and the many, between privilege and democracy, between aristocracy and the rest. . . . There is no case for a quarrel between wealth and poverty; it is a quarrel between methods of government and themes of government. . . .

Although Churchill's class had become Shaw's own by wealth and achievement, he seldom saw Churchill personally because Shaw avoided luncheons and dinners and country-house weekends. While these encounters were useful for politicians, they did not help him to get on with his writing. Exceptions were sometimes made for visiting authors and artists, and at Lady Lavery's home—Hazel was Sir John Lavery's wife and favorite model—in June 1925 Shaw came to meet playwright Luigi Pirandello, who had written, the year before, in praise of *Saint Joan*. But since Shaw knew Italian largely from opera librettos he was seated prudently next to Churchill. What they talked about is a mystery, but it was more likely politics than plays. In Churchill's letter to his wife the year before, after filling her in with political bulletins, he postscripted, "In Bernard Shaw's *Methuselah* Adam after being 1,000 years in Heaven wanted to come back to earth for a spell. He asked St Peter for the necessary pass. 'Certainly,' said Peter, 'I suppose you want to take Eve with you.' 'No,' said Adam, 'I am going to turn over a new leaf.' " No such exchange appears in *Back to Methuselah*, which the risqué joke appears to spoof.

Hurling deflating jibes at each other continued to be associated with Churchill and Shaw, not all of them as grounded in reality as the evidence of their own letters. One, claimed to have been overheard in 1924 during a performance of the vastly successful and popular *Saint Joan*, concerned the third scene, during which Dunois is pacing restlessly along the banks of the Loire. If the wind would shift, his boats could cross, and that shift would be ascribed to the ability of Joan to invoke heavenly aid. "West wind, west wind, west wind," Dunois invokes—and at the performance attended by Churchill, allegedly he could be heard to follow Dunois's plea with "Pong!"

The middle 1920s were the heyday of the game *mahjong*, and many in the audience understood that "Pong!" meant that the player held three of a kind. The outburst was said to have stopped the show.

1924 was also the year of the Shaw-Churchill debate, played out in the Sunday papers. The *New York Tribune* gave the middle of its front page on 11 May to the combatants, complete with photographs, headlined, "A Debate on the Principles of Socialism: Winston Churchill vs. George Bernard Shaw." Neither combatant gave any quarter, and the "debate"— actually opposing views in parallel columns, with Shaw having the last word—was heightened by the existence of something new in politics—a Socialist (Labour Party) government in power in Britain for the first time.

It is easy to be a Socialist polemicist, Churchill began. All one needed to do was to take the world as it is, "painfully and gradually built up from barbarism. From this you pick out every evil, every injustice, every inequality, every misfortune that catches the eye. These you say are the fruits of the Capitalist system." The new order, "where everyone will receive more and give less, where sublime wisdom and godlike efficiency will inspire the rulers, where self-interest, personal profit, private possession will play no part in human action, and where all will dwell together side by side in perfect equality and brotherhood," was easy to contemplate. All one had to do was to "put a cross on a voting paper and enter broadly and swiftly into a serene and glorious existence." It was, he warned, the "Socialist Fraud."

"Selfishness, self-seeking, self-interest," Churchill warned, made such utopian dreams impossible of fulfillment. A new Socialist member of the

Labour Cabinet, Churchill noted, had immediately asked to have his salary doubled, a fair warning of what could follow. So were the "glittering dreams . . . reduced to practice." A better strategy was to reward enterprise, "the right of the individual to make the best for himself, or, within limits, the worst of himself, if he chooses. . . ."

Capitalist evils, Shaw rejoined, were real, and had been documented over the years by Owen, Marx, Lasalle, the Fabians, and "the departmental reports of the Labour Party." The "wretched Capitalist panacea of unbridled selfishness," he charged, which had promised to trickle down, at the least, "a bare subsistence wage for everyone," deserved to be discarded. It had "not only failed to keep that pitiful promise for a single instant, but produced such a blasting disfigurement of nature and degradation of humanity that it will stink in the nostrils of history so long as we can bear to be reminded of so contemptible and disastrous an episode in the records of political quackery and corruption." Socialism was "the way out of it."

The machinery of Parliament "as it exists at present" was useless to effect change. "As Dickens pointed out when I was born (but without reference to that event), the object of governments was to prevent things from being done, not to do them." What Churchill foresaw as a "terrible bureaucracy ordering every detail of our lives and drawing huge salaries at public expense is a bugaboo that could hardly frighten an ex-minister. . . . He had the job of bringing up the British fleet to scratch for the war. He now assures us by implication that it would have been done much better by, say, the Thames Steamboat Company." If Socialism in practice meant Big Government, Shaw was for it.

Churchill had been offered no opportunity for rebuttal, but both men kept at the debate in other ways over the years. Whether Labour or any other political combination could govern became the basis of Shaw's next book, a lengthy between-plays treatise that he called, in a reference to his sister-in-law's plaint that the new political ideologies were confusing, *The Intelligent Woman's Guide to Socialism and Capitalism*. On publication in mid-1928, with the flyleaf observation, "It is a sure way to prevent you [from] reading it," Shaw sent a copy to Churchill, who appeared on several of its pages, once as the origin of the allegation about Labour's unfitness for governing. Shaw's contention was that no party could govern so long as Capitalism was "a runaway car."

Thanking Shaw, Churchill agreed with "the simple-brutal style and treatment" that might awaken "the thoughtless complacent propertied person." Although, he added, his son Randolph was neither thoughtless nor propertied, he was buying a copy for him since Randolph was "far too ready to take the existing system and situation as axiomatic." He agreed with Shaw

> in condemning not only Capitalism and Socialism, but every other conceivable intermediate variant—so long as men—and intelligent women—remain what they have so long been. Everything they try will fail—owing to their deplorable characteristics and their liking for these very characteristics. The only world fit for them is a Hugger Mugger world. Ants or Bees would be worthy of better things—tho' even they have some bad habits. The real fault lies with the Creator; and there is no apparent way of bringing it home to him. "He just keeps rolling along."
>
> About this equalization of income—I was much relieved to find that there were not going to be any immediate changes. I am writing a book—of enormous value (indirect) to mankind and of very considerable value (direct) to me; and I should certainly not persist in this labour if I thought the tax collector was going to take the whole instead of 2/5ths of its yield.
>
> Let me once again tell you how very much honoured I am to have received this great courtesy at your hands, and how highly I shall prize its embodiment, and with all good wishes to you and your wife, believe me,
>
> > Yours very sincerely,
> > Winston S. Churchill
>
> PS. My wife is now about to take the treatment (as an intelligent woman) and begs to be remembered to you.

Churchill was engaged in writing more than one book, but the intended money-spinner was A Roving Commission: My Early Life, an engaging autobiography. He was also writing a series of personality sketches for Nash's Pall Mall, eventually, as Great Contemporaries, to become another book, and in the August 1929 issue he published his profile of Shaw. In it Churchill noted that he had recently taken his family to see the revival of Major Barbara, which had opened at Wyndham's Theatre that March. "Twenty years had passed since I had seen it. They were the most terrific twenty years the world had known. Almost every human institution had undergone decisive change. The landmarks of centuries had been swept away. Science has transformed the conditions of our lives and the aspect of town and country. Silent social evolution, violent political change, a vast broadening of the social foundations, an immeasurable release from convention and restraint, a profound reshaping of national and individual opinion, have followed the trampling march of this tremendous epoch. But in *Major Barbara*, there was not a character requiring to be redrawn, not a sentence nor a suggestion that was out of date. My children were astounded to learn that this play, the very acme of modernity, was written more than five years before they were born."

Coincidentally that year, perhaps as a private joke, it is possible that Churchill made an unrecognized appearance in the Cabinet of Prime Minister Proteus in Shaw's political play *The Apple Cart*. Largely aiming his barbs at the hapless governments of the later 1920s, and particularly Ramsay MacDonald and his Labour Party apostates, Shaw nevertheless had his Minister represent both past and prophecy—tough, futuristic women and flabby, ineffective male bureaucrats of failed administrations. It would have been too obvious to give Churchill, Chancellor of the Exchequer from 1924 through 1929, his familiar post, but it may be that Balbus, the Home Secretary, described in Shaw's stage directions as *"rude and thoughtless,"* is part Winston, who was the bully behind the breaking of the General Strike of 1926. (The Prime Minister calls him "the bully" of the Cabinet.)

Ironically, too, the grand periods in the speeches by King Magnus about governing have the cadences of Churchillian rhetoric. One can almost hear the Churchill of the Woodford address of 1924 in Magnus, who sees in monarchy values coordinate with representative government—continuity, experience, nonpartisanship, symbolism—and who declares his unconcealed distaste for mobocracy. As he wrote about "the witty scenes and dialogue of *The Apple Cart*" in a *Great Contemporaries* profile of the deposed Spanish king Alfonso,

> our Fabian dramatist and philosopher has rendered a service to monarchy which never perhaps could have been rendered from any other quarter. With his unsparing derision he has held up before the Socialists of every land the weaknesses, the meannesses, the vanities and the follies of the trumpery figures who float upwards and are borne forward upon the swirls and eddies of so-called democratic politics. The sympathies of the modern world, including many of its advanced thinkers, are powerfully attracted by the gay and sparkling presentation of a king, ill-used, let-down, manipulated for personal and party ends, yet sure of his value to the mass of his subjects, and striving not unsuccessfully to preserve their permanent interests, and to discharge his duty.

Fiction anticipated history in *The Apple Cart* and involved both Shaw and Churchill. The crux of the play is the King's threat to get his way by abdicating and then running for a seat in parliament as head of his own party. If he could then translate his popular appeal into votes, he would be Prime Minister, unseating the government in power. Seven years later came an authentic abdication, with Churchill suggesting that Edward VIII first threaten abdication and the formation of a "King's Party" if he were not permitted to marry the twice-divorced Wallis Warfield Simpson and make her his queen.

When the news, kept from the newspapers for months by a cabal of press barons, finally broke in England, Shaw published a spoof playlet—"a fictitious dialogue," he called it—in the *Evening Standard* on 8 December: "The King, the Constitution and the Lady." Few more lighthearted lines have been written by playwrights aged eighty. The situation in the "Kingdom of the Half-Mad" replicated the Edward and Wallis predicament almost exactly. Shaw's king was forty, unmarried, and in need of a queen. What better choice than Mrs. Daisy Bell, an American who "had been married twice before and was therefore likely to make an excellent wife for a king who had never been married at all."

"I shall be crowned in May," says the King to the Prime Minister, "and in April I shall marry Daisy."

PRIME MINISTER (*almost shrieking*): Impossible! Madness!
ARCHBISHOP (*whose pulpit voice is a triumph of clerical art*): Out of the question. You cannot marry this woman.
KING: I had rather you called her Mrs Bell. Or Daisy, if you prefer it.
ARCHBISHOP: If I were to officiate at your proposed marriage, I should have to speak of her as "this woman." What is good enough for her in the House of God is good enough for her here. But I shall refuse to officiate.
PRIME MINISTER (*shouting*): And I shall resign.
KING: How awful! Would it be too brutal to remind you that there are others? Sandy McLossie will form a King's Party for me in no time. The people are behind me. You may have to resign in any case long before the Coronation.

It was Shaw's update on *The Apple Cart*, fact having approached perilously close to fiction. But the real king opted out of history instead, with Churchill helping to draft the "woman I love" farewell address that is now all that is remembered about the eleven-month reign of Edward VIII. His accepting the title of a Royal Duke in settling his future precluded any candidacy for a seat in Commons, and thus any designs suggested in Shaw's play—and in life by Churchill.

What Churchill had perceived in the Shaw of *The Apple Cart* was a monarchist in Fabian disguise, yet if anything, Shaw was the stauncher royalist, as would become even more apparent in his 1939 "true history that never happened," *"In Good King Charles's Golden Days."* Like Churchill a believer in strong prime ministers and admirable but figurehead sovereigns, the strongminded Balbus is pleased about the possibility that the Prince of Wales of the play would become King. "He wont interfere with you as long as you dont interfere with him. Just the right king for us. Not pig-headed. Not meddlesome." Deflecting any identification with Churchill by placing Balbus in a Birmingham constituency dominated by a confectionery works, Shaw nevertheless has Balbus boast about his boozing, which could suggest Churchill's already legendary bibulousness—or perhaps 400 other members of the House. In name, Balbus suggests the Roman general and consul, a favorite of Caesar, who, when tried for assuming the rights of a Roman citizen although born an alien, was defended by Cicero, Pompey, and Crassus. Churchill, son of an American mother, not only served in half a dozen Cabinet offices, but commanded the 6th battalion, Royal Scots Fusiliers in France in 1916. Although he saw and enjoyed the play, very likely he never perceived a part of himself disguised in Balbus. Shaw kept his own counsel and, clearly, had done his homework.

If Balbus in any way was Churchill, Winston got his own back in the good-humored barbs of *Great Contemporaries*.

> Few people practise what they preach, and no one less so than Mr. Bernard Shaw. Few are more capable of having the best of everything both ways. His spiritual home is no doubt in Russia; his native land is the Irish Free State; but he lives in comfortable England. His dissolvent theories of society have been sturdily banished from his personal conduct and his home. No one has ever led a more respectable life or been a stronger seceder from his own subversive imagination. He derides the marriage vow and even at times the sentiment of love itself; yet no one is more happily or wisely married. He indulges in all the liberties of an irresponsible Chatterbox, babbling gloriously from dawn to dusk, and at the same time advocates the abolition of Parliamentary institutions and the setting up of an Iron Dictatorship, of which he would probably be the first victim. It is another case for John Morley's comment upon Carlyle, "the Gospel of silence in thirty volumes by Mr. Wordy."

Churchill perceived, too, the Achilles heel in Shaw. "The clown in me trips me up," Shaw once confessed. And Churchill observed that Shaw seemed to derive "equal pleasure" from any and all of his "contrary habits, poses and attitudes, . . . exploding by his own acts or words every argument he has ever used on either side of any question, teasing and bewildering every public he has ever addressed, and involving in his own mockery every cause he has ever championed." It was amusing to watch "the nimble antics and gyrations of this unique and double headed chameleon, while all the time the creature was eager to be taken seriously." Shaw, Churchill thought, was chief victim of his own gift for paradox. "He pays an incomparable tribute to the work of the Salvation Army, and leaves it a few minutes later ridiculous and forlorn. In *John Bull's Other Island* we are no sooner captivated by Irish charm and atmosphere than we see the Irish race liveried in humbug and strait-jacketed in infirmity of purpose. . . . The intense emotions aroused in our breasts by the trial and martyrdom of Joan of Arc are immediately effaced by the harlequinade which constitutes the final act. . . ."

Shaw, Churchill charged, depended crucially for his effects on such "contradictions" that belied the fact that he was "at heart sincere," with a "life's message" that remained consistent. The Shavian strategy, he concluded, left Shaw's audiences bewildered as well as beguiled. "The greatest master of letters in the English-speaking world" was jester as well as thinker—"saint, sage, and clown."

A master at extracting mileage from his material, Churchill later published a variation on his G.B.S. essay in the Manchester *Sunday Chronicle*, enabling the paper to cajole a reply from Shaw, printed on 13 April 1930. Because portraits, the one-time art critic explained, are often "much more authentic as portraits of the painter than of the sitter (and as only the excuse for the picture and not really the subject for it), I am glad to find Mr. Churchill endowing me with such generous, and brilliant, qualities. They are his own. The guess-work and rumour in the sketch are sometimes wildly off the prosaic truth, but that is inevitable and does not matter."

The exchanges might have ended with Shaw's evasion and with the aborting of Churchill's next scheme. That Churchill had a soft spot for serious clowns was obvious, for soon he was thinking of Shaw again with another journalistic project in mind. Writing to Professor Frederick A. Lindemann at Oxford, his consultant on ideas of every sort, he tried out a concept for another series—"*If they had lived long ago?*" He wanted Lindemann to imagine the careers of famous contemporaries in past times—

"Henry Ford in Cromwellian days, . . . Mussolini with Henry VIII, Ramsay MacDonald in the French Revolution, Bernard Shaw with the ancient Greeks, and so on." (Churchill may have had the fifth playlet of *Back to Methuselah* in mind, placed in the future but in a setting suggested by Greece in 5th Century B.C.; or he may have been thinking of Shaw as modern Aristophanes.) The idea teased Churchill but did not amuse Lindemann, and Shaw failed to reappear in the quickly forgotten project.

In mid-1931 the confusion of thinker and clown in Shaw alleged by Churchill was reinforced by a junket G.B.S. took, at seventy-five, to Soviet Russia, which for the benefit of the great publicist was turned by Stalin everywhere Shaw went into a huge Potemkin Village. As he crossed the border from Poland into Russia by train Shaw threw away, to the horror of bystanders, the food packed for him for the journey, remarking that in the Soviet paradise nothing would be wanting. For him nothing was, and he would return convinced that he had seen, and sampled, Utopia.

Russia was literally a nine days' wonder to Shaw, who announced on arrival at the Moscow railway station, "I was a Socialist before Lenin was born." Lenin had died seven years earlier but was still physically available, in his Pharaonic mausoleum in Red Square, for Shaw to venerate. Lenin's successor, Stalin, invited Shaw to the Kremlin for a chat between interpreters in which the Premier's chief question was why Churchill was so violently anti-Russian. "I said," Shaw reported, "he had a bee in his bonnet and was hopelessly old-fashioned. But Stalin was not satisfied with this reply. He has a high opinion of Mr. Churchill's ability."

To Lady Astor's contention that Churchill was "finished, finally," Stalin had answered, "I am not so sure. If a great crisis comes, the English people might turn to the old war horse."

"We told him," Shaw said confidently, "he need not worry, because Churchill would probably lose his seat at the next election and anyhow would never be prime minister." Three months later, Churchill renewed his hold on his seat in Commons, and when, as prime minister, he visited Stalin in Moscow in August 1942, the Russian premier reminded him of the exchange with Shaw and Nancy Astor.

As Stalin knew, and as Shaw put into a post-1931 revision of his *Guide*, Churchill had saved Sovietism by attempting to finance a Capitalist counter-revolution. In 1919 he had arranged, as Secretary of State for War, to have British forces still mobilized, and "stocks remaining from the Great War" worth a hundred million pounds, "to back up a series of royalist raids into Russia led by generals and admirals of the old dynasty. At first it seemed as if the Soviet [state] must fall. . . . Yet within two years the raiders were completely defeated; and the victorious Red Army was clothed in the British boots and khaki, and armed with the British weapons which Mr Churchill had supplied for their destruction."

It was accomplished, Shaw explained to Stalin, "without a single vote being taken in the House of Commons," and when Churchill had to bring the matter, finally, to an unhappy House, "he crumpled up." Despite such stubborn opposition to Communism, Shaw asked whether Churchill would be welcome in Russia, and Stalin "replied enigmatically that he would be delighted to see Mr Churchill in Moscow, as they had every reason to be grateful to him."*

It was a story that Shaw, with his taste for irony, never tired of repeating in letters-to-the-editor and in radio talks, in one of which he joked that "Churchill proposed, but Providence disposed." Providence, he insisted, was "sick of Capitalism," and the thought, he wrote in *The Times*, kept Churchill awake nights. Rejecting charges that the Soviet system was kept in place by Stalinist terror rather than by popular enthusiasm, he explained, "Only when Communism is conceived, as by Mr. Churchill, to be a tyranny which all its subjects would denounce if they dared, does it seem reasonable to believe that the Russians must be gagged to prevent them from clamouring to be reduced to the condition of the inhabitants of this highly perplexed island."

Always on the alert, in his years out of office, for money-spinning journalism, Churchill found Shaw's pilgrimage to the East opportune. In the *Sunday Pictorial* for 16 August 1931, with G.B.S. hardly back from Russia, Churchill weighed in with a long "Personalities" piece, set against a photograph of Lady Astor and Shaw strolling in the shadow of the turreted Kremlin. Despite the differences in sex, class, and almost everything else that counted in England, Churchill began, the pair had one crucial characteristic in common. "They like to have everything both ways. Thus Mr. Bernard Shaw is at once a wealthy and acquisitive capitalist and a sincere communist. His spiritual home is in Russia, but he lives comfortably in England, which he derides and abuses on every occasion. . . . He couples the possession of a mild, amiable and humane disposition with the condonation and even glorification of the vilest political crimes and cruelties. . . ."

---

*"Have you forgiven me?" Churchill asked Stalin in 1942. "Premier Stalin, he say," replied the interpreter, Pavlov, as Stalin smiled amiably, "all that is in the past, and the past belongs to God."

Churchill provided a catalogue of paradoxes about how the captains of the "grim domains" of communism anticipated the Shavian "merry harlequinade." The Russians, fond as they were, Churchill claimed, of "circuses and travelling shows, . . . had imprisoned, shot or starved most of their best comedians." The Shaw-Astor pair "might fill for a space a noticeable void. And here was the world's most famous Clown and Pantaloon in one, and [in the other] the charming Columbine of the capitalist pantomime."

The "well-drilled" crowds unfurled their banners, well-rehearsed bands blared, and "loud cheers from sturdy proletarians rent the welkin." Despite the desperate food queues "in the back streets," the visitors were banqueted sumptuously, and Stalin, "pushing aside his normal budget of death warrants and *lettres de cachet*, received his guests with smiles of unaffected comradeship."

Churchill's icy satire seemed partisanship at its most extreme, but history would vindicate all of it, while validating Shaw's naïveté. Eager to believe, Nancy Astor and Bernard Shaw believed with complete faith, ignoring, as Churchill put it, that their claimed mission was "investigatory." Their public service to Britain in furnishing first-hand data, he observed, consisted only in permitting Stalin's eager guides "to show them *the right things to see*."

There was "a serious moral" to the "comical" scenes, Churchill went on, acidly. "Here we have a State . . . whose intelligentsia have been methodically destroyed, a State nearly a half-million of whose citizens, reduced to servitude for their political opinions, and rotting and freezing through the Arctic night; toiled to death in forests, mines and quarries for indulging in that freedom of thought which has gradually raised man above the beast." Was it not strange, he questioned, that decent and even intelligent observers could be so "airily detached" from the unpleasant realities—"that they have no honest word of indignation for such crimes, no word of sympathy for all these agonies?" The venality of the system was too vast to be hidden. How could one account for the "moral and intellectual myopia?"

In the same paper the following week, Shaw offered a smugly brief reply blaming Churchill's "Russophobia," which was international "mischief" and thoroughly false—"full of sound and fury, and signifying nothing." Stalin—a monster to Churchill—would have been described by Louis XIV, Shaw suggested, as "well-bred, unaffected, charmingly good-humoured." Elsewhere, when Churchill and others accused Shaw of ignoring the wholesale brutality in totalitarian regimes that he was praising throughout the early 1930s for their efficiency, in contrast to the torpor of parliamentary democracies, Shaw responded that positive social change had its price. And at the start, even Churchill confessed, in another *Great Contemporaries* essay, to admiring Hitler for restoring German national pride in the aftermath of military defeat and economic depression. Shaw, meanwhile, found Hitler on the evidence of his *Mein Kampf* to be, paradoxically, "the greatest living Tory." Both would regret the remarks, Churchill much sooner than Shaw.

As the European dictators swelled in arrogance, Shaw's stage satires continued to prophesy the demise of democratic institutions, his *On the Rocks* (1933) closing with a revolutionary mob gathering outside No. 10 Downing Street. In the political wilderness, Churchill, out of power and shorn of influence in the ramshackle "National" governments, continued writing—to maintain his lifestyle and to make his voice heard. Among his books was a life of his famous ancestor John Churchill, first Duke of Marlborough. Britain would soon need another of his like, Churchill implied. Shaw took a copy of *Marlborough* with him on a long voyage to New Zealand, and on board the *Rangitane* in May 1934 he wrote to Churchill begging forgiveness "for meddling; but the book interested me so much that I could not keep quiet."

Although Shaw described the biography to Churchill as "very good reading," he felt compelled to take issue with Churchill's "Macaulayisms." Macaulay "did not reckon with genius." No one really understood the nature of genius, Shaw observed, but some writers, at the least, recognized it, among them Macaulay's contemporary, Carlyle. Yet Macaulay's Byron "is a writer of fashionable skits in verse: his Bunyan is a patronized tinker. He could not hit even the vulnerable spots in Marlborough, whose love letters, which you quote so effectively, are the love letters of a booby (Thackeray might have invented them to depict a typical military booby) and whose outlook in youth is that of a flunkey. Mac would have him a melodramatic villain. . . ." But, Shaw continued, turning his letter into a Fabian lecture, the "really dangerous side" of Macaulay was his Whiggery, his "idolatry of Parliament, of public opinion, . . . of an underlying divinity in the British character," all smashed by Karl Marx. Whiggery had given rise to "the Party System, though [King William and Marlborough] never understood it," or recognized that it destroyed parliamentary government just as the revolution that had brought William III in had destroyed the monarchy. The "anarchy of Capitalism" had been substituted, a condition in which "all the able political adventurers achieve their irresistible successes . . . by denouncing Liberty, Democracy, Opposition as putrefying antisocial superstitions . . . and calling for those betes noires of the Whigs: Discipline, Loyalty, State Supremacy, Control, Silence, Obedience, Absolutism."

Even you, Shaw told Churchill, floundering in the Conservative Party, are "wondering what the devil you are doing [in league] with the comrades and nobs. . . ." An up-to-date book on Marlborough, then, should trace the "amazing results" of the introduction of political parties, which substituted original genius in government with third-rate party careerists and the anomaly that "Whig William had to work with Tory Cabinets and Tory Marlborough with Whig ones," for only in that way could parliaments be prevented from voting on the merits of an issue. The wars against France, then, virtually imposed the "Party System" on England; yet "identifying it with the Cause of Liberty (which it has utterly destroyed) was preparing the way for Fascism and Bolshevism just as clearly as for the French Revolution."

The lessons of that history were clear to Shaw, he explained, fourteen years before Lenin had learned them, because Shaw had read Marx that much earlier, and "got Macaulay out of my blood forever." But you, he admonished Churchill,

> having had class education, swallowed the poison without the antidote. Hence the amazing, and, believe me, hopelessly obsolete passages in an otherwise splendid book which might have been written by Tom [Macaulay] himself.
>
> Have you finished the second volume, or is there still time to bring it into its historical relation with the present thrilling situation, and incidentally and frankly, with your own personal struggle with the Party System, in which your crossings of the floor* and Ramsay [MacDonald] are such a puzzle to the party ridden public? After all, Winston is a live wire and John [Churchill] a dead one.
>
> Think it over. A bigger book than your first Macaulayish volume is quite easily within your grasp. . . .
>
> > faithfully—really
> > G. Bernard Shaw

Shaw's continuing disenchantment with parties and parliaments may have exasperated Churchill, who responded warmly—but firmly—late in May

---

*Churchill's changing of party affiliations from Conservative to Liberal and from Liberal to Conservative.

1934, "I believe that freedom for the individual to succeed or fail, in spite of all the resulting irregularities, gives the best climate for culture, happiness, and material well-being. I think the English constitution and Parliamentary system, expressing English character, has produced results superior to those now existing in any [other] country, and I hope I shall die before it is over-turned."

The pivot of Shaw's concerns to Churchill was the same as that of the Shavian plays of the 1930s—unresponsive governance and unclear national direction. Although Shaw publicly referred to Churchill as a representative of "the robber class," he recognized the need, in a society he identified as class-ridden, and in a world he saw as drifting into a repetition of 1914, for leadership of a Churchillian order. And both men thought they saw in T. E. Lawrence, self-reduced to the ranks, a possible future leader. Teased himself by the idea, Lawrence, a Shavian surrogate son who had legally changed his name to Shaw, vacillated, as he chose retirement early in 1935, between his Clouds Hill cloister in Dorsetshire and emergence into public life. From 1920 to 1922 he had worked for Churchill, when Winston was Minister for the Colonies, in rearranging the map of the Middle East. Then he had gone underground as a private soldier while publishing his *Seven Pillars of Wisdom*.

The Shaws, who had been among his closest confidants while "Shaw" hid very visibly in the ranks, took seriously none of his hints that he might return to active life, and in the mid-1920s they lobbied for a Civil List pension for him. But when Lawrence threatened to commit suicide if he were not permitted to leave the Army and rejoin the Air Force, from which he was expelled when his identity became known, Shaw pressed Stanley Baldwin, then Prime Minister, to approve the transfer. Baldwin discussed the matter with Churchill, Lawrence's former chief at the Colonial Office, and the Air Ministry was lobbied to relent.

In the early 1930s, although holding no office, Churchill nevertheless had a large following among those who pressed for rearming Britain to prepare for inevitable European war. Lawrence might be his man to reorganize "Home Defence," T. E. confided to his Clouds Hill neighbor Pat Knowles in March 1935, and there may have been a scheme, promoted by Churchill, to plant Lawrence as deputy to Sir Maurice Hankey, an invisible power in government who was both Secretary of the Cabinet and Secretary of the Committee of Imperial Defence. "Hankey has too much to do," Lawrence intimated to his architect friend Sir Maurice Baker.

Disoriented by the publicity attendant upon his discharge from the

R.A.F. in February 1935, and by his need to put his private life back together—"something is broken in the works," he told Lady Astor— Lawrence did little to encourage the idea that he was up to doing important national work. When he died in a motorcycle accident that May, the Shaws were in South Africa. At the burial ceremonies at Moreton Church, near Clouds Hill, Winston Churchill walked apart from the pallbearers. The eight names on the committee for a Lawrence memorial at St. Paul's would include both Churchill and Shaw.

Despite such things as they had in common, when Churchill updated his Shaw portrait for *Great Contemporaries*, he used the opportunity to respond to Shaw's allegations about the Russian-intervention fiasco of 1918–20 and to reiterate the paradox of Shaw as "at once an acquisitive Capitalist and a sincere Communist." Shaw was stirred into rebutting some of the harmless inaccuracies in the profile, paragraphs that he gathered together only when, in his nineties, he needed padding to eke out into a book what became his *Sixteen Self Sketches*. To Churchill's assertion that Shaw "was dragged to Low Church and chapel" as a child, Shaw replied, "Never"; far from being Dissenters, his family members were "derisive free-thinkers," and Shaw himself was an atheist as a matter of deliberate choice at an early age. As for Churchill's statement that Shaw "speaks at hotels and at street corners," Shaw insisted that he never spoke at hotels. Churchill's pseudo-scholarly pinpointing of 1889 as the year when Shaw "shows for the first time a little Marxian influence" was, Shaw insisted, off by more than six years, for a Shavian novel of 1883 "is pure Marx." Churchill's following sentence, "Later on he throws Marx over for Mr. Sidney Webb," was flatly denied: "I never threw Marx over. In essentials I am as much a Marxist as ever." There was more, none of it crucial to either writer's reputation. Shaw dated it "Sidmouth, September 1937."

As T. E. Lawrence anticipated, Churchill was back in the Cabinet as soon as war broke out in 1939, as First Lord of the Admiralty—a reprise of his Great War post—and then in May 1940 as Prime Minister. Shaw, at 84, coached from the sidelines. As early as February 1940 he advised Churchill via a letter in the *Daily Telegraph* to make better provision than in 1914–18 for the recreation of servicemen when on leave. "What I want to know," he inquired, "is whether . . . irreplaceably rare and highly skilled [theatrical] artists, providing a most delectable entertainment of the highest class for our 50,000 soldiers on leave every night, are to be sent into the trenches to fill 30 places which could be better filled by 30 unskilled labourers?"

The German blitzkrieg in the Low Countries and France did in the

Neville Chamberlain government and brought Churchill to Downing Street. "The moment we got a good fright, and had to find a man who could and would do something," said Shaw, "we were on our knees to Winston Churchill." Without the war, Shaw assessed when it was over, "Churchill would not have had a dog's chance of crowning his Parliamentary career as Prime Minister; for he had always been suspected of wanting to do something; and he was known to be capable of crossing the floor of the House on the merits of a Parliamentary measure instead of invariably voting on the one question that is ever before the House in one disguise or another: to wit, whether the Party Government is to remain in power or to be ousted by the Opposition."

When the shooting war came closer, Shaw's physician at Ayot, C. B. Dansie, remembered, "I was with him when Churchill's famous 'blood and sweat and tears' speech was about to be broadcast. . . . He called out to Mrs Shaw but she didn't come into the room to hear it; she hated Churchill." Shaw, however, had now passed through his admiration-of-Hitler phase and was out—in his fashion—to help Churchill win the war. After the capitulation of France in June 1940, Shaw offered advice directly to Churchill, whom he had just heard on the radio (so he wrote to Beatrice Webb). Winston was "evidently badly floored" by the surrender ordered by old Marshal Pétain, and "should have said more or said nothing; but it is impossible to blame him; for what can any of us say until we know the terms obtainable by Pétain?" To Churchill himself he offered some Shavian strategy:

> Dear Prime Minister
>   Why not declare war on France and capture her fleet (which would gladly strike its colors to us) before A. H. recovers his breath?
>   Surely that is the logic to the situation?
>
> > tactically
> > G. Bernard Shaw

Churchill—presumably on other advice than Shaw's—did attempt to seize or cripple the French fleet, which did not go over as easily as expected to the British side. In a fever of Anglophobia, commanders and crews scuttled the precious warships.

Every evening Shaw had his wireless tuned to the war news and heard nearly every Churchill speech, deploring the "House of Commons style, with long pauses between every word to think out what . . . to say next." It was "pitiful through the mike," he felt, especially when prepositions and conjunctions were pronounced as if the speakers were "oracles." For radio audiences, the Churchillian pauses represented *gravitas* rather than anything else, and they worked, but Shaw felt that the microphone required a different venue of address than the echoing chambers of Westminster. Further, the Puritan in Shaw was appalled, as he wrote to Gilbert Murray in October 1940. "Churchill," Shaw observed, "occasionally tells as much of the truth as he safely can over the wireless. Then he takes an audible gulp of his favorite stimulant and, with a preliminary yell, gives the gallery a peroration and denounces Nazi scoundrels who actually bomb civilians, women and children. He is immediately followed by the news announcer, who begins by describing how the R.A F. has rained bombs on the railway stations of Berlin etc. etc." As a result Shaw claimed to lack "moral indignation"—but Churchill would have blamed Shaw's outlook on another strained attempt at airy detachment.

Basically—the handling of Ireland was an exception—Shaw approved the way Churchill conducted the war, and when the Prime Minister discussed war aims, Shaw read about the address to the Conservative Party in *The Times* on 28 March 1941 (it was not broadcast) and applauded the Prime Minister's honesty.

"Churchill was absolutely right the other day," Shaw wrote to H. G. Wells, ". . . when he said that if he declared his war aims the united nation behind him would split into fifty irreconcilable factions" (15 April 1941). Since Ireland had retained relations with Germany and was covertly aiding the Nazi war effort, he added, England might "have to re-occupy Ireland militarily; or at least take over the ports, for the duration . . . if the battle of the Atlantic continues to go against us."

The strategy appealed to Shaw despite his professed satisfaction with the independent-minded Irish president, Eamon De Valera, and he had already written in the Leftist Glasgow *Forward* (7 December 1940) that he disapproved of the idea of servicing German subs from Irish ports, however furtively. Churchill must say, he suggested, "I will not allow forty million Britons to be starved and defeated to save the paper neutrality of a few million hostile Irish. . . . Local patriotism with all its heroic legends is as dead as a doornail today. The ports do not belong to Ireland; they belong to Europe, to the world, . . . and are only held in trust by your Government in Dublin."

Although Shaw realized that Irish politics was a factor in American politics and that Churchill needed the United States, the idea reappeared in his correspondence with Lord Alfred Douglas. One of Shaw's more persistent correspondents in the war years was the doddering Lord Alfred, a relic of Oscar Wilde's downfall but once, as a result of a libel action during Churchill's tenure as Home Secretary, a resident of one of His Majesty's prisons. Eager now for a Civil List sinecure as aging poet, he applied for help to Shaw, enclosing verses he had penned to Churchill. Shaw was sufficiently astounded to try a pair of spoof couplets of his own on Douglas:

> You have certainly performed an extraordinary feat. I tried to imagine how you could possibly make Churchill the addressee of a sonnet. Ridiculous rhymes jingled in my head.

> Churchill: both blessed [St] Jude and Christian God,
> Bid me forgive you putting me in quod

and

> Just one last thing I hardly like to mention
> But it must out. Say: what about that pension?

Douglas had ideas, too, about winning the war, and called De Valera "a skunk" for closing Irish ports to British warships and maintaining relations with Hitler. Shaw suggested—but only to Douglas—"a very private letter to the P.M. as follows[:] 'Dear Churchill: I cannot give you the ports because I should provoke an I.R.A. rising and lose such power for good as I have. I cannot prevent you from taking the ports, as I have only four millions to your forty, and you have America at your back this time. So for God's sake *take* the ports as nicely as you can as a temporary forced loan, promising to give them back when our common enemy the atheist Hun is disposed of. Faithfully, Eamon De Valera.' "

Nothing happened. To Churchill the price was too high, whatever the temptation. Shaw understood how futile was the advice of an octogenarian amateur and left the idea a facetious literary exercise. However his good friend Nancy Astor was close to Churchill, and to her Shaw tried out a different idea because he was concerned that talk of unconditional surrender, voiced at the Churchill-Roosevelt conference in Casablanca, would unnecessarily prolong the war. "Tell Winston," he wrote to Lady Astor on 13 February 1943, "to stop talking alarming nonsense about unconditional surrender. Make him explain that the surrender cannot be unconditional, but that we shall dictate the conditions. As to whether 'we' includes Uncle Jo[e Stalin], the less said just now the better."

A year later, in a letter to Gilbert Murray following the D-Day invasion of France, Shaw professed pleasure "with General Eisenhower's military disregard of Churchill's unconditional surrender slogan in his offer of a detailed list of conditions to the German soldiers." By then Shaw was deep into his last long political treatise, *Everybody's Political What's What?* (1944), in which he found Churchill happily less explicit about other war goals.

> This apparently millennial harmony was shattered by the Prime Minister, Mr Winston Churchill, who said, in reply to certain sceptics who were pressing him for a more explicit declaration of our war aims, that "if you try to set forth in a catalogue what will be the exact settlement of affairs you will find that the moment you leave the area of pious platitude you will descend into the arena of heated controversy."

> With this deadly sentence Mr Churchill knocked down all the skittles with a single throw, leaving us in the region of abstraction, in which we appear a united nation. Such unanimity is useful in war time, when we all have to fight for our lives whether we like it or not; but anyone who supposes that it will continue when the war is over, and we have to start rebuilding and cleaning up, is deluded by phrases as useless for legislative purposes as algebraical symbols which represent quantities but give no information as to quantities of what.

Shaw regularly offered Churchill advice in the press, largely because reporters and editors exploited G.B.S. as provocative copy. In January 1941 the *Sunday Graphic* offered Shaw's "My Advice to Winston Churchill." In March, in the *Sunday Dispatch*, appeared "The Amazing Winston Churchill." In *Cavalcade* in November came "G.B.S.—If I Were Churchill! Shaw Discusses War Strategy." The Leftist *Cavalcade* had asked Shaw to examine ways of aiding embattled Russia, and Shaw came up with ambitious moves for Churchill that involved "launching an Indian army, potentially 30 millions strong, at the Germans from the east." Even much smaller numbers of Indians, had they wanted to fight, which was doubtful indeed, could not have been armed and would have had nowhere to go. Would the "financial and economic system" of Britain, *Cavalcade* asked, "survive the war"? Churchill and Eden, Shaw responded, characteristically, were "for private property and oligarchy" while Stalin "is for public property and democracy." Although Churchill had been reminding Shaw for a decade that Stalin's utopia was a large prison camp, Shaw was not listening. Churchill's system would vanish with the victory, he predicted for *Cavalcade.* "There will be wigs on the green."*

After a public hiatus in 1942, Shaw analyzed Churchill's war speeches in a *New Leader* article in April 1943, and in the New York *Journal-American* he furnished guesses about what would be discussed when Roosevelt and Churchill met with Stalin. An admirer of Churchill's grand prose, Shaw could not believe that a ringing speech in Algiers delivered by Free French General Henri Giraud was anything but ghost-written because it was "of the finest literary and rhetorical quality in our Prime Minister's best style. It was a staggering performance. . . . Nobody in authority is capable of it but Mr. Churchill. . . . As it is my profession to write speeches for players, and I have incidentally written them for orators, it seemed to me quite natural and politically very prudent to write an important and badly needed speech [for somebody else]. It is exactly what I would have done myself."

Caught up in his old enthusiasm for Churchill, Shaw closed by suggesting how useful it would be for the nation to keep the inspirational leader in office for ten years after the war. Churchill, he noted, had observed that idleness was out of fashion and hoped that it would remain so in the immediate postwar years. In Shaw's summary of Churchill's state of mind, "The feudal aristocrat and the middleclass plutocrat are to be put to work as ruthlessly as the proletarian pubcrawler."

The suggestion was too much for Fenner Brockway, the editor. After all, the *New Leader* was the organ of the socialist Independent Labour Party. In a box on the same page the shocked Brockway dissented. "We refuse to contemplate the continuance in office of Mr. Churchill for a further ten years after the war. . . ."

The next year the Sunday *Reynolds News*, a Labour weekly, published "G. B. Shaw Gives Churchill a Tip about India," which the Prime Minister, eager to hang on to the seething subcontinent, would have ignored had he seen it. To the question *"What advice would you give to Mr Churchill concerning India?"* Shaw replied in block capitals, TO KEEP OUT OF IT. To the question about what to do with postwar Germany, Shaw answered in the *Sunday Pictorial* that breaking Germany's impulses to dominance was a proposal that came badly from a government so "completely imbued with

---

*G.B.S. was reaching back for his metaphor to the image of wigs of fallen aristocrats on embattled village greens.

the idea of its [own] dominance" as the British Empire. "Even the word Commonwealth as a substitute for the word Empire sticks in Mr Churchill's throat every time he tries to utter it." In the *Sunday Express*, after responding with scrupulous realism to the necessary place of Japan and Germany in a postwar international organization, he was led again—as the press loved to do with Shaw—to Churchill. *"What is the next thing you would do [in prosecuting the war] if you were Mr Churchill?"* the *Express* asked. "I would secretly guarantee Hitler," G.B.S. advised the Prime Minister, "a palatial residence free of rent and rates, and £20,000 a year free of Income Tax, to begin when Germany surrenders, not unconditionally, but on conditions dictated by* me."

None of the Sunday sage's barbs affected what was clearly seen by Winston as a cranky admiration. On 3 October 1944, in the midst of his preparations to fly to Moscow to confer with Stalin, Churchill took Clemmie to the theater—the Old Vic—to see Olivier and Richardson and Margaret Leighton perform in Shaw's *Arms and the Man*, the play that had disturbed him so many years earlier.

In the last year of the war, Shaw adhered to the editorial biases of the Leftist papers that solicited his views, explaining in the Glasgow *Forward* in February that Stalin could get his way at the Yalta conference because, as a Communist, he has "a made-up mind," while Churchill and Roosevelt were "muddled with Cobdenist superstitions, Tory Democracy, Monroevian isolation, and all sorts of nineteenth-century odds and ends." His supporting Communist candidate Palme Dutt in the 1945 General Election led to a *New York Herald Tribune* piece, "Shaw Indorses a Red and Tilts at Churchill." Meanwhile, again in the Glasgow *Forward*, he gave Churchill a left-handed compliment. "I protest," he wrote, "against Mr. Churchill being dismissed as a hypocrite and a humbug by his Labour critics. Hypocrisy and humbug are no disqualifications for political leadership; on the contrary, they are necessary accomplishments for ministers who have to govern fools according to their folly. No! What makes Churchill dangerous is that he sincerely and honestly believes what he says. . . ." But Churchill lost, and although he would return to office five years later, the "continuance" that Shaw had once suggested and then opposed in the ballot box was not to be.

When it came to morality and money, Shaw was a realist—like Churchill, he claimed, supporting Winston's ideas when it seemed useful. In 1943 he

---

*The *Express* printed *to,* but the sense suggests a typographical error for *by.*

had announced that at 88 he had made a new will. (Charlotte Shaw had just died.) He was hanging on to his considerable fortune and not giving it away while he remained alive. Several groups, including the Workers' Educational Association, complained about provisions in the will, and Shaw's answer was, "They want money like every other organization in the country. Mr. Churchill's attitude is my attitude—what I have I hold."

With the war over in Shaw's ninetieth year, he could not escape becoming, once more, a public figure, however much he evaded the public in his tiny Hertfordshire village of Ayot St. Lawrence, to which one could not make a pilgrimage by bus even after fuel rationing had ended. When his birthday came around in July 1946, processions of postmen and telegraph boys brought gifts and cards and cables. Waspishly rejecting the homage, Shaw ordered all the greetings destroyed unread, but the "two strong men" who followed Shaw's instructions pulled a batch with significant return addresses from the heap, including one from the Irish president, a gift golden shamrock from a Dublin dustman representing the Bernard Shaw Branch (Dublin) of the Irish Labour Party, a poem from Poet Laureate John Masefield, prayers from his old friend at Stanbrook Abbey, Dame Laurentia McLachlan, and a telegram from Winston Churchill.

Out of office since July 1945, Churchill remained, Shaw wrote in thanking Winston for "the cordially personal feeling," the only "eminence" other than De Valera to have sent birthday greetings. It gave Shaw another opportunity to bring up the perennial leadership question. "No man of action," he commiserated to Churchill, "has any chance of being a British prime minister until a war frightens the electorate out of its chronic dread of government interference and preference for guaranteed *fainéants** like Ramsay and Baldwin and their like." Churchill, he felt, represented "Disraeli's invention and your father's creed: Tory Democracy."

Shaw's shorthand draft ended, "You have never been a real Tory: a foundation of democracy and a very considerable dash of the author and artist and the training of the soldier has made you a phenomenon that the Blimps and Philistines and Stick-in-the-Muds have never understood and always dreaded."

Churchill replied to Shaw at length, confiding that he would treasure the letter "among my extending archives" and hoped that his papers would be "enriched by several more as time passes." He also asked, "Ought we not try

---

*The word, misspelled in the published Shaw *Letters*, means *do-nothings* and refers to the Merovingian kings of early France who were notorious for their laziness.

and settle the Irish question? Could we not call it quits in the long tragedy? We succeeded in exercising remarkable forbearance about the Irish ports [during the war]." And he closed with a tribute to one of his favorite Shaw plays—and an acknowledgment that there were issues on which they never would agree.

> I have always been much stirred by Joan. Anatole France is pretty good about her. She is indeed a gleaming star. I am taking your play about her away with me to read on my "holiday." Like you, my work and my holidays are the same.
>
> It must be agreeable to enjoy such a prolonged view of the dissolving human scene and to be perennially rejuvenated by the resilience and permanence of what you have written.
>
> We do not agree about Communism. The impending division or collision will be Communism v The Rest. I read with some sympathy Maeterlinck's *Life of the Bee*. At any rate the bees have preserved the monarchical principle! I am not attracted by "The soul of the white ant." To hell with all static ideals of human society. What matters is the behaviour of individuals under an infinitely varying and, we must hope, on the whole improving atmosphere and surroundings.
>
> Do you think that the atomic bomb means that the architect of the universe has got tired of writing his non-stop scenario? There was a lot to be said for his stopping with the Panda. The release of the bomb seems to be his next turning-point.

The atomic bombs had been dropped just a year earlier. Churchill was writing on 18 August 1946. The world into which both men had been born had been irrevocably altered by them.

Shaw had mellowed at ninety and was not eager to argue politics with his old acquaintance—or even whether the world had a future. He had always seen Churchill, whatever their differences, as thoughtful activist rather than as amiable nullity. He appreciated being linked with him in history, writing in June 1948 to retired prizefighter Gene Tunney, an old friend, that when heavyweight champion Joe Louis arrived in England for an exhibition tour, "it was announced that the only people he wished to visit were myself and Winston Churchill. The whole British Press made a rush for me (probably also for Churchill) to learn the date and place and hour and minute of the visit. I said I had not heard from Mr Louis; but two comparatively unknown

persons like myself and Mr Churchill could not but feel flattered by a visit
from a world-famous head of his profession."

The announcement was a press agent's publicity stunt. "I have no reason
to believe," Shaw concluded to Tunney, "that J. L. knew about the stunt at
all, or had ever heard of me or of Winston."

In the preface to his last full-length play, *Farfetched Fables* (1948), Shaw
paid his final—and paradoxical—tribute to the Churchill of World War II,
recalling his post-birthday words to Winston. G.B.S. threw few ideas away.
"When Mr Winston Churchill, as a man of action," Shaw wrote, "had to
be substituted for the *fainéants* when the war [of 1914–18] was resumed, his
big cigars and the genial romantic oratory in which he glorified the war
maintained his popularity until the war was over and he opened the [1945]
General Election campaign by announcing a domestic policy which was a
hundred years out of fashion, and promised nothing to a war weary
proletariat eager for a Utopia in which there should be no military controls
and a New World inaugurated in which everybody was to be both employed
and liberated."

The Tory strategy failed. "The Utopians carried the day triumphantly.
But the New World proved the same as the old one, with the same
fundamental resistance to change of habits and the same dread of government interference surviving in the adult voter like the child's dread of a
policeman." For Shaw this was a dose of realism about the mass of people
he had long considered his own constituency and an indulgent retrospective
look at Churchillian politics. One could not re-make people from without.
But G.B.S. in his nineties, despite his outward cantankerousness, had his
temperate moments. Even his lean lifestyle was not for everyone. "Winston
Churchill," he told Ayot St. Lawrence neighbor Stephen Winsten, "smokes,
drinks, and eats meat and has managed to survive. Of course if we stop
killing animals and insects, they'd kill us. It's a matter of who is to survive,
after all."

Just before the 1950 General Election, Mrs. Alice Laden, Shaw's house-
keeper at Ayot, a confessed "true blue" Tory, stuck a campaign poster—a
large bulldog-like Churchillian head—in her kitchen window. "I'm Red—
you're Blue," Shaw assured her when he noticed it. "It's your part of the
house—you can do whatever you like in it." The next day Shaw discovered
it attached to the front gate and festooned with blue ribbons and forget-me-
nots. "It makes a joke—and a very good one," he said. After it hung there
the rest of the day, Mrs. Laden had enough of her joke and took it down.

The last observation on Churchill by Shaw as Sunday sage came in the *Reynolds News* on 6 August 1950 in an "interview" with Hayden Church written, except for an opening query, by Shaw himself. There was at long last no quarrel. The war in Korea had begun a little more than a month before, and Shaw did not want to see it spread into a general war. Pandit Nehru in India, Shaw declared, "would go to any length" to avert that catastrophe. "So would I. Winston Churchill says virtually the same. No greater calamity could be conceived." Churchill had actually supported military intervention and would send token troops, but Shaw had seized on his old adversary's professed anxiety about confining the struggle to Korea. They had almost agreed on something.

In September, Shaw fell while pruning a tree, fracturing his thigh. He was ninety-four and frail. The damaged bone was pinned, but Shaw would never walk again. Flowers and fruit and other gifts arrived from well-wishers worldwide, including roses from the Churchills. In return, Shaw sent his newest book, *Sixteen Self Sketches*, with its long-dormant rebuttal to *Great Contemporaries*. "You need only read 'Am I an Educated Person' as you and I," Shaw explained to Churchill, who shared his lack of an Oxbridge degree, "are officially classed as ignoramuses." It was their last exchange. Weakened by his immobility, and by subsequent kidney failure, Shaw died on 2 November.

There would be, as seemed appropriate for such persistent and friendly combatants, a posthumous interchange. At the urging of Charles Eade, Shaw had written some fragmentary additional notes as a further rejoinder to *Great Contemporaries*, which Eade published in 1953. In them, Shaw called Churchill (who as Prime Minister was officially the First Lord of the Treasury) "the most brilliantly talented Minister on the Treasury Bench." And he remained impressed that even Churchill's "recreations" were "civilized": "painting and bricklaying, not hunting and shooting." Had peace prevailed, Shaw observed from the beyond, Churchill would never have made it in politics—he was "suspected of wanting to do something." If Churchill had his life to re-live, Shaw wondered, would he again "waste it in the British House of Commons as it has been wasted by the party system"? That it was the only way to reach what Disraeli called the top of the greasy pole was lost on the nonagenarian Shaw. One took the route to the goal that was available. And without it, England in 1940 might have emerged differently.

Churchill continued to summon up his old antagonist, recalling in several books and speeches what he claimed to have learned from Shaw. To a meeting of the Honourable Artillery Company on St. George's Day in 1953—in memory of a very different George—Churchill talked of the times

> when our artillery really came boldly out on to the battlefield. George Bernard Shaw—if I remember—said about Napoleon that his dominant theme and master thought was "Cannons kill men"— well, I must say that rather stuck in my mind and in August 1941, on my way to Placentia [, Newfoundland], where we signed the North Atlantic Pact [with Roosevelt], I had a little time to think about things, and I did write in a memorandum "Renown awaits the commander who first in this war restores artillery to its prime importance upon the battlefield" from which it had been ousted by heavily armoured tanks. It was left, I think, to General Montgomery in the Battle of Alamein to show the power of a thousand or more guns all firing in a regular system to enable an army to advance.

Churchill was remembering, inexactly but colorfully, Shaw's Napoleon play of 1896, *The Man of Destiny*.

Three years after Shaw's death, Churchill received the Nobel Prize for Literature, and on 15 October 1953 he issued a statement from 10 Downing Street reacting to the award. Two earlier Nobel laureates from England, he observed, had been Kipling and Shaw, writers with whom, he felt, he could not compete. "I knew them both quite well and my thought was much more in accord with Mr. Rudyard Kipling than with Mr. Bernard Shaw. On the other hand, Mr. Rudyard Kipling never thought much of me, whereas Mr. Bernard Shaw often expressed himself in most flattering terms." Bringing G.B.S. into the picture made Churchill the politician feel more comfortable about the Prize.

Notes

Most sources are in the text itself. Churchill correspondence not directly taken from the press is from Martin Gilbert's eight-volume *Winston S. Churchill* and companion documentary volumes, its first volume only by Randolph S. Churchill with Gilbert's research assistance (Boston: Houghton Mifflin, 1966–88). Extracts from Churchill's speeches are from the eight-volume *Winston S. Churchill: His Complete Speeches, 1897–1963*, ed. Robert Rhodes James (New York: Chelsea House Publishers, 1974). Churchill's recollections of the early Shaw, beginning on the first page of the essay, are from his article in *Nash's Pall Mall* (magazine) as reprinted in *Great Contemporaries* (London: Butterworth, 1937), pp. 47–60. Shaw's letters, with the exception of one to Lord Alfred Douglas, are from the four-volume Laurence edition cited elsewhere in this volume, or from the Gilbert biographical volumes. Shaw's letter of 31 July 1941 to Douglas fashioning a spoof sonnet to Churchill is from Mary Hyde, ed., *Bernard Shaw and Alfred Douglas: A Correspondence* (New York and New Haven: Ticknor & Fields, 1982), p. 145.

Acknowledgments

Although all the essays in this volume have been revised, updated, or entirely rewritten following their original appearances, the reader may wish to know where the originals appeared. These sources are cited in order of appearance in this volume:

"Exasperated Admiration: Bernard Shaw on Queen Victoria," *Victorian Poetry* 25 (Autumn–Winter 1987): 115–32.

" 'The Hibernian School': Oscar Wilde and Bernard Shaw," SHAW: *The Annual of Bernard Shaw Studies* 13 (1993): 25–49.

"Bernard Shaw in Darkest England: GBS and the Salvation Army's 'General' William Booth," SHAW: *The Annual of Bernard Shaw Studies* 10 (1990): 45–59.

"Apostate Apostle: H. L. Mencken as Shavophile and Shavophobe," *Educational Theatre Journal* 12 (October 1960): 184–90.

"A Jennifer from Australia: Edith Adams and *The Doctor's Dilemma*," SHAW: *The Annual of Bernard Shaw Studies* 6 (1986): 77–80.

"Uneasy Friendship: Shaw and Yeats," YEATS: *An Annual of Critical and Textual Studies* 1 (1983): 125–53.

"A Respectful Distance: James Joyce and His Fellow Townsman Bernard Shaw," *Journal of Contemporary Literature* 13 (March 1986): 61–75.

["The Playwright and the Pirate: Bernard Shaw and Frank Harris"], introduction to *The Playwright and the Pirate. Bernard Shaw and Frank Harris: A Correspondence* (University Park: Penn State University Press, 1982); pp. vii–xx.

" 'Lawrence of Arabia': Bernard Shaw's Other Saint Joan," *South Atlantic Quarterly* 64 (Spring 1965): 194–205; and "The Two Sides of Lawrence of Arabia: Aubrey and Meek," *Shaw Review* 7 (May 1964): 54–57.

"Shaw's Other Keegan: [Sean] O'Casey and G.B.S.," in *Sean O'Casey Centenary Essays*, ed. David Krause and Robert G. Lowery (Totowa, N.J.: Barnes and Noble, 1980), pp. 212–16.

"Indulging the Insufferable: Shaw and Siegfried Trebitsch," developed from a review of *Bernard Shaw's Letters to Siegfried Trebitsch*, ed. Samuel A. Weiss (Stanford: Stanford University Press, 1986), in *English Literature in Transition* 30 (1987): 333–36.

"Jesting and Governing: Shaw and Churchill," developed from a paper read at the annual meeting of the International Association for the Study of Anglo-Irish Literature, University of Leiden, Netherlands, July 1991.

Index